The Bread Makers

Jared T. Benton

The Bread Makers

The Social and Professional Lives of Bakers in the Western Roman Empire

palgrave
macmillan

Jared T. Benton
Old Dominion University
Norfolk, VA, USA

ISBN 978-3-030-46606-0 ISBN 978-3-030-46604-6 (eBook)
https://doi.org/10.1007/978-3-030-46604-6

This Palgrave Macmillan imprint is published by the registered company Springer Nature Switzerland AG.
The registered company address is: Gewerbestrasse 11, 6330 Cham, Switzerland

Contents

List of Figures

List of Tables

CHAPTER 1

Introduction: *Chaînes Opératoires* and the Making of Roman Bread

Bread was the staple food of the ancient Mediterranean diet.[1] It was present in the meals of emperors and it was on the tables of the poorest households. In many instances, a loaf of bread probably constituted an entire meal. As such, bread was something that unified society; it was a commonality linking people from the most modest backgrounds with those with the highest social status. But bread, because it was present on every one's table, is also something upon which the social divisions in society played out. Certain types of bread were associated with higher or lower social status; for Juvenal 'to know the color of one's bread' meant knowing one's place in Roman society[2] and jokes about giving darker bread to sub-elite guests were common.[3] It is easy to imagine that some bakeries made finer grain flour and produced bread for elite customers, while others made courser, browner breads, serving a more modest clientele. We should imagine the world of bakers being equally diverse, marked by social stratification and tinged by inequality. Much recent work on craftsmanship has focused on the interwoven professional and social lives of craftspeople,[4] but most of that work has been done by historians and remains grounded in epigraphic, juridical, and literary evidence. In tandem, a growing number of studies have taken a more material approach to Roman industry and craftsmanship, using archaeological methods and documentation to detail the nature of production in the actual remains of workshops.[5] Such studies have been very interested in expanding our understanding workshop operation to include the social lives of bakers, but have struggled to

J. T. Benton, *The Bread Makers*,
https://doi.org/10.1007/978-3-030-46604-6_1

integrate industrial processes with social habits from the material remains alone. A third category of scholarship is beginning to use economic theory and models to help bring the evidence together to make inferences that perhaps extend beyond what can be deduced directly from the evidence, addressing social strategies of Roman economic actors.[6] Each approach faces problems unique to its discipline and its body of evidence. Literary approaches tend to highlight elite perspectives and activity or the curated self-presentation of craftspeople, rather than sub-elite contributions or the practical realities of industry. Archaeological approaches, on the other hand, tend to emphasize processes with material consequences and technological innovation over social behaviors which leave little or no material footprint; the results are almost entirely synchronic and localized in the city or region in question, with an undue amount of attention to well-preserved cities in central Italy. The mode-driven approaches tend to focus on large urban centers, pushing a neo-Classical economic bent that underscores the economic complexity of high-population centers such as Rome or Ostia, neglecting production and economic maneuvering of small-scale producers in towns and villages, which comprised the vast majority of Roman urban centers.

The purpose of this book is not to create a comprehensive catalog of Roman bakeries throughout the Mediterranean. Instead, my goal is to provide a framework—or frameworks—for our understanding of the production of bread in the Roman world that can encompass the material remains and the textual evidence to provide a coherent model of how bread was produced across time and place, what strategies were enacted by bread producers, and what values or aspirations were held by bakers. Specifically, two theoretical models are used to assist in our understanding of the production of bread in Roman or pre-Roman contexts: cultural heritage as a way to model diachronic changes in the production of bread and 'modes of production' as a backdrop against which both industrial processes and social systems can be set. Chronologically, the scope of the book begins in the middle Iron age and includes evidence from the end of antiquity as late as the sixth century CE, but the heart of the book consists of the bakeries in cities and towns of the first century BCE to the third century CE. The scope of the book is restricted to the western half of the Mediterranean and the Roman empire, with evidence from the eastern half only brought in to enrich or substantiate our understanding of the bakeries in the west. There are definite drawbacks to approaching the evidence in this way, most notably that the western Mediterranean was never defined as a geographic or cultural locus in antiquity. On the other hand, if we restrict ourselves to synthesizing evidence from a single site or from a single culture with defined geographic parameters, we will never arrive at a broader understanding of the Roman world which was by its very nature eclectic. Moreover, I would contend that there are some reasons to think of the two halves of the Mediterranean basin as distinct and for the west to be thought of as a region with shared historical and cultural trends, if not languages and genetics. The linguistic divide between a Latin west and a Greek east aside, the cultures of the east including those of Egypt, the Levant, Anatolia, and Greece had long histories of urban development and infrastructural complexity, dating back into the Bronze Age in some cases. The cities of the western Roman empire, most of which had their roots in the first century BCE, lacked the same population sizes and complexities of their eastern counterparts. One of those complexities was specialization. Specialized bakers are evident in the Bronze-Age texts of Egypt, Mesopotamia, and even Linear-B tablets in Mycenaean citadels.[7] The Iron-Age *poleis* of greater Greece and throughout the east attest to a wide variety of craftspeople. In the west, such specialization seems to be taking place much later in the last few centuries CE and was coeval with other phenomena such as rapid urbanization, acculturation associated with Roman rule, and the unique social stratification of urban centers. In other words, the inhabitants of Arsinoë in Egypt were unlikely to link commercial baking and bakers with the advent of the Roman Empire, but the pre-Roman peoples of Lusitania at a place such as Augusta Emerita would probably have seen those two phenomena as contemporaneous, if not interconnected.

One of the difficulties that the study of industries has faced is how we frame production in such a way that allows us to account for the immense variety and obvious social symbolism of production in Roman and non-Roman, Mediterranean cultures alike. For example, we tend to call Roman bakers *pistores* and debate the etymology, but our epigraphic evidence suggests that there was a wide variety of terminology for Roman-period bakers, including *pistor*, *pistrix*,[8] *pistorium*,[9] *pisstoricus*,[10] *pistor magnarius*,[11] *clibanarius*,[12] *pistor siliginiarius*, *pistor candidarius*,[13] or *negotiator pistoricius*[14] in Latin. *Pistor* also appears in Hellenized form, but the traditional word in Greek was *artokopos*, but also attested are *artokreas*[15] *artopolos*,[16] *artopoios*,[17] *artopolikon*,[18] *artokopadios*,[19] *katharourgoi*,[20] *aleurokathartis*, and *abakitais*.[21] In addition to baking titles, there are also a number of milling professionals, in both Greek and Latin, such as *molitor*,[22] *mulothriaios*,[23] and *mularchontes*.[24] This is only a fraction of such terms and the variation in terminology was very likely grounded in regional dialects or idiosyncrasies of cultural eating habits, but others reflect the different economic realities of different cities and regions, such as *negotiator pistoricius*. Some probably indicate what type of bread was being made, in the case of *siliginiarius* or *candidarius*, suggesting something about the social status of their customers or the quality of the product.

This diversity in the industry is not reflected in scholarship on Roman baking, which has a tendency to default toward the legal definitions provided by jurists[25] or to epigraphy,[26] which is inclined toward Latin and regions with intense epigraphic habits, such as central Italy. One of the ways that archaeologists and historians are redressing regional variation in craft production is to look closely at how production was actually occurring in Roman workshops or how specific objects were made. For baking, the workspace and the technologies associated with the production of bread are more readily available than the final product, bread, but there are instances of preserved loaves carbonized by heat and fire. Variation in technology has traditionally been cast in a chronological light; less efficient technologies become replaced with more efficient ones.[27] For example, less productive millstones, such as hopper rubbers, are replaced with rotary-action millstones, each iteration of which is larger than the last. The situation is significantly more complicated than that. Moreover, antiquated technologies, the hopper rubber in particular, occasionally remained in use despite the existence of more efficient technologies such as rotary-action, ass-driven millstones.[28] Rather than focusing on innovation, more recent studies of production and commerce in Roman cities have tended to frame technologies in the sequence of operations (or *chaînes opératoires*) to which they contributed and were used.

Chaînes Opératoires *and the* Tools of Bread Making

The application of *chaînes opératoires* is grounded in the belief that knowing the necessary processes and their order facilitates an understanding of production. Such sequences of operations, when linked to specific features or technologies, can provide a critical link between industrial processes and the spaces that hosted them. Most commonly, the *chaîne opératoire*—and the technologies used to accomplish it—is derived from a combination of modern observation, ancient iconographic representation, and textual description. Then that sequence of operations is grafted onto—or identified within—the archaeological remains. The concept of the *chaîne opératoire*, as a means to understand the past and production, was initially envisioned by André Leroi-Gourhan, whose primary interest was lithic production in Paleolithic archaeology.[29] The concept, growing out of Leroi-Gourhan's work, took on renewed significance within a broader field: materiality studies. Tim Ingold, an anthropologist and ethnographer whose work focuses on husbandry in northern Scandinavia, has become the champion of the use of *chaînes opératoires* to frame and understand ancient industries.[30] Ingold laments the increasing distance between the theorists and the material as evidence, particularly in studies of materiality, and thus for him *chaînes opératoires* serve as a way to bridge theoretical concepts of how humans interact with objects and the real-world praxis of the study of materials and making of things.[31]

For the study of ancient Roman industries, the growing use of *chaînes opératoires* in our understanding of production has resulted in a shift away from the identification of workshops within the urban fabric of a city[32] to a focus on processes and outcomes inside workshops. A series of recent publications have begun to examine more closely the nature of the operation of Roman workshops. Miko Flohr's work on the fulleries of Pompeii was the first to really examine comprehensively the interior of workshops of a city. Flohr isolates the processes that comprise fulling through a combination of ancient textual and iconographic evidence, combined with historical comparanda. He then isolates those processes in workshops as a means of understanding materially the operation of fulleries.

For Roman baking, Betty Jo Mayeske, Robert Curtis, and Jan Theo Bakker conducted some of the initial work on how ancient bread was made and what technologies were required to accomplish them.[33] These scholars, in identifying the technologies associated with the various processes in the production of bread, were significantly aided by the Roman iconographic depiction of bakery scenes, for example the frieze on the Tomb of the Baker, Eurysaces, in Rome (Fig. 1.1). The core processes as identified by Curtis are milling, sifting, mixing and kneading, forming loaves, leavening, and baking.[34] The tomb, just outside the Porta Maggiore in Rome, originally had four sides, though only three remain extant in fragmentary form.[35] Bakker similarly uses that same understanding of the operational sequence and its associated technologies, derived

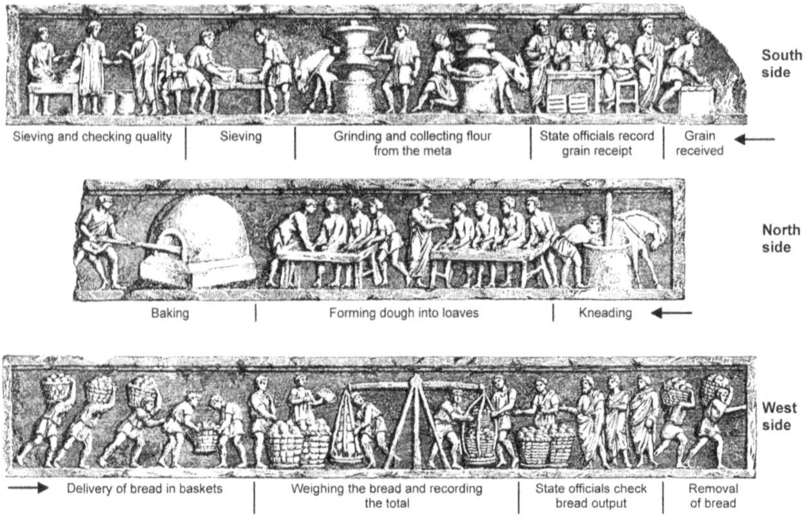

Fig. 1.1 Frieze with various Processes Indicated courtesy of Robert Curtis (2001, fig. 28)

from the frieze on Eurysaces' tomb, to identify the bakeries at Ostia, noting areas where millstones exist and places where mixing occurred, as well as places where baking occurred.[36] Nicolas Monteix, who has studied most fully the bakeries of Pompeii and Herculaneum, goes beyond the simple identification of spaces with regard to the bakeries in Pompeii, noting that previous literature "has failed to go further than providing a synthetically designed description of the main features of bakeries; the first step beyond this would be to insert each operation into the space of the workshop. This should lead to an understanding of how technical challenges have been solved – or not – within a peculiar spatial layout."[37] What this allows Monteix to do is align process to space and begin isolating choices made by those who built or worked and lived in the space. His forthcoming book on bakers and bakeries in central Italy should reveal much more granular analysis of these craftspeople and further detail their lives.

One of the strengths of the *chaînes opératoires* approach is that the production of bread is governed by—or perhaps guided by—certain natural processes that circumscribe it. As such, modern bread production is not unlike that of ancient bread production and it is worth briefly reviewing the processes involved in the production of bread. W.P. Edwards, in his work on modern commercial baking, reduces bulk fermentation—and the sourdough method—to the processes that comprised them, in essence the sequence of operations or *chaîne opératoire* (Fig. 1.2).[38] His sequence is mixing, kneading, bulk fermentation, dividing, molding, panning, proofing, and baking. Edwards' sequence of operation can be further reduced to four processes: mixing and kneading, loaf-formation, proving, and baking. Furthermore, ancient bakers milled their own grain, compelling the inclusion of milling and sifting to the operational sequence. Thus the *chaîne opératoire* in ancient bread production is (1) the grain is milled into flour; (2) the flour is sifted to remove impurities; (3) wet and dry ingredients are mixed and the first rising of the dough occurs; (4) the dough is formed into loaves; (5) the seconding rising of the loaves occurs, ideally at a controlled and rather warm temperature; (6) and finally, the loaves are baked into bread.

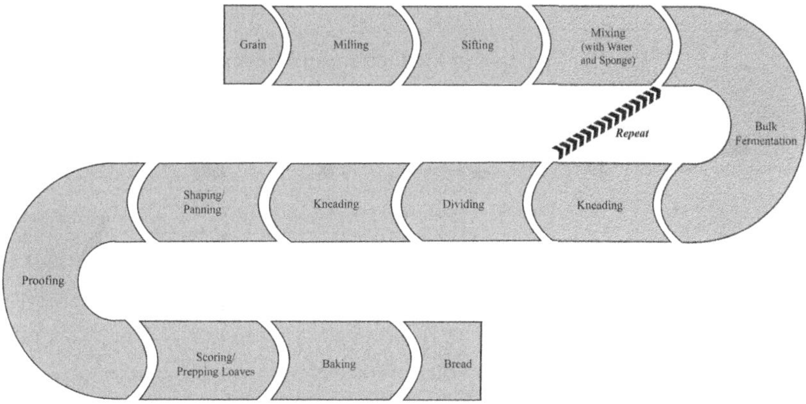

Fig. 1.2 The Sequence of Operations in the Production of Bread. (Adapted from Edwards 2007, 169 fig. 1)

Milling and Millstones

No matter what type of grain used or what type of bread produced, the first process is milling grain into flour. The type of grain could vary widely, ranging from millets to barley and naked-grain wheat.[39] Of the technologies involved in the production of bread, the millstone is without a doubt the best studied in part because of the durability of its material composition, usually of some type of porous volcanic rock, but always of some type of stone. The variety of millstones is innumerable, but they range from small saddle and rotary querns and hopper rubbers (Olynthus mills) to massive hourglass millstones known from around the Mediterranean (Fig. 1.3). In general, millstones consist of two parts one of which is moved in some fashion and while the grain is ground into flour between the two elements. The upper portion that moves is usually referred to as a *catillus* and the lower portion is a *meta*.[40] Porous, volcanic stone is often the preferred material because its porosity allows the stone to renew its ability to cut and grind grain even as its initial surface is worn by the contact between the *meta* and *catillus*.[41] But stone used for millstones ranges

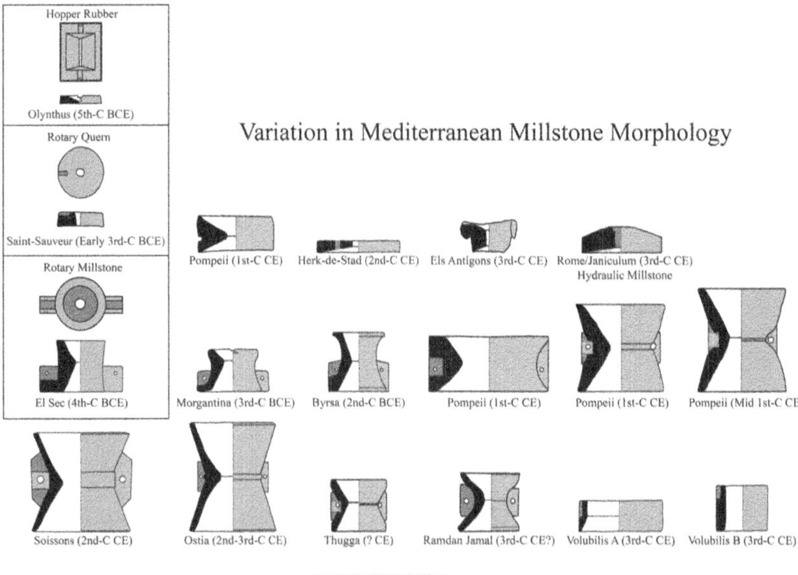

Fig. 1.3 Variation in Western Mediterranean Millstone Morphology

from basalts to puddingstone, sometimes using local stones and importing millstones from far away.[42] For commercial baking, we are often given the impression that Pompeian style millstones were the norm throughout the Mediterranean, but this is not the case. A wide variety of millstones existed and even within the hourglass-shaped, rotary millstone type that is associated with Pompeii, there exists a wide variety.[43] Such variation was often cast in terms of innovation and a desire for increased productivity, emphasizing a linear or taxonomic approach to the variation in millstone morphology.[44] Innovation-focused studies yielded some important data and conclusions, including that the millstones were clearly getting larger from the fifth century BCE to the third century CE. The steady increase in size is almost assuredly coeval with other phenomena that would incentivize increased productivity, such as population increases, urbanization, and specialization of craftspeople.

There are some problems with framing millstone variation strictly within the context of innovation; there is good evidence that antiquated technologies could continue to be used well after the innovation of millstones capable of higher productivity and different types were also contemporaneous with a degree of regionalized uses. The Hopper Rubber or 'Olynthus' millstone, for example, has been discovered throughout the Mediterranean and is associated largely with the sixth to the third century BCE.[45] But despite the invention of more efficient technologies, older mills sometimes continued to be used, particularly in domestic production or in rural areas disconnected from the trade routes that proliferated new technologies.[46] Moreover, chronological change and innovation can account for much variation in millstone technology, but some is also grounded in regional difference. The annular millstone, for example, is attested only in Mauretania Tingetana, Baetica, and Lusitania during the third and fourth centuries CE.[47] The hourglass millstone or 'Pompeian' millstone,[48] although often treated as a single type, actually consists of a vast array of different shapes and sizes that all happen to share the hourglass shape. Those of Pompeii and Ostia seem very much the same in shape, but the millstones at Ostia are significantly larger. The hourglass millstones of North Africa tend smaller and wider, proportionally, and they often have a stone trough or vat for catching the flour.[49] At Pompeii, and presumably at Ostia, the masonry base of the millstone supported a lead catchment basin.[50]

There is another way to cast this evidence: the hourglass millstone represents standardization and the growing political and economic unity of the Roman Empire. The mechanism for its spread was long-distance trade of millstones.[51] Because specific types of stone were preferred, hourglass millstones were sourced from select quarries in the Mediterranean, including examples from Orvieto, Sardinia, and Etna.[52] The millstones were then exported, serving as ballast on trade ships that replaced them with goods from the places of export. In fact, the first known hourglass shaped Morgantina-style millstone is known from the mid fourth century shipwreck off the coast of el Sec, an island near the Baleares.[53] The stone has been sourced to Sardinia. Similar stones in Sicily have been sourced to quarries on Etna. Many of the hourglass millstones in later periods, from Pompeii to Gaul, have been sourced to a quarry near Orvieto.[54] Because the millstones were exported and traded widely, they one of the few components of Roman commercial baking that were relatively standardized with a relative degree pan-Mediterranean consistency. Even the millstones in Gaul that were sourced to local quarries were clearly of the same form, if somewhat different, as the technologies imported from other regions influenced local habits.

Sifting and Sieves

Sifting accomplished a number of important things for bakers of bread; it removed impurities from the flour, such as bits of millstone or other unwanted elements. It could also be a way to evenly mix dry ingredients. If salt were added to bread, it might be at this stage in the process that one might add it and sifting would provide an easy way to ensure it was evenly distributed throughout the flour. It was also evaluated for its quality, with flour made from certain grains preferred over others, but the acts of milling and sifting were also important to the perceived quality of bread and white bread made from finely ground flour was preferred above others. Sifting was also a means of quality control; it allowed a bakery to make sure that the particles comprising the flour had been ground into a consistent grade without larger bits of germ or husk that might decrease the perceived quality of the loaf.

Sieves, the technology associated with commercial production of bread, are not well attested in the archaeological record probably because they were made of materials that did not lend them to preservation. Small metal sieves are known, but they are too small for commercial production and likely served cosmetic purposes. Sieves in the form of baskets and other ephemeral materials are preserved in certain places, such as Egypt,[55] but it is unclear to what extent the same technologies were implemented throughout the Mediterranean. Despite being a critical process in the production of flour and bread, sieves are known largely from iconographic depictions of them, probably because they were made from ephemeral materials such as wood and organic fibers. The iconography, at least, suggests that most sieves were round objects with rims, possibly of wood, with some sort of grate or screen made of fibers or metal which filtered the impurities or inadequately milled grain, while allowing the flour to pass through (Fig. 1.4). On Eurysaces' tomb, just left of the milling, four

Fig. 1.4 Men Using Sieves on the Tomb of Eurysaces, Rome. (Courtesy of Nicolas Monteix)

men in short tunics hold sieves upright over tables or vats. On the Bologna plaque, in a fragment now lost, a man dumps the impurities or inadequately milled grain, ensuring a finer flour and higher quality bread.[56] The qualitative aspect of sifting is evident in the iconography from Eurysaces' tomb: one of the men in tunics turns back to a fifth, togate individual who rubs the flour between his fingers, testing the fineness. The sieve, even just as a technology, is often displayed even alone, as though hanging on a wall. On the funerary monument of P. Nonius Zethus, in addition to ***modii*** and millstones, baskets and sieves appear hanging from nails and resting on shelves. The funerary plaque of the bread seller from Isola Sacra near Ostia depicts sieves hanging on a wall behind the vendor and the man seems to be holding what might be a sieve, but it could be a basket with bread. The prominent display of the sieve in the iconography of bakers is surely a reference to the quality that sieves insured and, by extension, to the skill and quality work of the baker himself. The iconography, however, is largely born of Rome and Ostia and such devices surely differed significantly across the Empire; it is doubtful, given the limited evidence, that we will ever recover even a percentage of the variation in sieve morphology.

Mixing and Mixers and Bulk Fermentation

After milling and sifting the grain into flour, it needs to be mixed with the other ingredients and, for leavened bread, those included active yeast in some form. There is some debate as to how leavened ancient Roman bread would have been,[57] but the carbonized loaves of Pompeii and certain literary descriptions of bread making clearly describe a leavening process. Pliny details the use of fermented grape juice (***mustum***), a soured barley cake, or even beer foam, but he makes clear that these were abnormal or antiquated in his time. The most popular in his day was to use a fermented mixture of bread and water from the days before, commonly called a sponge, a starter, or a preferment.[58] The normal method, says Pliny, was to save some dough before salt is added. This was mixed with water and allowed to ferment into a sourdough starter (a sort of fermented slurry) and added to the next day's dough to serve as the leavening agent. Although sourdough bread was probably the norm,[59] what characterizes Pliny's description of Roman bread is the variety of types, made from different grains and taking myriad forms; but the basic recipe necessitates three main ingredients: flour, water, and a leavening agent.

On the other hand, ancient grains likely contained less gluten than their modern counterparts and so such bread may not resemble modern spongey breads.[60]

Almost any vat or trough could serve to mix the various ingredients and begin the process of aligning the glutens so the bread can leaven. In fact, in both the physical remains of workshops and in the iconography of central Italy, we see the process occurring with a variety of technologies and features, including wooden barrels as seen on the Villa Medici sarcophagus, bowls as identified by Monteix at Pompeii,[61] and troughs of some sort as seen on the Romolo relief (Fig. 1.5).[62] By the first century CE, a new technology was invented to mix the various ingredients and knead the resulting dough. This device is referred to as a kneading machine or a kneader, but in this work it is referred to as a mixer to encompass its full range of purposes.[63] The mixer, as a specific technology, is attested from around the Mediterranean as early as the second century BCE,[64] but it varies in precise form and petrological analyses have shown that they are usually made of more local stones than millstones (Fig. 1.6).[65] The mixers of Pompeii are largely unfixed features that do not appear in every bakery. The mixers of Ostia are fixed, embedded into paved floors and their rims flair out. The mixers at Volubilis come in two types: some have rectilinear exteriors, others are cylindrical.[66] Despite regional variation in form and material, mixers all operate in much the same way. They consistently have a cylindrical vat with a volume of about 50–100 liters. Holes on the sides of the vat had stationary elements that provided resistance to the central element that could rotate (Fig. 1.7). That central rotating element had phalanges that served to stir the ingredients in the vat. Monteix suggests that the first rising of the dough, also known as autolyze, may have occurred in the mixers, at least for those bakeries that leavened their bread.

Fig. 1.5 The Romolo Relief from Rome. (Courtesy of Andrew Wilson and Katia Schorle)

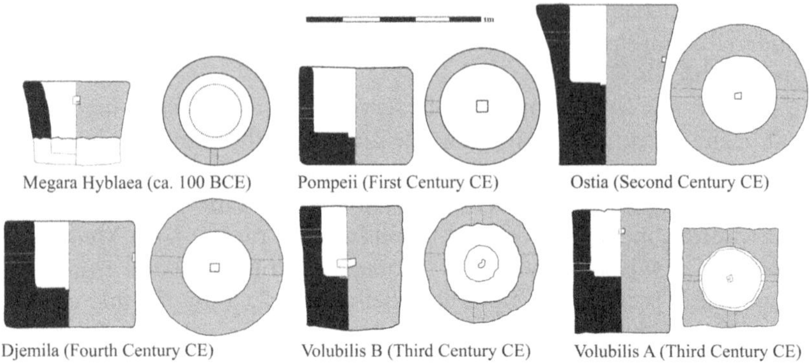

Fig. 1.6 Development of the Mixer in the Western Mediterranean

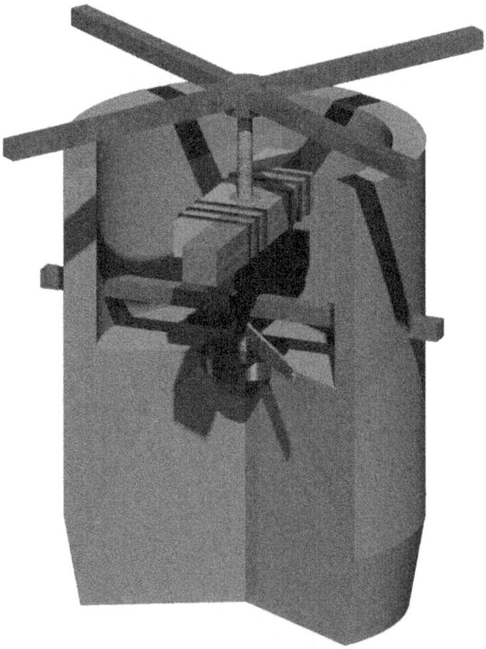

Fig. 1.7 Reconstruction of a Mixer from Volubilis (design by Giancarlo Filantropi)

Kneading, Dividing, Shaping, and Tables

After mixing the ingredients and the bulk fermentation, the dough needed to be formed into loaves and kneaded. Some kneading or folding occurred in the mixers, but a secondary kneading would occur for bread that was leavened. Kneading aligns the glutens in the dough, creating a structure for the loaf and creating a surface tension that allows the bread to keep its form and to hold the fermentation so that the gasses produced can leaven the bread.[67] For the production of entirely unleavened flat bread, the process of kneading would be largely superfluous and the formation of loaves would involving rolling out of dough into flatter pieces.

This task requires a surface and a fair bit of flour to prevent sticking. In Pompeii, at least, there are definitely supports for tables preserved in a number of bakeries, even standardized as two piers which surely supported wooden planks (Fig. 1.8). Tables are evident in iconography as well on the tomb of Eurysaces and on the Romolo relief (Fig. 1.9). There is little

Fig. 1.8 Table Supports from Pompeii (I.12.1-2)

Fig. 1.9 Shaping of Loaves from the Frieze on the Tomb of Eurysaces. (Courtesy of Nicolas Monteix)

archaeological evidence for tables outside of Pompeii and Herculaneum or from the iconographic evidence at Rome. One could imagine that kneading and shaping of the loaf would look very different from culture to culture, but even within one region or community bread types differ. Conversely, tables were probably very much like sieves, made from wood and not preserved to the extent that stone technologies were.

Proofing and Shelves

After the dough was kneaded and shaped into loaves, it would need to rise again, often referred to as the proof by bakers. This process would not be necessary for unleavened breads. The yeast in the dough would begin consuming the natural sugars in the flour, creating gasses that would be trapped by the aligned glutens, thus the bread would attain its crumb or the patterning of cavities in the dough. The lower gluten content of the wheat would make this process take longer than for modern breads and many breads were probably much denser than modern iterations made industrially. The fermentation process, however, would have been sped up in warmer conditions, ideally between 26 °C and 30 °C (79 and 86 °F).[68] As such, modern bakers tend to set loaves aside near ovens to facilitate the proof.

Medieval and early modern depictions of baking depict leavening and offer some indication of what features might have facilitated this process. The medieval tradition of handbooks often addresses various trades, like baking and milling. Manuscript illuminations frequently accompany textual descriptions of the trades. One such handbook was the *Tacuinum Sanitatis*, the Maintenance of Health. Two scenes from Vienna 2644, a manuscript of the *Tacuinum* in Austria dating to the last decades of the 14th century CE, show men and women making bread (Fig. 1.10). Already baked bread is stacked in baskets and depicted with a slightly darker hue. The unbaked loaves are stacked on shelves or planks of wood that may follow the loaves from their shaping and kneading from the tables to the shelves and the fronts of the ovens as a means to mitigate handling of the loaves once shaped.

In fact, shelves are known in bakeries, usually found near the ovens, or at least they can be inferred from postholes in walls (Fig. 1.11). Most of the shelves are known from Pompeii, where the walls are preserved to abnormal heights; most of the physical remains of bakeries do not survive to an elevation that would allow for the shelve postholes to be preserved.[69] Shelves are also known in the Bakery in the Maison à la Citerne in Volubilis near to the oven. Their proximity to the ovens reinforces the hypothesis that they served for proofing the bread, which would occur more efficiently in warm controlled conditions. It also explains why shelves might not be known in certain areas, such as the bakeries of central North Africa, where there are some indications that flat, unleavened bread was preferred to the leavened bread clearly preferred in central Italy and farther west in North Africa. Flat breads would not require the second rising (or the first for that matter).

Baking and Ovens

Baking is the process by which the uncooked dough is dehydrated by exposure to high heat, no less than 100 °C (212 °F) (the temperature at which water boils), but really no less than 180 °C (285 °F) (the temperature at which the Maillard reaction occurs) caramelizing sugars to produce a crust.[70] During the baking, the bread will experience an 'oven spring' as the last of the yeast continues to produce carbon dioxide before it dies in the heat. Bread needs relatively uniform heat to bake consistently and

Fig. 1.10 Scene of baking and use of Shelves from the Tacuinum Sanitatis Vienna 2644. (Courtesy of the Österreichischen Nationalbibliothek Cod. Ser. n. 2644, fol. 63v)

there are three main ways to create such conditions: convection, conduction, and radiation. Convection requires the circulation of hot air from a heat source. Conduction is the transfer of heat from a hot object to a cold one, so placing a loaf directly on a hot rock or surface would be conduction. Radiation is the transfer of heat from one object to another without direct contact. Most bread produced in antiquity would have been baked using a combination of conduction and radiant heat.

Fig. 1.11 Shelves at Pompeii House of the Baker (I.12.1) and the Maison a la Citerne at Volubilis

Ovens are the most recognizable component of the ancient bakery, at least those of central Italy which so closely resemble their modern counterparts in service at pizzerias and bakeries throughout Campania. The reality is that baking could occur in a variety of ways and via a wide range of technologies. Even in what we call an oven, there is a wide range of technologies, ranging from small terracotta vessels[71] to vertical aperture *tannūr*-style ovens[72] (Fig. 1.12). But even among masonry ovens of the type at Pompeii and Ostia, there is a wide range of forms that are predicated on regional traditions and the availability of new technologies. They vary from rubble platforms and adobe domes cobbled together on floors to masonry ovens integrated into the building around them (Fig. 1.13). Such ovens can be small, less than a meter in average diameter, but they can also be quite large, up to more than five meters, such as the massive ovens of Ostia.

The ovens of Pompeii have a domed space, but also a ***praefurnium*** or front chimney that would funnel smoke up and out of the bakery. Additionally, most of the bakeries in Pompeii have a chute that allowed access from a room with shelves, presumably for leavening, to the front of the oven. Monteix speculates that the chutes facilitated the transfer of loaves from the kneading tables to the oven. His excavations at Pompeii revealed olive pips in remarkable numbers throughout the bakeries, which Erica Rowan interprets as evidence of the fuel used in Pompeii's bakeries, detritus from olive-oil production called pomace; similar results have been found outside of Pompeii and Herculaneum.[73] Nevertheless, a wide

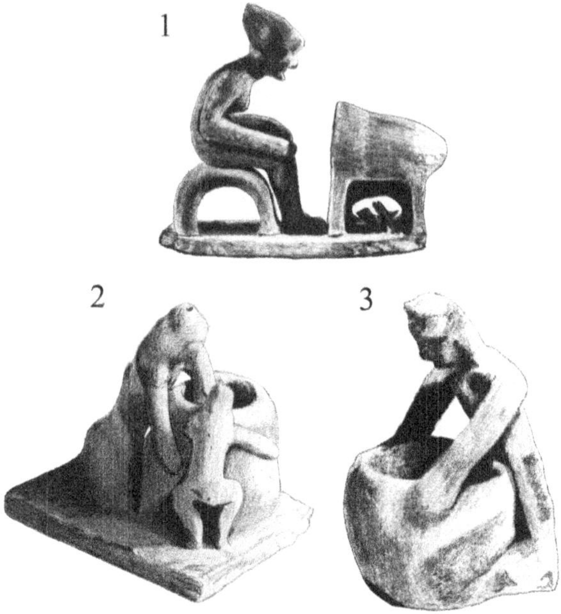

Fig. 1.12 Terracotta Figurines Depicting the Use of Other Types of Ovens: (1) Woman using an ἰπνός (Berlin, Staatliche Museen inv. 31.644 after Sparkes 1962, fig. 4), a *tannūr*-style Oven, on the left (2) from Borj-el-Jedid in Tunisia (after Hoyos 2010, pg 110, ill. 15), and on the right another (3) from Megara Hyblaea on Sicily (Syracuse, National Museum. Inv 9957 Sparkes 1981, Pl. 4b) Drawing by Dan Weiss

variety of combustibles could probably have been used as fuel, including wood and charcoal, especially in areas where olive cultivation was not widely practiced, such as central Europe or Britain.

Problems with Process-Oriented Approaches

The application of *chaînes opératoires* revolutionized how we approach Roman industries, providing a framework for the production of objects for which we have no workshops. It has also allowed us to isolate the details of production in the material record, thus linking process with space. Part of its success has relied on the fact that the method has largely

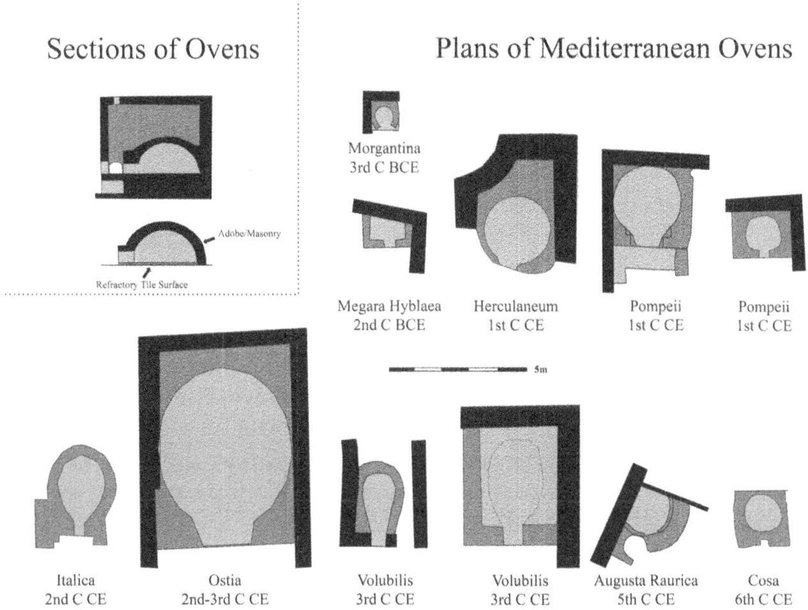

Fig. 1.13 The Development of the Domed Oven in the Western Mediterranean

been applied in cities with exceptional preservation, such as Pompeii or Ostia in central Italy, where technologies and infrastructure are often still intact. The reasons that make the central Italian cities an ideal body of evidence to apply *chaînes opératoires* also make the region a poor touchstone for understanding ancient baking in other areas of the Mediterranean. First, the preservation of Pompeii, Herculaneum, and Ostia are unique. The vast majority of Roman cities and towns were not covered by a volcanic eruption. Second, few regions of the Roman Empire enjoyed the infrastructural advantages of Ostia, as Rome's port, or even that of the Campanian cities as tax-exempt Italian communities near a hub of production and manufacture in Latium. In fact, an increasing body of scholarship is showing that, despite the political unity of the Roman empire, regional variation predicated on local customs and familial traditions was more the rule than homogeneity.[74]

There are other problems with the *chaîne-opératoire* approach that extend beyond where they have been applied. The conceptualization of production as a series of interrelated processes all leading to a single product are, in the long run, fundamentally synchronic. It provides no framework to model change in production across time periods, often leading scholars to seek diachronic datasets in the comparison of one city to the next, which has not proven fruitful largely because such remarkable variation existed from city to city even at the same point in history. Moreover, the *chaîne-opératoire* approach has not lived up to its intended purpose. From its origins, as outlined by Leroi-Gourhan, it was intended to bridge processes of production with direct material consequences with social behaviors.[75] This is also a preoccupation that is regularly encountered with the scholarship on Roman industries. But in both cases there is a disjoint between the operational sequences drawn on the plan and the description of life in the workshop, despite that being one of the intended purposes of the *chaîne opératoire* approach. Indeed, one of the criticisms of the *chaîne opératoire* approach is that it never actually accomplishes the integration of industrial processes with social habits.[76]

Elizabeth Murphy directly engages with this very problem. Growing out of recent developments in Roman household studies, she conceives of workshops and "work groups" as separate entities just as houses and households are treated separately. This reconceptualization allows Murphy to move past a simplistic view of production as strictly speaking commercial and economic. She writes that "just as the household was part of larger social spheres, workshops were also part of larger communities that reinforced the nature of relations among workers. Furthermore, as evidenced archaeologically, workshops could be venues, not only of work tasks, but also ritual activity."[77] This is obviously a vast improvement on the idea that somehow chains of operations would magically link into social processes, but even empowered by Murphy's reconceptualization of social space in workshops, we still lack a means of bridging commercial processes and social habits. The following chapters are a series of attempts to provide a diachronic framework for understanding change in Roman baking, through its reconceptualization as a form of cultural heritage, and a theoretical backdrop (modes of production) against which to place both the production of bread and social habits of bakers to integrate them both into a single model of ancient baking.

Chapter Summaries

Commercial baking—and really most ancient industries—was largely born of domestic production.[78] As such, the baking traditions of the Roman Empire were as diverse as the peoples that occupied the Mediterranean basin. In fact, an increasing body of scholarship is showing that, despite a unified empire and some cultural consistency, regional variation was more the rule than homogeneity. Like many aspects of the Roman world, there exists a tension between the almost gravity-like inertia of pre-Roman traditions and the homogenizing force of being part of the Roman Empire. Focus on process might be able to indicate what types of bread were made and what technologies were used, but bread production was not a series of processes, it was an enactment of knowledge and experience that existed as bodies of knowledge in the minds of producers, both domestic and commercial. At the heart of Chap. 2 is the premise that craftsmanship is a body of human knowledge that is enacted or performed, not a process. It is passed down from one individual to the next, informed by familial and cultural habits and traditions. Viewing the production of bread as something inherited culturally not only allows us to account for regional variation in commercial baking; but it also provides a diachronic framework that allows us to explore the homogenizing impact of living in a politically unified Roman empire. It has become increasingly clear that local, pre-Roman traditions played a greater role in determining regional habits and material culture than early scholarship recognized. There is no reason why we should assume pre-Roman traditions were not informing commercial baking in every part of the empire. Indeed, food is at its heart a form of cultural heritage and ways of making and eating it are often passed down from one generation to another. Moreover, bread, its production, and its consumption are frequently imbued with symbolism and entangled in belief systems. Chapter 2 begins with an analysis of domestic bread production that is grounded in kinship and cultural units, such as *tannūr*-style ovens in North Africa and Spain, or clay-chamber ovens in central Europe. Following the second century BCE, ovens across the western Mediterranean homogenize, moving toward the familiar domed, masonry ovens, but there are also indications that local traditions continued to inform the baking process, such as clay ovens used in Roman forts on the *limes* or the continued use of *tannūr*-style ovens in parts of North Africa.

None of this is to say that nothing can be derived from a broader, synthetic analysis of commercial baking, particularly one informed by models of production from other time periods. Roman bakeries tend to combine milling and baking, a habit later abandoned in the Middle Ages, and they tend to be small spaces, no more than one or two rooms. There are also anomalies, such as the bakeries at Ostia and certain other large cities, which are massive bread factories with up to eight millstones and as many mixers. The ovens in Ostia's bakeries can be over 5 m in diameter. This, in itself, is not a new observation, but what has been lacking in previous analyses is a means of interpreting the dichotomous nature of this evidence. In Chap. 3, the different types of bread production are recast as 'modes of production' per the Marxist legacy of social historical materialism in archaeological thought.[79] Combined with comparanda from the Industrial Revolution, different modes of production are deployed to expand our conceptualization of 'the bakery' beyond process to include the relationship of production to dichotomies such as home and work, family and workforce, and craftsman and businessman. The modern data are derived from nineteenth century New Jersey largely because the state kept methodical records of the employers' names and the number of employees and their genders, but also because many of the structures still exist or were meticulously documented by surveyors.[80] Most bakeries in nineteenth century New Jersey were small-scale producers, but there was also a small number of mass-producers who employed hundreds in factories. The small workshops were clearly grounded in families, supplemented by a few employees, and their successes were predicated on the skill and charisma of the 'master craftsman.' The factories, on the other hand, were conceptually removed from both the home and the family. Their owners had no social ties or obligations to their employees, who were often poor and vulnerable. The evidence from Roman cities, both large and small, parallels many of the phenomena in both modern workshops and factories, particularly the relationships between home and work and the family and workforce.

Much of the documentation of New Jersey's bakeries comes in the form of fines and regulations, focusing on the housing and treatment of workers and the employment of children. Scholars of craftsmanship, such as Richard Sennett, have identified the growing distance between businessman and laborer or household and workspace in the shift from workshop production to factory production as one of the leading causes of exploitation of labor.[81] Chapter 4 uses the modes of production deployed in Chap. 3 to explore the evidence for exploitation and violence in the Roman bakery. The evidence for this inequality has been identified before, most comprehensively by Boudewijn Sirks, but he made no effort to parse the various phenomena, such as mistreatment of slaves versus the abduction and forced labor of free people, nor how such phenomena would align with different types of production.[82] The modes facilitate this discussion and allow one to begin providing context and meaning to such anecdotes, whether it be the impersonal systemic oppression of a businessman or the very personal brutality of a cruel master craftsman.

Chapter 5 incorporates evidence for voluntary associations of bakers from the eastern Mediterranean to help explore the evidence for collectivity among Roman bakers in the west. In the study of voluntary associations of Roman craftsmen, *collegia* have loomed large.[83] These formal trade associations are not, however, ubiquitous and it is unclear whether they played an important role in determining training standards.[84] Moreover, there is no reason to assume that phenomena such as cooperation, shared risk management, and collectivity writ large could not have existed outside the presence of formal trade associations and *collegia*. In fact, we have some good evidence that some forms of collectivity did exist independent of formal associations, including *rogatores* inscriptions[85] and collective fines of *pistores*[86] in places where we have no evidence for *collegia*. Small-town collectivity of bakers took a very different form and function than the associations of large cities; members tended to be more homogenously modest in their means and their aims were more about managing social perceptions and providing social benefits for the bakers than creating opportunity or mitigating operating costs.

In the sixth chapter, I explore how the workshop bakers and bread factory owners presented themselves to the public and how they constructed not only a collective identity but also a communal ideology. Chapter 6 relies heavily on the iconography commissioned by commercial bakers for their tombs, shop signs, and visual culture in general. In the past, such iconography has largely been read as a document of workshop activity, but such images are in fact visual expressions of how the bakers wanted to be perceived, what they valued about their occupations, and what they aspired to for themselves and their progeny. As such they offer unique evidence, not for what bakers did or how they lived, but for what they believed. Consistent with the reliance of the workshop bakeries of Newark on the skill and charisma of the master craftsman, the iconography of Roman commercial bakers in small urban centers tends to focus on the quality of their work and their family. Similarly, in the iconographic evidence from large Roman urban centers where factory-like bakeries existed, one sees not only larger compositions, such as the famous tomb of the bakery Eurysaces, but also a strong emphasis on management, expression of status, and trustworthiness.

In concluding remarks, the lessons learned from each chapter are deployed to address the question of the middle class, reinvigorated by Emanuel Mayer. At the heart of the debate is whether class and social mobility are useful ways to frame our understanding of sub-elites in the ancient world. Craftsmanship and trade certainly produced profits and some of that wealth was accumulated by sub-elites, but class also carries with it the connotation of solidarity and class consciousness. Criticisms of Mayer's methods and conclusions abound, but the questions he poses are having a lasting effect. One of the more structural critiques of class analysis, at least when applied to the Roman world, has been that it treats Roman sub-elites as a monolith, ignoring their prosaic nature. Bakers, as commercial actors, offer an interesting opportunity to examine – at a detailed level – the lives of Romans who were neither social elite, nor poor and destitute, revealing some of that rich diversity that comprised ancient society, particularly among sub-elites.

Notes

1. Heinrich (2019, 102).
2. Juvenal *Sat.* 5.74–5.
3. Moritz (1958, 153); Martial IX.2.4; Petronius 64.8.
4. Verboven (2002), Tran (2006), Venticinque (2016) and Ellis (2018).
5. Monteix (2009, 2010, 2016), Flohr (2013), Mauné et al. (2013), Salido Domínguez et al. (2014), and Amraoui (2017).
6. Silver 2009; Broekaert 2012; Hawkins 2016.
7. *ar-to-po-qo*. Arto- (bread) -poqos (maker). Chadwick (1970, 91) and Ventris and Chadwick (1973, 130).
8. *ILAlg-02-01*, 3181.
9. *CIL* IV 10150.
10. *CIL* XIII 8255.
11. *CIL* VI 1739.
12. *CIL* IV 677.
13. *CIL* XIV 2302.
14. *CIL* XIII 8338.

15. *Didyma* 438.
16. *IG* I^3 546.
17. *IG* II^2 10.
18. *IG* II^2 1707.
19. Lefebvre, *IGChrEg* 3.
20. *P.Cair.Masp.* II 67147.
21. *SEG* 33, 1165.
22. *AE* 1993, 1139.
23. *ID* 456.
24. *P.Oxy.* 1899.
25. Sirks (1991).
26. Fujisawa (1995) and Liu (2008).
27. Moritz (1958, 1–74).
28. The continued use of hopper rubbers in the third century is to be expected; there is evidence that they continue to be used in some places well into the first century BCE. Williams-Thorpe (1988, 256).
29. Leroi-Gourhan (1964, 164).
30. Ingold (2007, 2).
31. There are, of course, other traditions of tracing series of procedures. Carl Knappett (2012, 196–7) identifies two inferential frameworks from within 'materiality' studies: behavioral chains and *chaînes opératoires*. Knappett sees the distinction between the two schools of thought as breaking down on geographic (and linguistic) lines. Behavior chains dominate in the Anglophone literature of the United States and *chaînes opératoires*, as the name might suggest, is the product of Francophone scholarship in France. David and Kramer (2001, 140–1), on the other hand, see the difference between behavioral chains and *chaînes opératoires* as an epistemological difference. Behavioral chains emerge from James O'Connell's 'behavioral ecology' (1995, 206), more in the determinist camp of archaeology, while *chaînes opératoires* comprise part of the French school of *technologie culturelle*, a somewhat more relativist tradition.
32. This is well-tread ground and does not require further exploration, see Robinson (2005) and Flohr (2013) for a discussion of early studies of Roman industries in Pompeii.
33. Mayeske (1972), Bakker (1999) and Curtis (2001).
34. Curtis (2001, 359).
35. Petersen (2006, 87).
36. Bakker (1999, 4–9).
37. Monteix (2016, 171); see also Monteix (2011, 2012, 2013, 2014, 2017).
38. Edwards (2007).
39. Moritz (1955).

40. Moritz (1958, 74–96).
41. Moritz (1958, 55, 79, and 91).
42. Jaccottey and Longepierre (2011) and Peacock and Cutler (2011).
43. De Vos et al. (2011).
44. Moritz (1958, 1–74) presents millstones chronologically, beginning with saddlequerns (fig. 2a and 3a) advancing unitl the donkey mill becomes the millstone "*par excellence*".
45. Frankel (2003).
46. Wefers (2011) and Walthall et al. (2018).
47. Akerraz and Lenoir (2002) and Ponsich (1974, 1979).
48. Peacock (1989).
49. De Vos et al. (2011, 142–143) and Amraoui (2017, 191).
50. Monteix (2010, 277).
51. Peacock (1980, 1989), Thorpe (1988), Thorpe and Thorpe (1990, 1993), Antonelli et al. (2000, 2001, 2010), Frankel (2003) and Jaccottey and Longepierre (2011).
52. Santi et al. (2013, 2015).
53. Thorpe and Thorpe (1990).
54. Antonelli et al. (2000, 2001).
55. Hamdy and Hadidi (2009, fig. 2).
56. Blümner (1912, 44 fig. 19).
57. Heinrich (2019, 105) observes that modern leavened bread contains artificially added gluten proteins, which make for a lighter more porous crumb, but fermentation, developing of glutens, and leavening were processes evident in the making of some Roman-period bread.
58. Pliny *Naturalis Historia* XVII.xxvi.102–4. Pliny (*Naturalis Historia* XVIII.xii.68) also describes the use of foam from the production of beer to leaven bread in Gaul and Hispania.
59. Thurmond (2006).
60. Heinrich (2019, 105).
61. Monteix (2016, 163).
62. Wilson and Schorle (2009).
63. Wilson, A., 2008. Dough-Kneaders. In J.P. Oleson (ed.), Engineering and technology in the Classical World. Oxford, 358.
64. Tréziny (2018, 264–266) (*Megara Hyblaea* 7).
65. Benton (2020).
66. Leduc (2008, 2011).
67. Edwards (2007, 218 and 239).
68. Edwards (2007, 218).
69. Monteix (2016, 164).
70. Edwards (2007, 14).
71. Banducci (2019, 43–44).

72. Campanella (2009, 469–98), Helas et al. (2011), 98–102, Russenberger (2016, 235–36) and Docter (2019, 447).
73. Monteix (2009, 331) and Rowan (2015, 2018). Concentrations of carbonized olive-pips were also found in the bakery in the Maison a la Citerne in the space behind the oven identified as storage by early excavators. Benton (2020).
74. Woolf (1998); Oltean (2008), Sinner (2015) and Haeussler (2016).
75. See Soressi and Geneste (2011) for a fuller discussion of the history of the approach.
76. Graves (1994, 440).
77. Murphy (2016, 143).
78. Brun (2016, 81).
79. Rosenswig and Cunningham (2017, 1–20).
80. New Jersey, Inspector of Factories and Workshops, 1889–1902; https://library.princeton.edu/libraries/firestone/rbsc/aids/sanborn/essex/newark.html
81. Sennett (2009).
82. Sirks (1991, appendix A).
83. Waltzing (1895–1900), Sirks (1991) and Tran (2006).
84. Liu (2005), Venticinque (2013) and Hawkins (2016).
85. Mouritsen (1988).
86. Ordóñez and Chamizo (2009).

References

Akerraz, A., and M. Lenoir. 2002. Instruments de broyage en Maurétanie Tingitane à l'époque romaine: Le cas de Volubilis. In H. Procopiou, R. Treuil (eds.), *Moudre et broyer. L'interprétation fonctionnelle de l'outil¬lage de mouture et de broyage dans la Préhistoire et l'Antiquité [actes de la Table ronde international "Moudre et broyer" qui s'est tenue à Clermond-Ferrand du 30 novembre au 2 dé cembre 1995*, 197–207. Paris: CNRS.

Amraoui, Touatia. 2017. *L'artisanat dans les cités antiques de l'Algérie: 1. siècle avant notre ère – 7. siècle après notre ère*. Oxford: Archaeopress.

Antonelli, Fabrizio, and Lorenzo Lazzarini. 2010. Mediterranean Trade of the Most Widespread Roman Volcanic Millstones from Italy and Petrochemical Markers of Their Raw Materials. *Journal of Archaeological Science* 37: 2081–2092.

Antonelli, F., G. Nappi, and L. Lazzarini. 2000. Sulla "pietra da mole" della regione di Orvieto: Caratterizzazione petrografica e studio archeometrico di macine storiche e protostoriche dall'Italia centrale. In *Proceedings of I Congresso Nazionale di Archeometria*, ed. M. Martini et al., 195–207. Patron Editore: Verona.

———. 2001. Roman Millstones from Orvieto (Italy): Petrographic and Geochemical Data for a New Archaeometric Contribution. *Archaeometry* 43 (2): 167–189.

Bakker, Jan Theo. 1999. *The Mills-Bakeries of Ostia: Description and Interpretation*. Amsterdam: J.C. Gieben.

Banducci, L.M. 2019. Material Evidence on Diet, Cooking and Techniques. In *The Routledge Handbook of Diet and Nutrition in the Roman World*, ed. Paul Erdkamp and Claire Holleran, 36–50. London: Routledge, Taylor & Francis Group.

Benton, J. 2020. The Social Construction of Roman Industrial Space: The Limits of Chaînes Opératoires and the Nature of Roman Baking. In *Designating Place. Archaeological Perspectives on Built Environments in Ostia and Pompeii*, ed. Kamermans, H., and L.B. van der Meer, 153–167. Leiden: Leiden University Press.

Blümner, Hugo. 1912. *Technologie und Terminologie der Gewerbe und Künste bei Griechen und Römern*. Leipzig: B.G. Teubner.

Broekaert, W. 2012. Vertical Integration in the Roman Economy. *Ancient Society* 42: 109–125.

Brun, J.-P. 2016. The Archaeology of Ancient Urban Workshops in Southern Italy: A French Approach? In *Urban Craftsmen and Traders in the Roman World*, ed. A. Wilson and M. Flohr, 77–94. Oxford: Oxford University Press.

Campanella, L. 2009. "I forni, i fornelli e i bracieri fenici e punici." In *Nora: il foro romano: storia di un'area urbana dall'età fenicia alla tarda antichità, 1997–2006, Volume II.1*, a cura di Jacopo Bonetto, Andrea Raffaele Ghiotto, Marta Novello, and Giovanna Falezza, 469–597. Padova: Università degli Studi di Padova – Dipartimento di Archeologia.

Chadwick, John. 1970. *The Decipherment of Linear B*. Cambridge: University Press.

Curtis, Robert I. 2001. *Ancient Food Technology*. Leiden: Brill.

David, Nicholas, and Carol Kramer. 2001. *Ethnoarchaeology in Action*. New York: Cambridge University Press.

de Vos, M., R. Attoui, and M. Andreoli. 2011. Hand and 'Donkey' mills in North African Farms. In *Bread for the People: The Archaeology of Mills and Milling: Proceedings of a Colloquium Held in the British School at Rome*, ed. David Franklyn Williams and David P.S. Peacock, 131–150. Oxford: Archaeopress.

Docter, Roald. 2019. Residential architecture. In *The Oxford handbook of the Phoenician and Punic Mediterranean*, ed. Brian R. Doak and Carolina López-Ruiz, 435–452. New York: Oxford University Press.

Edwards, W.P. 2007. *The Science of Bakery Products*. Cambridge: Royal Society of Chemistry.

Ellis, S.J.R. 2018. *The Roman Retail Revolution: The Socio-Economic World of the Taberna*. Oxford: Oxford University Press.

Flohr, M. 2013. *The World of the Fullo*. Oxford: Oxford University Press.
Frankel, Rafael. 2003. The Olynthus Mill, Its Origin, and Diffusion: Typology and Distribution. *American Journal of Archaeology* 107 (1): 1–21.
Fujisawa, A. 1995. I 'Pistores' nel Primo Impero. *Acme* 48 (2): 169–181.
Graves, P.M. 1994. My Strange Quest for Leroi-Gourhan. *Antiquity* 68: 457–460.
Haeussler, R. 2016. *Becoming Roman? Diverging Identities and Experiences in Ancient Northwest Italy*. London: Routledge.
Hamdy, R.S., and E.N.M.N. Hadidi. 2009. *"Identification of plant materials used in the coiled basketry collection at the agricultural museum (Giza, Egypt)", windows on the African past: Current approaches to African Archaeobotany*. London: Reports in African Archaeology.
Hawkins, Cameron. 2016. *Roman Artisans and the Urban Economy*. Cambridge: Cambridge University Press.
Heinrich, F. 2019. Cereals and Bread. In *The Routledge Handbook of Diet and Nutrition in the Roman World*, ed. Paul Erdkamp and Claire Holleran, 101–114. London: Routledge, Taylor & Francis Group.
Helas, S., O. Hofmeister, A. Werner, J. Schumann, G. Zuchtriegel, and G. Mammina. 2011. *Selinus II. Die punische Stadt auf der Akropolis*. Wiesbaden: Reichert.
Hoyos, B.D. 2010. *The Carthaginians*. Milton Park: Routledge.
Ingold, Tim. 2007. Materials Against Materiality. *Archaeological Dialogues* 14 (1): 1–16.
Jaccottey, L., and S. Longepierre. 2011. Pompeian Millstones in France. In *Bread for the People: The Archaeology of Mills and Milling: Proceedings of a Colloquium Held in the British School at Rome, 2009*, ed. D.F. Williams and David Peacock, 97–116. Oxford: Archaeopress.
Knappett, C. 2012. Materiality. In *Archaeological Theory Today*, ed. Ian Hodder, 176–195. Polity: Cambridge.
Leduc, M. 2008. Les Pistrina Volubilitains, Temoins Majeurs du Dynamisme Economique Municipal. In *L'Africa Romana. Le Ricchezze dell'Africa Risorse, Produzioni, Scambi. Atti del XVII Convegno di Studio. Sevilla, 14–17 Dicembre 2006*, 475–505. Rome: Carocci.
———. 2011. L'artisanat au Coeur de la ville: l'exemple des pistrina de Volubilis. In *La ville au quotidien: regards croisés sur l'habitat et l'artisanat antiques: Afrique du Nord, Gaule et Italie: actes du colloque international, Maison méditerranéenne des sciences de l'homme, Aix-en-Provence, 23 et 24 novembre 2007*, ed. Souen Fontaine, Stéphanie Satre, and Amel Tekki, 181–189. Aix-en-Provence: Publications de l'Université de Provence.
Leroi-Gourhan, A. 1964. *Le Geste et la Parole – I. Technique et langage*. Paris: Albin Michel.
Liu, J. 2005. *Occupation, Social Organization, and Public Service in the Collegia Centonariorum in the Roman Empire (First Century BC-Fourth Century AD)*. Ann Arbor: University of Michigan Press.

———. 2008. Pompeii and *Collegia*: A new appraisal of the evidence. *The Ancient History Bulletin* 22 (1–2): 53–69.

Mauné, S., N. Monteix, and M. Poux. 2013. *Cuisines et boulangeries en Gaule romaine. Gallia*. Paris: Revue Gallia, CNRS Editions.

Mayeske, Betty Jo B. 1972. Bakeries, Bakers, and Bread at Pompeii: A Study in Social and Economic History. Ph.D. dissertation, Ann Arbor.

Monteix, N. 2009. Pompéi, Pistrina – Recherches sur les boulangeries de l'Italie romaine. *Les Mélanges de l'École française de Rome* 121 (1): 323–335.

———. 2010. *Les lieux de métier: boutiques et ateliers d'Herculanum. Collection du Centre Jean Bérard, 34*. Rome: École française de Rome.

———. 2011. "Pompéi, Pistrina—Recherches sur les boulangeries de l'Italie romaine." en collaboration avec S. Aho, A. Coutelas, L. Garnier, V. Matterne-Zeck, S. Zanella. *Les Mélanges de l'École française de Rome* 123, 1: 306–313.

———. 2012. "Pompéi, Pistrina—Recherches sur les boulangeries de l'Italie romaine." en collaboration avec S. Aho, L. Garnier, C. Hartz, É. Letellier, S. Zanella. *Chroniques des activités archéologiques de l'École française de Rome.*

———. 2013. "Pompéi, Pistrina: Recherches sur les boulangeries de l'Italie romaine." *Chroniques des activités archéologiques de l'École française de Rome.*

———. 2014. "Pompéi, Pistrina. Recherches sur les boulangeries de l'Italie romaine." en collaboration avec S. Aho, A. Coutelas, S. Zanella. *Chroniques des activités archéologiques de l'École française de Rome.*

———. 2016. Contextualizing the Operational Sequence: Pompeian Bakeries as a Case Study. In *Urban Craftsmen and Traders in the Roman World*, ed. Miko Flohr and Andrew Wilson, 153–182. Oxford: Oxford University Press.

———. 2017. Urban Production and the Pompeian Economy. In *The Economy of Pompeii*, ed. Miko Flohr and Andrew Wilson, 209–2242. Oxford: Oxford University Press.

Moritz, L.A. 1955. Corn. *Classical Quarterly* 5 (3–4): 135–141.

———. 1958. *Grain-Mills and Flour in Classical Antiquity*. Oxford: Clarendon Press.

Mouritsen, H. 1988. *Elections, Magistrates, and Municipal Elite: Studies in Pompeian Epigraphy*. Rome: L'Erma di Bretschneider.

Murphy, E.A. 2016. Roman Workers and Their Workplaces: Some Archaeological Thoughts on the Organization of Workshop Labour in Ceramic Production. In *Work, Labour, and Professions in the Roman World*, ed. K. Verboven and C. Laes, 133–146. Boston: Brill.

Oltean, I.A. 2008. *Dacia: Landscape, Colonisation, and Romanisation*. New York: Routledge.

Ordóñez Agulla, S., and J.C. Saquete Chamizo. 2009. Una Dedicacion Votiva *ex mvltis pistorvm* hallada en la Betica. *Habis* 40: 197–204.

Peacock, D.P.S. 1980. The Roman Millstone Trade: A Petrological Sketch. *World Archaeology* 12 (1): 43–53.

———. 1989. The Mills of Pompeii. *Antiquity* 63: 205–214.
Peacock, D.P.S., and L. Cutler. 2011. The Earliest Rotary Querns in Southern England. In *Bread for the People: The Archaeology of Mills and Milling: Proceedings of a Colloquium Held in the British School at Rome, 4th–7th November 2009*, ed. D.F. Williams and David Peacock, 77–80. Oxford: Archaeopress.
Petersen, L.H. 2006. *The Freedman in Roman Art and Art History*. New York: Cambridge University Press.
Ponsich, M. 1974. *Implantation rurale antique sur la Bas-Guadalquivir I*. Madrid: Casa De Velázquez.
———. 1979. *Implantation rurale antique sur la Bas-Guadalquivir II*. Parigi: Casa De Velázquez.
Robinson, D. 2005. Re-thinking the Social Organisation of Trade and Industry in First Century A.D. Pompeii. In *Roman Working Lives and Urban Living*, ed. A. MacMahon and J. Price, 88–105. Oxford: Oxbow Books.
Rosenswig, R.M., and J.J. Cunningham. 2017. *Modes of Production and Archaeology*. Gainesville: University Press of Florida.
Rowan, Erica. 2015. Olive Oil Pressing Waste as a Fuel Source in Antiquity. *American Journal of Archaeology* 119 (4): 465–482.
———. 2018. Sustainable Fuel Practices in Roman North Africa and the Contemporary Mediterranean Basin. *Interdisciplinaria archaeologica* IX (2): 147–156.
Russenberger, C. 2016. Punier am Berg. Archäologische Szenarien punischer Präsenz im Binnenland des frühhellenistischen Westsizilien am Beispiel des Monte Iato. In *Karthago Dialoge. Karthago und der punische Mittelmeerraum–Kulturkontakte und Kulturtransfers im 1. Jahrtausend vor Christus*, ed. F. Schön and H. Töpfer, 227–251. Tübingen: Eberhard Karls Universität Tübingen.
Salido Domínguez, J., M. Bustamante Álvarez, and E. Gijón Gabriel. 2014. *Pistrina Hispaniae: panaderías, molinerías y el artesanado alimentario en la Hispania Romana*. Montagnac: Editions Monique Mergoil.
Santi, P., A. Renzulli, and R. Gullo. 2013. Archaeometric study of the hopper-rubber and rotary Morgantina-type volcanic millstones of the Greek and Roman periods found in the Aeolian archipelago (southern Italy). *European Journal of Mineralogy* 25: 39–52.
———. 2015. The volcanic millstones from the archaeological site of Morgantina (Sicily): Provenance and evolution of the milling techniques in the Mediterranean area. *Archaeometry* 57: 803–821.
Sennett, R. 2009. *The Craftsman*. New Haven: Yale University Press.
Silver, M. 2009. Glimpses of Vertical Integration/Disintegration in Ancient Rome. *Ancient Society* 39: 171–184.

Sinner, A. 2015. Cultural Contacts and Identity Construction: A Colonial Context in NE Spain (2nd–early 1st c. B.C.). *Journal of Roman Archaeology* 28: 7–37.

Sirks, A.J.B. 1991. *Food for Rome: The Legal Structure of the Transportation and Processing of Supplies for the Imperial Distributions in Rome and Constantinople*. Amsterdam: J.C. Gieben.

Soressi, Marie, and Jean-Michel Geneste. 2011. The History and Efficacy of the Chaîne Opératoire Approach to Lithic Analysis: Studying Techniques Toreveal Past Societies Inanevolutionary Perspective. *PaleoAnthropology*: 334–350.

Sparkes, B.A. 1962. The Greek Kitchen. *The Journal of Hellenic Studies* 82: 121–137.

———. 1981. Not Cooking, but Baking. *Greece & Rome* 28: 172–178.

Thorpe, O.W. 1988. Provenancing and Archaeology of Roman Millstones from the Mediterranean Area. *Journal of Archaeological Science* 15: 253–305.

Thorpe, O.W., and R.S. Thorpe. 1990. Millstone Provenancing used in tracing the route of a fourth-century BC Greek merchant ship. *Archaeometry* 32: 115–137.

———. 1993. Geochemistry and Trade of Eastern Mediterranean Millstones from the Neolithic to Roman Periods. *Journal of Archaeological Science* 20: 263–320.

Thurmond, David L. 2006. *A Handbook of Food Processing in Classical Rome: For Her Bounty No Winter*. Leiden: Brill.

Tran, N. 2006. *Les membres des associations romaines: le rang social des collegiati en Italie et en Gaules, sous le Haut-Empire*. Rome: École Française de Rome.

———. 2016. Ars and doctrina: The Socioeconomic Identity of Roman Skilled Workers (First Century BC-Third Century AD). In *Work, Labour, and Professions in the Roman World*, ed. K. Verboven and C. Laes, 133–146. Boston: Brill.

Tréziny, H. 2018. *Mégara Hyblaea. 7, 7*. Rome: École française de Rome.

Venticinque, P. 2013. Matters of Trust: Associations and Social Capital in Roman Egypt. *Center for Hellenic Studies Research Bulletin* 1: 2.

———. 2016. *Honor Among Thieves: Craftsmen, Merchants, and Associations in Roman and Late Roman Egypt*. Ann Arbor: University of Michigan Press.

Ventris, Michael, and John Chadwick. 1973. *Documents in Mycenaean Greek: Three Hundred Selected Tablets from Knossos, Plyos, and Mycenae with Commentary and Vocabulary*. Cambridge: Cambridge University Press.

Verboven, K. 2002. *The Economy of Friends: Economic Aspects of Amicitia and Patronage in the Late Republic*. Brussels: Editions Latomus.

Walthall, A., T. Souza, J. Benton, E. Wueste, and A. Tharler. 2018. Preliminary Report on the 2015 Field Season of the American Excavations at Morgantina: Contrada Agnese Project (CAP). *FastiOnLine Documents & Research* 408: 1–23.

Waltzing, J.-P. 1895–1900. *Étude historique sur les corporations professionnelles chez les Romains depuis les origines jusqu'à la chute de l'Empire d'Occident*, 4 vols. Louvain: Peeters.

Wefers, S. 2011. Still Using Your Saddle Quern? A Compilation of the Oldest Known Rotary Querns in Western Europe. In *Bread for the People: The Archaeology of Mills and Milling: Proceedings of a Colloquium Held in the British School at Rome, 4th–7th November 2009*, ed. D.F. Williams and David Peacock, 67–76. Oxford: Archaeopress.

Wilson, A. 2008. Large-Scale Manufacturing, Standardization, and Trade. In *The Oxford Handbook of Engineering and Technology in the Classical World*, ed. J.P. Oleson, 393–417. Oxford: Oxford University Press.

Wilson, A., and K. Schorle. 2009. A Baker's Funerary Relief from Rome. *Papers of the British School at Rome* 77: 101–123.

Woolf, G. 1998. *Becoming Roman: The origins of provincial civilization in Gaul.* Cambridge: Cambridge University Press.

CHAPTER 2

Baking as Cultural Heritage: Regional Variation in the Roman Production of Bread

The study of ancient production and craftsmanship is often viewed through the lens of the better preserved—and studied—evidence from central Italy, often within the false dichotomy of domestic versus commercial production. Publications about Roman industries of all kinds will frequently reference the workshops of Pompeii or Ostia as touchstones for understanding the material remains of similar industries in other places, even as far away as France or Spain.[1] The workshops in the central Italian cities are, in fact, much better preserved and more thoroughly studied than most places in the Mediterranean, but several assumptions underwrite this method: first, that craftsmanship and production are universal across the Mediterranean; and second, that better preserved remains at Pompeii and Ostia can fill in the blanks, so to speak, for the less well preserved workshops in other places. Over the last few decades, through the work of Greg Woolf and others, it has become increasingly clear that local, pre-Roman traditions played a greater role in determining regional habits and material culture than previous scholarship recognized.[2] There is no reason we should assume pre-Roman traditions were not informing commercial baking in every part of the empire, as this chapter shows; in fact, the evidence demonstrates that these pre-Roman traditions often informed the habits of later commercial bakers even if there is evidence for acculturation leading into the Roman period.

One of the other major assumptions that pervades scholarship about Roman baking—and production of all sorts—is that there existed a neat division between those who produced commercially and those that made

J. T. Benton, *The Bread Makers*,
https://doi.org/10.1007/978-3-030-46604-6_2

bread exclusively for household use. The reality of bread production was far more convoluted. For one thing, much bread sold commercially may have been household surplus sold locally as a side hustle to earn a bit of additional income. But the commercial baking of bread almost certainly grew out of household traditions, leading to high levels of variation in baking practices. Viewing households and families as central to baking practices helps us account for variation in the industry in general; the varieties of bread produced by humans are innumerable and no two cultures view bread in exactly the same way. Bread and its preparation, it has been observed, were ways in which ethnicity was constructed, performed and reinforced within such a multicultural world.[3] Moreover, bread is often imbued with symbolic meaning and the foodstuff can itself can be critical to funerary or religious rites. But it is not only the loaf that is culturally specific; the acts of making and consuming bread are also part of this performance of identity and belief. In this chapter, the production of bread is reconceived as a form cultural heritage, knowledge and traditions passed from one generation to the next, rather than as sterile pragmatic decisions. But like many things in the Roman world, local traditions were negotiated within the context of homogenizing forces, such as contact between cultural groups, inter-regional trade, or the political unity of belonging to an empire. A diachronic analysis of baking habits, region by region, reveals not only the pre-Roman traditions, but also how they continued to inform bakers and bakeries under the Roman Empire and into the end of antiquity.

The chapter consists of two parts, beginning with a discussion of pre-Roman baking among the various peoples of what will later become the western Roman Empire. In the second half of the chapter, the legacy of pre-Roman traditions is explored in the Roman-period evidence for commercial baking, region by region. Five broad regions are examined: Italy, Central North Africa, Western North Africa, the Iberian Peninsula, and the Northern Provinces (Gaul, Germania, and Britannia). These regions are in part artificial, but they are also reflections of shared or parallel histories and differences in technology and workshop operation. Even if the thrust of this study is the variation in baking traditions, there are some commonalities that allow for some broad discussion of trends. Commercialization of baking was coeval with Roman conquest and the homogenization of baking technology. The city and the family emerge as the two units of organization that determined the nature of commercial baking in workshops and across regions.

Pre-Roman Baking Traditions

The Tannūr *and Rotary Quern: The Phoenician Expanse to the West*

For the pre-Roman populations of the southern half of the Mediterranean, most bread was probably unleavened and it was, for the most part, baked in an upright, vertical aperture terracotta vessel or oven known by a variety of modern names, including the *tannūr* (Fig. 2.1). Modern iterations of this baking tradition persist throughout North Africa and the Arabian Peninsula. A variety of terracotta votive figurines depict the use of the *tannūr*, including sixth-century examples from the necropolis of Borj-el-Jedid in Tunisia and from a tomb at Megara Hyblaea (Fig. 1.12).[4] An adult figure leans over the pot and a smaller figure, perhaps a child, aids in the process. The scene almost certainly depicts domestic production of flatbread and similar figurines are known from Cyprus and Turkey.[5] Such ovens take a variety of forms, but in general their shape is cylindrical,

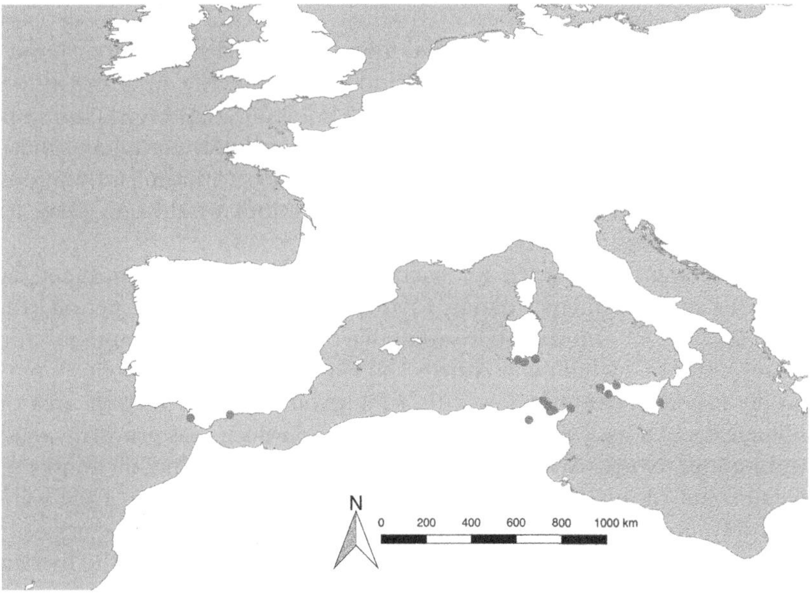

Fig. 2.1 Pre-Roman Communities with *Tannūr*-style Ovens in the Western Mediterranean (not a complete dataset)

broad at the base, and narrower at the top with an aperture of 70–100 cm.[6] The lower part serves as a combustion chamber; it is ventilated by a draft hole at the base of the oven. The upper part is the cooking space of the flatbreads. The *tannūr* works by baking unleavened bread dough, which is pressed against the inside walls of a large vessel and baked by coals or fire at the bottom of the *tannūr*.

The *tannūr*-style oven is attested early in the archaeological record, already in use in the Bronze Age and found in almost every house of the fourteenth century BCE workmen's village at Amarna.[7] How flat breads and *tannūr*-style ovens arrived in the western Mediterranean region is unclear, but should probably be taken case by case because there are at least three different possibilities. Recent genetic studies argue that peoples from the east migrated westward, possibly from the Near East, as early as 23,000 years ago, but that migration was pre-agricultural; fixed ovens seem like a possible, but unlikely, trait for such peoples to have brought to western and central North Africa. The lack of pre-Roman *tannūrs* in Morocco or western Algeria dating before the eighth century CE suggests that the oven was introduced later.[8] There was another migration in the seventh and eighth centuries BCE when Punic or Phoenician peoples expanded their influence to the west, founding Carthage and surely bringing traditions with them, baking included.[9] Finally, the Arab expansion westward in the seventh century CE could bring different bread traditions as well. None of these are mutually exclusive; one culture bringing similar baking habits to a new area might find communities with similar traditions more hospitable and in these cases, their traditions would only serve to reinforce pre-existing ones.

Archaeological evidence for such technologies have been found at Dougga and Kerkouane, dating to the so-called Numidian period (ca. 200–40 BCE).[10] *Tannūr*-style ovens have been found throughout the Mediterranean, including at Athens and Corinth, but they are most commonly found in communities with a Punic history or in a Punic area of influence, such as Cyprus, Southern Spain, Sardinia, eastern Sicily, and throughout North Africa.[11] Such ovens have been found in houses at Selinus and Monte Iato, both of which had Punic histories. They were probably introduced, like many things, to the Greeks by the Phoenicians.[12] Some have also been found in communities in the very south of the Iberian Peninsula at Cadiz and Cerra del Villar.[13]

The *tannūr* was not the only technology that Punic peoples proliferated around the western Mediterranean; they also seem to have invented the rotary action quern, small millstones that ground grain into flour through manual rotary action (Fig. 1.3).[14] The earliest known example was found at Carthage in a sixth-century context.[15] The stone employed was not the porous volcanic basalt that would be favored later, but rather a local limestone. It has been suggested that the rotary action of Punic mills and the use of porous basalt of the Greek hopper rubbers (see introduction for discussion of millstone types) led to the innovation of the so-called Morgantina millstone, the earliest example of which was found near a fourth-century shipwreck off the coast of Mallorca and sourced to Sardinia.[16]

Earthen Chamber Ovens and the La-Tène Culture

Baking in central Europe has largely been examined in terms of Gaul and two general narratives prevail about pre-Roman cereal processing there. Greg Woolf has suggested that the adoption of Pompeian red ware pottery signified the switch from the consumption of grain in the form of porridge to its consumption as bread.[17] Pliny the Elder, on the other hand, says that the peoples of Gaul and Spain brewed a drink from grain (beer), the foam of which they employed as a leaven for their bread, suggesting not only that the Gauls made bread, but also that it was leavened.[18] Pliny, as an officer in the army, may well have known such things first-hand, but his account—and perspective—is that of an outsider; he is probably describing his own time and not pre-Roman Gaul. But Woolf's hypothesis is also fraught with problems. First, it is unclear why *terra sigillata* ware would make good proxy data for the consumption of bread. Second, it is not established that pre-Roman populations in Gaul preferred porridge to baked breads. Much recent work on baking in Gaul during the pre-Roman and Roman periods has begun to define the nature of baking in the region under the Empire and to explore the role of pre-existing Gallic baking traditions in defining it.[19]

The pre-Roman baking traditions of central Europe should probably be understood within the context of the Urnfield/Hallstatt/La Tène culture. In central Europe during the Bronze and early Iron Ages, baking occurred in hearths, using earth and clay to create a chamber to bake unleavened bread loaves (Fig. 2.2).[20] A remarkably well preserved example, the Ovelgönne bread roll, has been dated the early Iron Age (900–600 BCE), associated with deposits of the Urnfield material culture (Fig. 2.3).[21] The loaf does not seem to have been leavened by artificially added yeasts, but

Fig. 2.2 Replica of a clay oven from the bronze age at the archaeological site in Nizna Mysla, Slovakia

it is a loaf. It was clearly baked on a hot surface because it has a crust below it and has wood charcoal inclusions in its underside.[22] Found in the fill of a small pit in a cave, with pieces of metal in it, the loaf has been seen as a ceremonial object rather than normal daily bread.[23] Similar loaves have been found in tombs in central European contexts, seemingly as votive offerings or as grave goods for the deceased and hearths often have a close association with funerary rites and tombs.[24] What remains unclear is the extent to which the loaves in ceremonial deposits or funerary contexts reflect the day-to-day bread eaten by normal people, but there is some clear indications that baking itself—and by extension the use of the oven—was an act of worship, which is corroborated by the elaborate decoration often evident on clay ovens and hearths.[25]

A fifth-century apsidal house excavated at Gailhan offers a unique window into early cereal processing in a pre-Roman household.[26] The house contained a modest kitchen, which included a small pit with concentrations of burnt grains and charcoal, in addition to burnt and fragmentary pottery. What exactly occurred to deposit the charcoal and carbonized

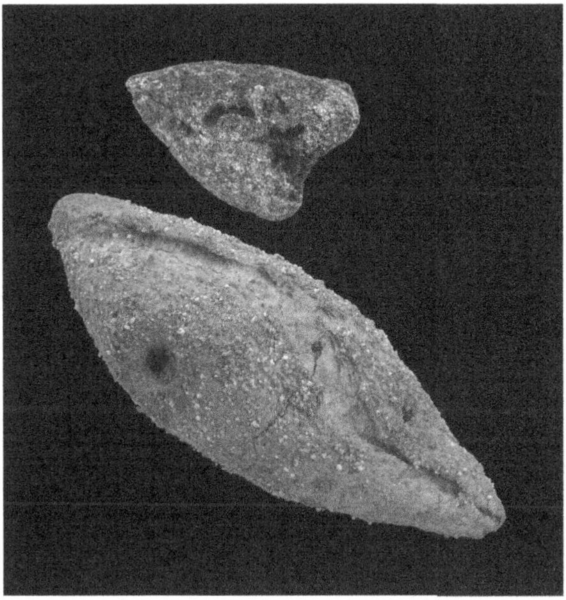

Fig. 2.3 The Ovelgönne Bread Loaf (courtesy of the Archäologisches Museum Hamburgund Stadtmuseum)

grain is unclear, but it does seem to suggest that cereal processing involved some form of baking, or at least toasting of grain, before consumption. There is, however, evidence at other La-Tène sites that suggests oven-like structures were carved into soil banks with super-structures of mud or adobe, some as far south as Sa Caleta in modern Spain (Fig. 2.4).[27] There is some speculation that these ovens were of the vertical-aperture *tannūrs*, rather than the horizontal types, suggesting contact between the La-Tène culture and the cultures of North Africa, which is not without historical corroboration. Michel Py, who did much of the early work on baking and industry in prehistoric France, equivocates on this point because the ovens are only preserved on their lowest elevation, but may have had domed or open tops.[28] However these round ovens were used, they were almost surely not used as *tannūrs* with flat dough slapped to the interior.

There were a variety of millstones available to the pre-Roman peoples of central Europe. The most common form is the simple and ubiquitous saddle quern, but hopper rubbers brought to the western Mediterranean on trade ships were also available. There is some indication that rotary

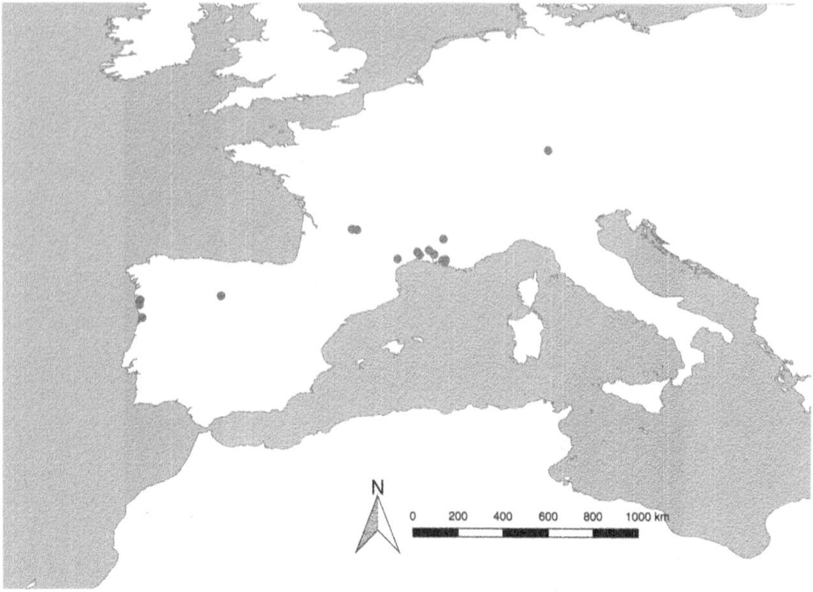

Fig. 2.4 Pre-Roman Communities with Attesting Earthen or Clay Ovens (not a complete dataset)

querns were also in use north of the Alps as early as the late Iron Age.[29] Early iterations of rotary querns dating to the sixth and fifth centuries BCE have been found along the Iberian coasts, which may suggest introduction by the Carthaginians, but there is a case to be made that the rotary querns were also used by the La-Tène inhabitants of the peninsula.[30] It may be that such mills were introduced into central Europe by contact with Punic peoples through the Iberian peninsula.

The Terracotta Baking Vessels in Italy and Magna Graecia

Tannūr ovens, despite their use on Sicily and Sardinia, were not the most common technology implemented on the Italian peninsula before the second century BCE. The *clibanus* or ἰπνός are much better attested in the Greek cities of southern Italy and the central Italian cities of Etruscan and Latin origin (Figs. 1.12 and 2.5). Although Pompeii and Ostia loom large in our understanding of commercial baking in Italy, there were clearly baking traditions, commercial and domestic, that continued to inform how

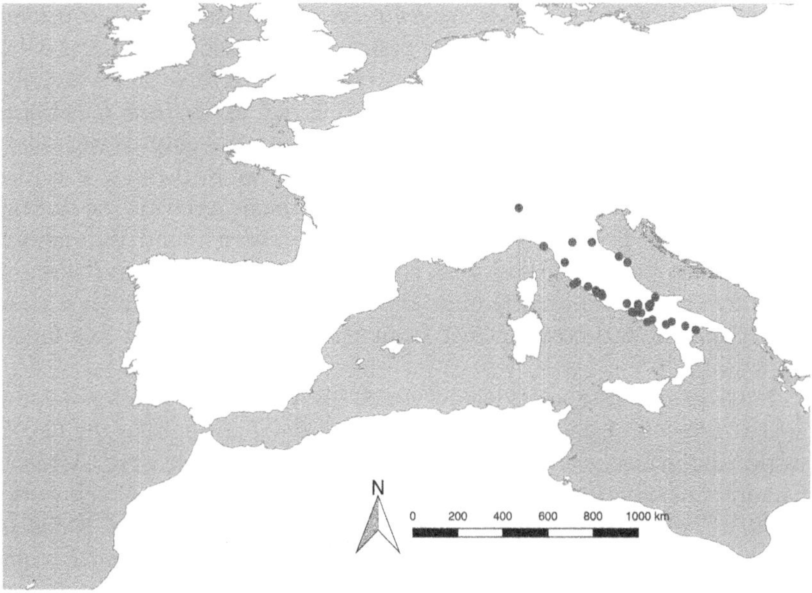

Fig. 2.5 Distribution of Testa and Clibani in the Pre-Roman and Early Roman Periods. (Adapted from Cubberley et al. 1988, fig. 3)

bread was made even as Rome went from a regional power to the capital of a pan-Mediterranean empire. The Italian peninsula was, as has been regularly commented, a multi-cultural region with Greeks to the south, Etruscans to the north, and Latin and Samnite populations in between. In the Bronze Age and early Iron Age, grain was milled with saddle querns and they continued to be used, probably in more domestic or rural contexts, even into the Roman period. The decline in the use of the saddle quern was precipitated by the advent of the Olynthus or hopper-rubber millstone. The earliest hopper-rubber millstone was found in a late fifth century context in Athens,[31] but by the fourth century, they were the most common millstone in Italy and Sicily, and common in many communities throughout the western Mediterranean.[32] Their presence is often equated with Greek communities or Hellenistic influence, but their use as ballast meant they were transported widely.

A variety of baking technologies appear to have been in use alongside the hopper rubber during the period from the fourth to the second century BCE. Cato, in his *de Agricultura*, refers to a method of baking bread under a pot (*sub testu*). The passage is brief and it is unclear what exactly is referred to here, but it is generally accepted that Cato is describing the use of technologies generally referred to as *testa* or *clibani* (Fig. 2.6). Loaves of dough are placed in such pots and covered with a lid. The entire vessel is then placed on coals, and covered by them, to bake the loaf. This method of baking bread, by whatever name, predates the Roman period; similar Bronze-Age technologies have been found throughout Italy, but also in Greece, Slovenia, and throughout the Balkans.[33] Even if the *sub testu* method persisted into the first century CE or later, it is clear that it and the technologies that facilitated it had their roots in a much earlier time.

In Greece, at least, small baking vessels likely led to the development of larger, terracotta baking devices which are known throughout the Greek world and which the Greeks probably called an ἰπνός (Fig. 1.12).[34] Examples of such technologies are known from around the Greek world and there are also depictions of their use in figurines and on vases. Nicholas Cahill, for instance, notes the presence of a large number of course wares in house A viii 8 at Olynthus, which he believes may have once been part of a large terracotta baking device, and one has been found Argilos.[35] Similar horizontal-aperture terracotta ovens have also been found in Etruscan contexts.[36] Both the actual remains of such technologies and the Tanagra figurines suggest that these larger terracotta baking devices were, at least initially, serving domestic purposes. This is not to say that a

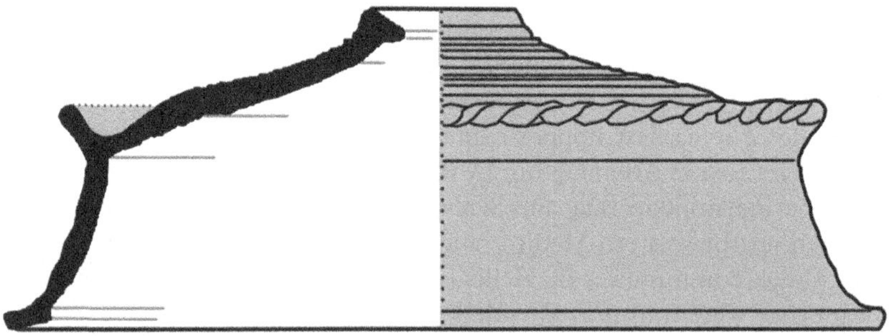

Fig. 2.6 A Line Drawing of a Clibanus. (After Cubberly et al. 1988, fig. 2)

household could not sell its surplus commercially, but that these technologies are largely found in spaces that are domestic in nature, rather than in shops.

Regional Baking under Rome

Italy and Sicily

The various terracotta baking technologies (*clibani*, ἰπνός, and *tannūrs*) continued to be used in Italy and on Sicily well into the first century BCE and even later in rural contexts. But they became extremely rare in urban ones following the first century BCE.[37] Some of our earliest possible material evidence for commercial baking in Italy comes, perhaps not surprisingly, from the Greek cities in the south. Recent excavations at Morgantina have revealed a building, interpreted by excavators as a modest house, which included an oven of shoddy masonry and two rotary millstones of the 'Morgantina' type.[38] Similar ovens are known elsewhere at Morgantina, including one installed in the North Baths after their abandonment.[39] A similar oven was found in a shop at Monte Iato by the Swedish team working there, although no millstones were found in that shop.[40]All of the ovens have been dated to the second half of the third century or the first half of the second century. An oven very similar to the ones found in the baths and the modest house can be found in a second-century shop southwest of the House of the Doric Capital on the hill east of Morgantina's agora (Fig. 2.7).[41] The same excavations found that the rotary millstones were in primary deposits on floors, while fragmentary hopper-rubber or 'Olynthus' millstones were always found in secondary deposits or reused in walls and floors. From this, excavators inferred that the rotary millstones were only being introduced to Morgantina during the third century BCE.

The first definitive bakery in Italy was also found in Sicily at Megara Hyblaea dating to the late second or early first century BCE (Fig. 2.8).[42] It contains a masonry oven much more elaborate than the rubble ovens at Morgantina and also has platforms that seem to have been used to raise rotary millstones, probably of the 'Morgantina' type. Furthermore, the bakery at Megara Hyblaea also contained a new technology, a mixer (*pétrin* in French) (Figs. 1.6 and 1.7). The bakery itself dates to the second or early first centuries BCE, making the mixer at Megara Hyblaea the earliest known example of such a technology in a workshop. By 20 BCE,

Fig. 2.7 Oven from Morgantina in a shop near the House of the Doric Capital. (Courtesy of Barbara Tsakirgis)

mixers appear on the Tomb of the Baker, Eurysaces, in Rome, both on the frieze depicting production and in the form of roundels decorating the sides.[43] The heavy emphasis of the mixer in the roundels has led a number of scholars to suggest that the mixer was a relatively recent innovation that Eurysaces' was touting.

Commercialization of baking in Italy dating to the second century BCE is not inconsistent with what ancient Romans themselves believed. Pliny states that there were no *pistores* (Latin for miller-bakers) in Rome until the war with King Perseus (171 BCE).[44] The earliest epigraphic and literary evidence in Latin offers further corroboration of a second-century date for commercialization of baking in Italy. The first mention of the word *pistor* in the collected body of Latin literature occurs in Plautus' *Asinaria*, ca. 200 BCE.[45] An inscription from Capua, dating to the late second century, attests a certain Marcus Ocratius, a freedman and *pistor*.[46] Fujisawa, among others, struggles with the discrepancy between a third or second century date for the specialization of commercial bakers and suggests that Pliny was referring to *pistores* as he knew them, miller-bakers,

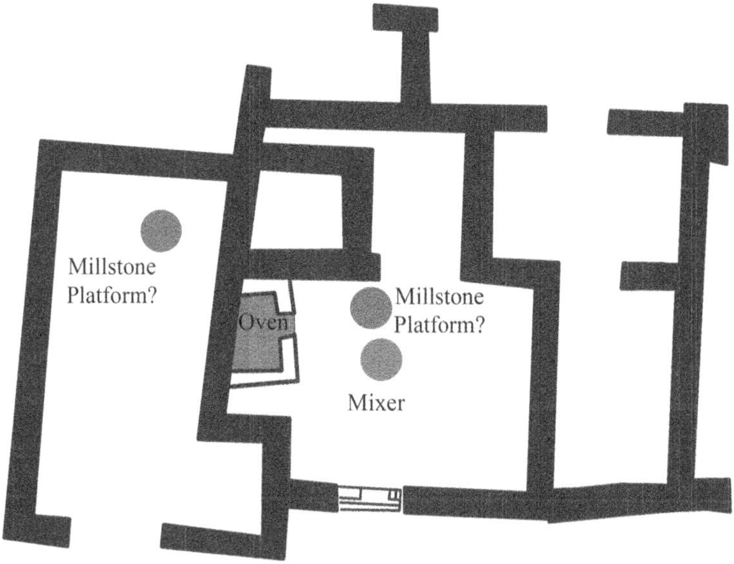

Fig. 2.8 Second-Century Bakery at Megara Hyblaea. (Modified from Tréziny 2018, fig. 393)

while the early incidence of the word in the *Asinaria* reflects an older definition suggested by the etymology of the word *pistor*, which derives from the word *pisere* or *pinsere* (to grind or mill).[47] This interpretation is refuted by the fact that Plautus writes, "*a pistore panem petimus*," indicating that at least some early *pistores* had already incorporated the production of bread into their repertoire. Pliny continues to explain that among the *quirites* of Rome's past, women baked the family's bread, an observation he bases on comparisons with contemporary non-Roman peoples.[48] This gendering of the domestic production of bread is almost certainly an oversimplification; modes of domestic production were probably as diverse as the families themselves and early terracotta figurines from the eastern Mediterranean, although not Roman, show women, men, and children all participating in the production of bread. Furthermore, the 30 years between Plautus plays and the war with King Perseus is not an irreconcilable period of time and it is very likely that the commercialization of baking occurred in Italian communities at different times, just as it occurred at different times in different regions of the Mediterranean.

Pompeii

For the first century CE, we have a great deal more information for commercial baking in Italy, though most of that information comes from Pompeii and Herculaneum. Betty Jo Mayeske identified 30 bakeries in Pompeii and one could probably question a few of the identifications or add to that number, but for the most part she identified the body of evidence for baking and bakeries at Pompeii (Fig. 2.9).[49] The actual number of commercial bakers and bakeries is hard to establish not only because the city is not fully excavated, but also because it is difficult to differentiate domestic bakeries from commercial ones and the distinction itself is probably a modern preoccupation more than a reality of ancient production.[50] Nicolas Monteix, picking up where Mayeske left off, shifts away from questions of domestic or commercial production and focuses instead on questions of production, process, and technology. He reconstructs the operational sequence of bread production in Pompeian bakeries.[51] He divides the various processes into three broad clusters of activities: (1)

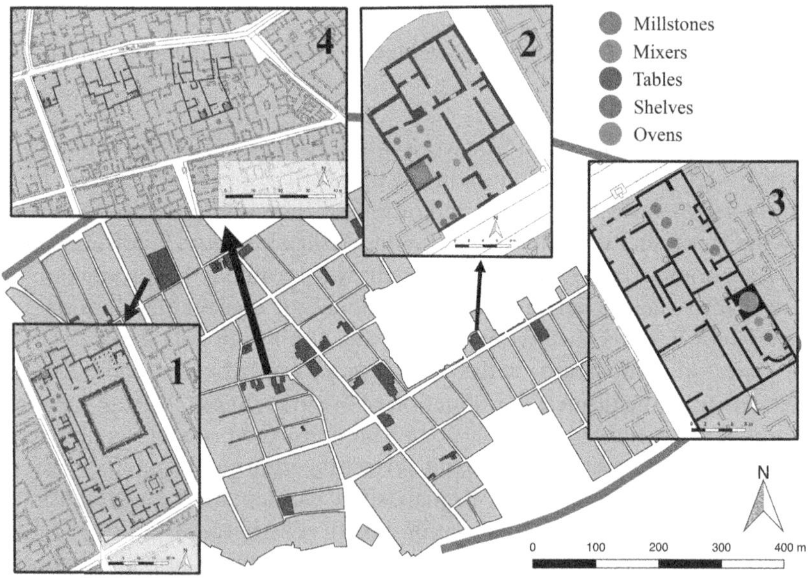

Fig. 2.9 Locations of the Bakeries in Pompeii, Illustrating the (1) House of the Labyrinth (VI.11.8-10), the (2) House of the Chaste Lovers (IX.12 6), the (3) House of the Baker (I.12.1&2), and the four Bakeries on the via degli Augustali (4)

tempering, milling, and sifting; (2) mixing, kneading, and forming loaves; (3) baking. The technologies that accomplish the various processes are, quite often, similar from one bakery to the next. The ovens have chutes that connect them to nearby rooms and their masonry is very similar. One type of millstone is more common than the others at Pompeii, a fact that has led to it being referred to as a 'Pompeian' millstone, and of the millstones many have been sourced to a few quarries in Italy.[52] Such heavy machinery and technology (millstones, masonry ovens, stone mixers) suggests a level of investment that exceeds the means of single households, at least those of a modest size, implying some form of debt or elite investement, although that cannot be substantiated from the material remains. All of this standardization among many of Pompeii's bakeries leads him to speculate that subindustries were catering to the needs of bakers, including building large masonry ovens or transporting mills of preferred stone from Orvieto.[53] There was, however, a great deal of variation: Monteix notes that the first rising or bulk fermentation may have occurred in bowls designated for just such a purpose, but that process could easily have occurred in the mixer. Furthermore, technologies such as shelves and rising bowls are not ubiquitously found in Pompeian bakeries and a variety of technologies could serve such functions, including barrels or other objects of ephemeral materials that are hard to see in the material record.[54]

Monteix also notes, however, that when the three clusters of activities and the operational sequence are considered in their spatial layout, a great deal of variation in baking is revealed. That is to say, even if bakers had similar resources available to them or used the same contractors, they put the bakeries together in ways that met their specific needs, according to their habits, whether grounded in family traditions or those of a workshop legacy. For example, the House of the Labyrinth (VI.11.10) contains a bakery very like the city's others, but hidden in the back of the house. In other bakeries the production is more obvious, but manifests in different ways. The bakeries at the House of the Chaste Lovers (IX.12.6) and the House of the Baker (I.12.1&2) both have three millstones surrounded by paving stones, a mixer, and nearly identical ovens made of brick with a chute connecting them to room with a table and shelves. The House of the Baker, on the one hand, is organized such that it is divided almost neatly in two, with indications of elite domesticity in the house, and the other side dedicated to production. In the House of the Chaste Lovers, on the other hand, production is interwoven with indications of elite domesticity; for example, the donkeys would have to pass through a garden and past a triclinium to get to their millstones. Still other bakeries have many of the same baking technologies, but have almost no relationship with elite markers of domestic space even if one cannot discount that they served as modest housing, such as those along the via degli Augustali. One might infer from such variation in bakery form heterogeneity in the social status of Pompeian bakers and surely some bakers in the city were slaves working for large elite households and others were free operating small workshops. At the very least, it would seem the exact way in which investment occurred could well have differed from one bakery to the next even within one community; some owned by modest craftsmen and others owned by wealthy landowners who rented the workshops or staffed them with slaves. Whatever types of investment in the industry, all the bakeries of Pompeii are small with a few millstones and a nice oven; there is no evidence for mass production and strategic investment aimed at generating profits or social capital.

Herculaneum

Herculaneum's two bakeries are both located in the city's *insula orientalis*, an area characterized by commercial and public spaces (Fig. 2.10). Excavation of the insula's façade began in 1932, under the direction of Amedeo Maiuri.[55] The area was the focus of intense investigation from 1933 to 1937, when both bakeries were unearthed. The proximity of the bakeries to the Grand Palaestra is frequently noted and the *insula orientalis* is thought to be a commercial zone.[56] Maiuri identifies the patron of the first bakery, off of Cardo V, as Sextus Patulcus Felix due to the discovery of a sigil, which may be a bread or wax stamp.[57] There are two millstones in the room that opens directly onto the street. Two doorways link the mill-room to a back room, where 25 circular baking tins were found. They range from 13 cm to 50 cm, but the bulk of them are between 20 cm and 31 cm. A small door northeast of the milling room leads to a series of back rooms. The first room contains an oven, with a diameter of 1.8 m. Above the aperture of the oven, two apotropaic *phalloi* are built into the dome. The space northeast of the oven-room is less well conserved, but Maiuri records a terracotta plaque in the southeastern wall depicting a phallus with legs, supports for a table, and shelves.

Bakery Two is part of a large complex with an entrance on Cardo V and another entrance off of a side alley. The side entrance gives access to a large room with an oven in the southernmost corner and two millstones, next to which was found the skeleton of a donkey. Its two millstones and a partly destroyed oven (2.4 m in diameter) are in a room that opens directly

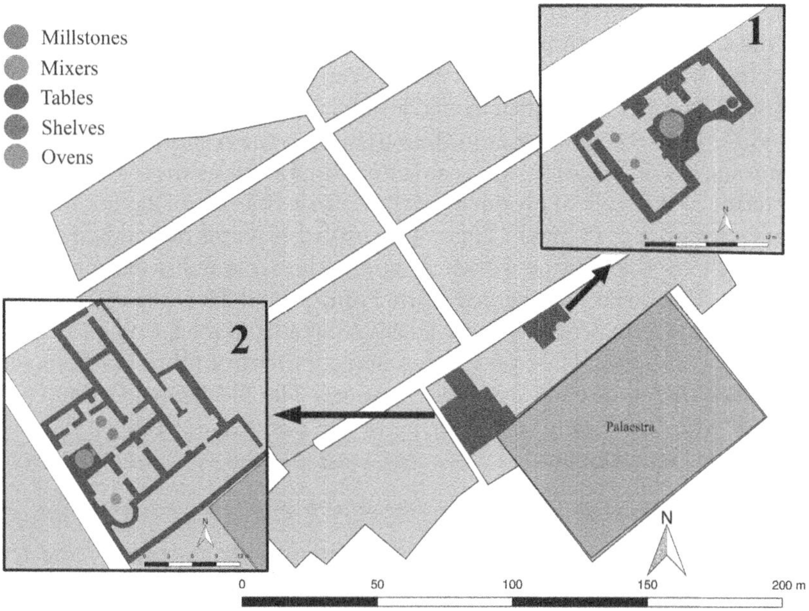

Fig. 2.10 Locations of the Bakeries in Herculaneum and the Proximity of Bakeries One and Two to the Palaestra

onto a narrow street perpendicular to Cardo V. A long room, probably a bathroom, resides to the northwest of the mill-room. To the northeast, the mill-room links to a long room with post-holes for shelves and a half-buried stone vat in the northern corner, maybe a *catillus*. The fine decoration of the complex lead Maiuri and Esposito hypothesize that the complex was once an "abitazione signorile."

In some ways, the bakeries of Pompeii and Herculaneum are quite similar. The scale of production is similar with 2–4 millstones and an oven with a diameter between 2–3 m and there are indications that some bakeries have a relationship with elite domesticity and some that do not. They both have domed ovens, probably driven by a cultural tradition of certain type of leavened bread baked in just such a way. But there are differences as well. The oven with a chute is not attested in either of the two bakeries at Herculaneum and neither oven has the so-called *praefurnium* that would double as a masonry chimney. No paving stones are found under millstones, but the millstones themselves are of the same stone and morphology as those at Pompeii. The mixers are also similar, and possibly of the same quarry, though that has not been demonstrated.

The differences and similarities between Herculaneum's bakeries and those of Pompeii are instructive. The similarities in scale and equipment, in addition to the similarities in the variation in the relationship with elite domestic space, suggests similar investment patterns as those of Pompeii. In terms of the scale of production, the bakeries of Herculaneum do seem similar to those of Pompeii. There were probably points of standardization driven by overlapping networks of supply; the same millstone trader, for example, may well have served both Pompeii and Herculaneum. Other components were probably more locally sourced and reliant on more local networks of supply. The ovens, for example, differ from those of Pompeii; they lack the chutes and extensive masonry. The local construction contractor who had clearly served many of the bakeries in Pompeii did not also serve Herculaneum.

Ostia and Rome

Regional variation in Italian commercial baking was not only predicated on local baking traditions and the infrastructure, resources, and economic complexity of individual communities. Some urban centers, such as Rome and Ostia, differed from most Roman urban centers in the sizes of their populations and their unique political circumstances as the capital of the empire and its port. The first archaeological evidence for commercial baking in Rome dates to the late first century BCE, discovered just outside the Porta Maggiore.[58] This bakery, if it was in fact a *pistrinum*, is very poorly preserved; indeed little material evidence for commercial baking remains extant in Rome from any period. But it is a pretty large structure, as large as any bakery in Pompeii, and its location outside the city walls implies a separation of commercial and domestic space characteristic of high production levels and complex economic systems, a topic further explored in Chap. 3.

Rome was, in many ways, unique as the capital of the Empire. Evidence from Rome and Ostia in the second and third centuries CE, when the state took a much greater interest in the provisioning of Rome (a topic picked up in Chap. 5), show that high levels of production in individual bakeries persisted into late antiquity. Emperors from Trajan to Aurelian took steps to incentivize higher production in bakeries by making legal concessions to those who operated a high-production bakery.[59] There is also evidence for some social stratification among the participants in the commercial baking industry, including some individuals who were not master craftsmen but instead participated via investment rather than direct engagement. Such men likely used their clients to manage their assets or even slaves acting as proxies (*institores*) for their masters, while others performed brutal physical labor.[60] Large workgroups, as Murphy might call them, and high levels of production are corroborated by the actual remains of the bakeries at Ostia and what little indications exist in Rome.[61] By the second century CE, at least some bakeries at Ostia, and probably at Rome, were approaching mass-production of bread. There are eight bakeries at Ostia (Fig. 2.11); some are quite large and others are more like the workshops at Pompeii and Herculaneum. The so-called Molino at Ostia (I.xiii.4) housed six millstones, maybe seven, four kneaders, and an oven 5 m in diameter. In fact, the oven in the Caseggiato dei Molini (I.iii.1) is

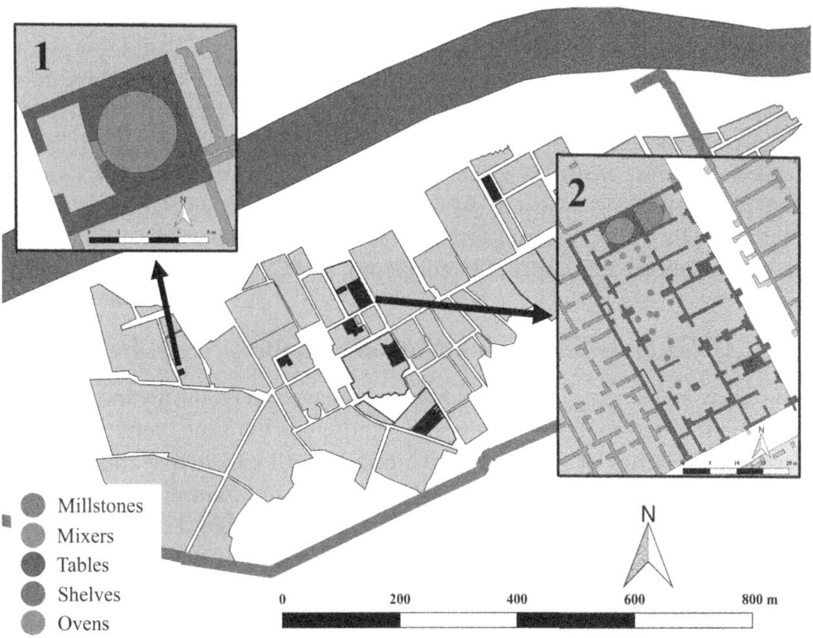

Fig. 2.11 The Locations of the Eight Bakeries at Ostia with Details of the (1) Caseggiato con Fornace per Laterizi and the (2) Caseggiato dei Molini at Ostia

so large that it has been suggested that it contained some sort of rotating lazy Susan so that the baker could utilize its entire capacity, as evidenced by a series of grooves in the sides of the oven.[62] Conversely, the bakery called the Caseggiato con Fornace per Laterizi (I.xvii.1) is a single room with one massive oven. But it is not a simple workshop, it is a single room with very large oven (over 4 meters). The Caseggiato con Fornace per Laterizi is still a mass producer, but the other processes are occurring elsewhere. Both the bread factories and the single room Ostian bakery evokes levels of investment and complicated economic strategies not evident at Pompeii or Herculaneum.

The third century CE witnessed the implementation of watermills in Rome, probably related to both the increased level of investment and the state's interest in the provisioning of the city. Some have argued that the introduction of this technology spurred specialization in the commercial baking industry and the creation of two separate crafts in the late fourth century CE: bakers and millers, a topic addressed more fully in the next chapter.[63] But it is clear that many if not most bakers in Rome and elsewhere continued to mill and bake well after the fourth century CE and that watermill technology was available from a very early time. Nevertheless, most Roman-era cities did not have watermills in them. The economic complexity that would allow for—and necessitate—technologies such as watermills distinguishes Rome from the other cities of late-antique Italy. At Cosa, for example, sixth-century ovens were found on the grounds of the town's church.[64] The ovens are small and lack the well-dressed masonry of the ovens in the workshops of Pompeii, Herculaneum, and Ostia a few centuries earlier.

Africa Proconsularis and Numidia (Central North Africa)

Any study of Roman bakeries of North Africa—and really any industry—is heavily indebted to Touatia Amraoui, whose work on the crafts and workshops in the cities of Algeria and Tunisia is both exhaustive and carefully presented.[65] She identifies bakeries throughout central North Africa, including examples at Djemila and Thibilis Announa. The evidence for commercial baking is largely third century CE and later, several hundred years after the *tannūrs* of the Numidian period, but there are some possible indications of continuity between the two traditions. No oven was found at Djemila, for example, only piles of rubble and ash in the corners of workshops that contained mills and mixers. It is entirely possible that those piles of rubble were *tannūr*-style ovens. Even if such ovens continued to be used, it was alongside seemingly domed, horizontal-aperture ovens. The hour-glass millstones, much as they did in Italy, continued to get larger and many of the mills have been sourced to quarries in Italy and in particular at Orvieto and Mulargia on Sardinia.[66] One of the unique features of millstones in central north Africa is the stone flour catcher, attested in small numbers on the Italian peninsula, but ubiquitous in north Africa. Mixers are also attested, but not as consistently as in Italy or further west in North Africa.

Djemila

Excavators at Djemila identified three bakeries at Djemila, known as Cuicul to the Romans. All three bakeries exist within the limits of the old city and inside the fortification walls and are on or near major thoroughfares leading to fora or other public areas (Fig. 2.12). Amraoui dates all three to the final phases of occupation at Djemila in the fourth or early fifth century CE. The operational sequence in the bakeries of Djemila is difficult to assess because all the features and technologies associated with different processes are located in a single room.

Bakery One at Djemila, located in the southeastern part of an insula north and east of the Severan Forum, consists of three rooms (7–9). Room 7 contains the features that led excavators to identify the space as a commercial bakery.[67] It contained the city's only mixer of the sort found at Pompeii and Ostia. The same room also contained a damaged hour-glass shaped millstone and a dolium, presumably for storage. Excavators interpreted a pile of bricks and charcoal (*vestiges dans un tas de briques et de charbons*) in the southeast corner of room 7 as an oven. Two front spaces were interpreted as shops or a courtyard and the western front room (8) contained a vat linked with a water pipe, possibly for mixing with flour.[68] Piers in Rooms 7–9 led Y. Allais to conclude the space was a courtyard with a bakery in it, but a link to the Decumanus to the south and the lack of communication with the houses on the insula suggest to Amraoui that rooms 7–9 should be viewed as a commercial workshop rather than a domestic kitchen for a large household.[69]

Bakeries Two and Three at Djemila are on the same insula. Bakery Two opens onto what one might call the Cardo of the city, north of the late-antique church in an area of modest houses and workshops. The preservation of the various spaces makes it difficult to identify the nature of production in the workshops, but for Allais the identification of Bakery Two as such was fairly secure. It contains a millstone of the hourglass type

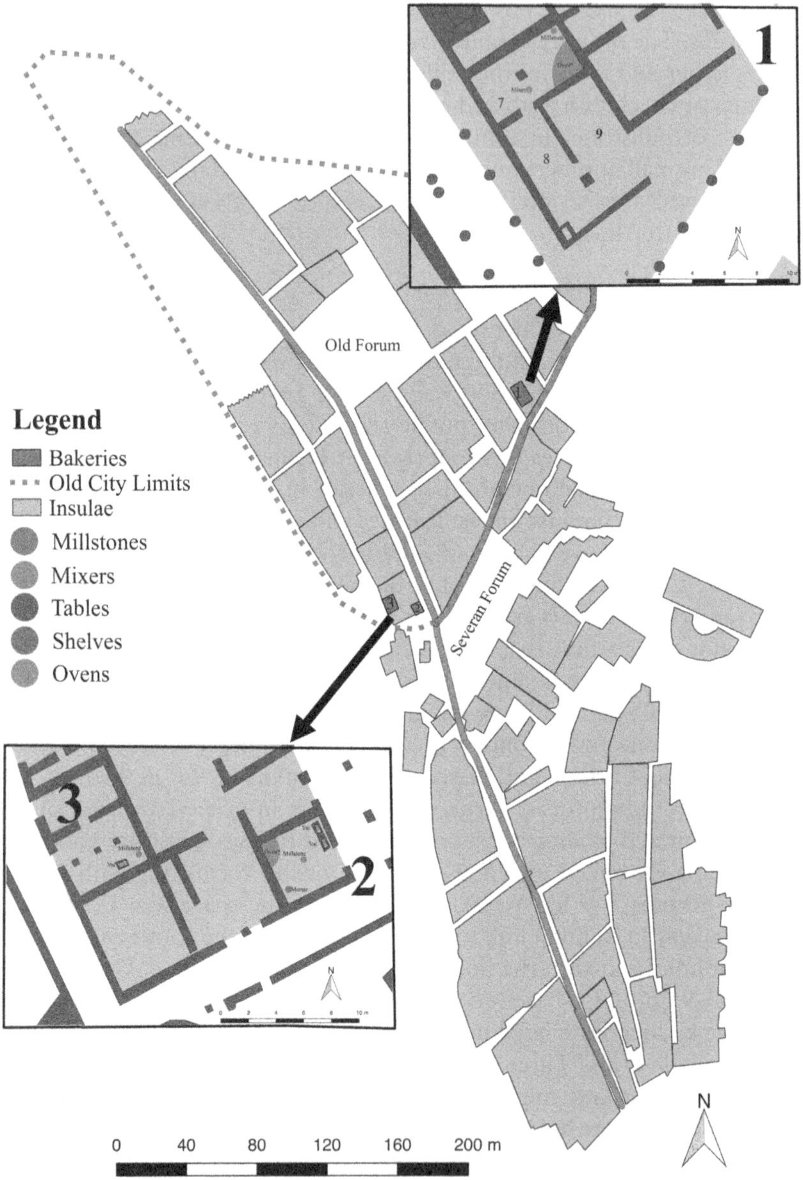

Fig. 2.12 The Locations of the Three Bakeries at Djemila and Details of Them

and two stone vats, which Allais interpreted as mixers or kneading basins. He also reports two mortars, which Amraoui did not find in 2017. On the south side of the room, Allais found a platform of stones that he interpreted as a base for the millstone.

Bakery Three is on the same insula as Bakery Two, but opens at the opposite side, onto Cardo West 1. The workshop consists of two rooms which are 0.80 m below the street level, leading Allais to conclude that the space may have been a basement for another building and the prevalence of millstones even in houses might suggest that many households made their own bread in Djemila. The first room contains a millstone, a masonry platform for it, and a stone vat fed by a pipe; the other room contains a terracotta vessel. Allais found no evidence for an oven, but the sparse evidence for ovens at Djemila suggests that baking may have relied on portable devices or that the ovens were made in such a way that they did not preserve well.

Thibilis Announa

The one bakery at Thibilis Announa is located in the north part of the city (Fig. 2.13), excavated in 1909 by A. Joly. The preservation at the site is such that delineation of rooms is difficult, but the bakery consisted of at least two rooms. The interior room is entirely occupied by a large oven, 3.1 m in diameter.[70] The exterior room opens onto the street and contains no other identifiable features. A millstone and a vat for mixing were found in rooms just to the west, which might imply that those rooms were also part of the bakery, but the millstone and mixer may have been moved to those other rooms after abandonment or maybe never belonged to the bakery in the first place.

The bakeries of Djemila and Thibilis Announa appear similar to the bakeries of Pompeii and Herculaneum in terms of scale: a few millstones and a vat or mixer. The lack of definitive evidence for an oven in the bakeries of Djemila is intriguing and one wonders if the search for domed ovens overlooked the possibility that a bakery could be furnished with a *tannūr*. If true, one imagines that the local bread preferences and baking traditions were somewhat different from one city to the next. On the other hand, the bakeries of both North African cities appear quite like those of Pompeii and Herculaneum in terms of investment: expensive equipment and workshops with occassional links to elite houses.

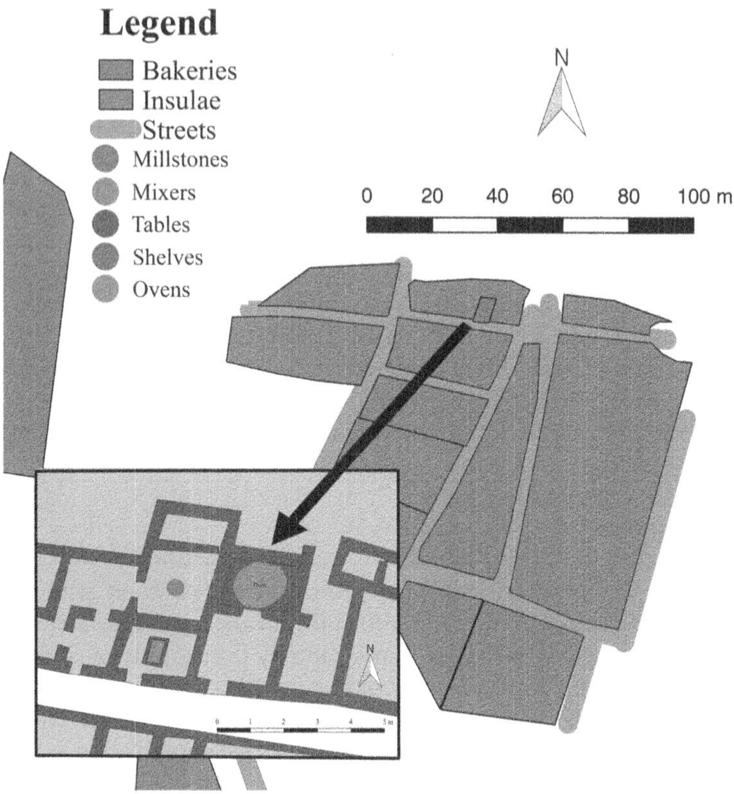

Fig. 2.13 Plan of Thibilis and Detail of the City's Bakery

Change at the End of Antiquity

At Timgad, a large number of ovens were found around the site. The ovens are all very large and made masonry and they seem to have a closer relationship with churches than readily identifiable workshops. Not one oven was found in a workshop with millstones or other technologies, but millstones are found in great numbers at the site. This raises the question for Amraoui of whether vertical specialization might have been happening, with milling and baking separating into separate professions.[71] She cites several funerary inscriptions dating to the late fourth or early fifth century CE which describe three men as *furnarii*, which is etymologically grounded in *furnus*, oven, rather than the more traditional *pistores*.[72] The shift in terminology might reflect a shift in operational practices; a *furnarius* might have made bread, but might not do some of the other processes involved in turning grain into bread, namely milling. Andrew Wilson and Claude Lepelley both parallel this lexical shift with a passage from St. Augustine, in which he recounts the refusal of a Donatist *furnarius* to bake the bread of a Catholic client in his home town of Hippo.[73] This seems to suggest that the *furnarius* only baked, but was not involved in milling or forming the loaves. One could see this as an example of oven-letting in which people brought goods from home to be baked by a commercial baker. The other hypothesis is that milling was happening elsewhere, particularly at watermills, and that the industry was vertically specializing into two separate professions. At the very least, one begins to see change and the semantic diversity probably reflects regional variation in baking traditions. Some towns, such as Setif or Carthage may well have had the economic complexity and infrastructure to allow for watermills and an industry specialized on baking bread from the four milled in them. The possibility of oven-letting might still have allowed a baking specialist to exist in smaller towns that lacked the advantages of the larger cities. Amraoui notes, however, that workshops that milled but did not bake may not be perceptible in the archaeological record because millstones move around a lot and the amount of flour produced domestically complicates the matter.[74]

Mauretania Tingitana (Western North Africa)

The bakeries have been found in three cities in Mauretania Tingitana: Volubilis, Banasa, and Thamusida. In many ways, the bakeries of Mauretania Tingitana share traits with those of Africa Proconsularis and Numidia in that they are small workshops. They also lack any real discernable relationship with elite housing. But the millstones in Morocco differ from those of Africa Proconsularis and Numidia in some important ways, most notably in millstone morphology. None of the millstones of Mauretania have the stone flour catcher that characterized the millstones of central North Africa. First and second century millstones appear to have been hourglass, 'Pompeian'-style mills, but in the third century CE the millstones are of an annular type that is specific to Mauretania and Baetica. But there are other differences as well. The ovens of Volubilis and Banasa are more elaborate and take a wide variety of forms, from oblong ovens to perfectly rounds ones, but they all tend to have stone substructures lined with tiles as a refractory surface. There is never any indication of a superstructure, which suggests that the dome was made of adobe or *pisé*. It is unclear what type of traditional household baking dominated Mauretania in the pre-Roman periods, but it may be that the pre-Roman Berber population built earthen ovens similar to those of central Europe and that domed ovens were a more natural fit for the inhabitants of the region.

Volubilis

Volubilis, a Roman-era city in central Morocco, contains some of the best preserved—and studied—evidence for commercial baking outside of North Africa (Fig. 2.14). A number of studies have addressed the bakeries and Mathieu Leduc conducted the first study of the bakeries at Volubilis. He explores the locations of baking equipment in the built environment of the city, finding eight bakeries with ovens and a number of other spaces with a millstone or a mixer, in total coming to 17 possible bakeries.[75] In addition to these more general analyses, Leduc estimates how many people could have been fed by the bakeries in the city by using the volume of the kneading machines.[76] My work at the city, with my colleagues, has begun to detail the interior operations of the bakeries in the city.[77] Unlike most of the bakeries in central North Africa, many of the bakeries at Volubilis are not single room spaces, but rather workshops with multiple spaces and a division of process by space, similar to the bakeries of central Italy. The operational sequences in the bakeries mirror those found at Pompeii; the direction of production moves from milling at the entrance toward baking in less accessible areas. The bakery (6) on the same insula as the Maison au Buste de Bronze has millstones in the front room and an oven in interior spaces with likely storage at the back of the building; the same configuration is evident in the bakery on the insula of the Maison a la Citerne.

In terms of scale of production, the bakeries of Volubilis are more akin to the smaller bakeries of Djemila, Thibilis, Pompeii and Herculaneum than they are like those larger bakeries of Timgad or Ostia; they have several millstones, usually a mixer, and an oven. None of the bakeries are integrated into large elite houses the way that some were at Pompeii, but Layla Es-Sadra observes that large courtyard houses dominate the insulae of Volubilis and that they tend to be surrounded by shop-like spaces, punctuated by monumental architecture, which open onto major thoroughfares, much like the other bakeries we have seen outside of Ostia.[78]

Fig. 2.14 Plan of Volubilis with Details of the Bakeries on Insula with the Maison au Buste de Bronze (6) and the one in the Maison a la Citerne (4)

There are two types of grain mills at Volubilis: hourglass millstones and annular ones. Aomar Akerraz and Maurice Lenoir delineated these into types one and two, respectively. Two two is subdivided by material; some of the annular millstones are made of vesicular alkali basalt (type 2a) and the others of a shelly limestone (type 2b). Nearly all millstones at Volubilis found in bakeries are made of a porous basalt and are annular, not unlike the stone preferred throughout the western Roman Empire since the Hellenistic period. It is the form of the millstone that makes it unique: its *catillus* is lighter and with less contact area between the upper and lower elements. Two things have been inferred from the form of annular millstones: first, they were almost certainly driven by humans, not beasts, and second, they had lower productivity than their hourglass counterparts. The mixers in the bakeries are similar to those of Pompeii and Ostia, but seem to be made of a local limestone. They come in two types: a rectilinear body and a cylindrical one (Fig. 1.7).

In the bakery (4) in the Maison à la Citerne, shelves are evident in the walls near the oven, much as they are in Pompeii and Herculaneum, implying that proofing was occurring and that the bread of Volubilis was leavened, not flat. The ovens of Volubilis are hard to reconstruct because often all that remains of them is a tile surface, sometimes raised on a platform and sometimes bedded directly onto a packed-earth surface. The form of the dome of the oven is sometimes preserved in the tile surface, but more frequently there is nothing left of the superstructure. The dome itself was probably adobe or *pisé*, as the early excavators suggested for the bakery in the Maison a la Citerne.[79] In general, the ovens of Volubilis do not share the masonry and complexity of Pompeii's ovens, but nor are they the mere piles of rubble at Djemila. An adobe oven has been found at Augusta Emerita (discussed below) and such ovens are frequently found in use today in Morocco. There are also many workshops at Volubilis with millstones and mixers, but no fixed oven feature. One wonders if the oven were simply destroyed because it was made of adobe, in which case the number of bakeries would need to be increased. No *tannūr* is known at Volubilis until the Islamic period, but they may have been overlooked and would account for the lack of ovens in certain workshops with millstones and mixers. The other possibility is that those technologies were moved into their current positions much later.

Cultural differences aside, the Roman-era bakeries of Volubilis are pretty similar in scale of production to those of further east in North

Africa and of the smaller cities of central Italy: they have a few millstones, a mixer or two, and an oven of moderate size. They also seem similar in regard to how investment occurred and the networks of supply. Volubilis' bakeries have expensive equipment, some of which is imported from afar and other technologies such as the mixers which seem to be made locally. Adobe ovens, one suspects, could be built and repaired by the baker, suggesting lesser economic complexity than in Pompeii and Ostia where subindustries are indicated by the homogeny in oven construction. That said, nearly all the bakeries of Volubilis are in or near larger elite homes, with a few exceptions in very public spaces or in areas of the city with an overall lower socio-economic profile, such as the southern part of the city. Furnishing the bakery likely followed much of the same patterns that has been inferred at Pompeii: the workshop is a lived in space with investment at modest levels by elite households or sub-elite families borrowing money.

Banasa

There are four possible bakeries at the site of Banasa, a Roman-era city north and east of Volubilis: the Macellum Bakery, the Bakery on Insula A, the Northeast-Quarter Bakery, and the Southwest-Quarter Bakery.[80] Preliminary work conducted by Sidi Mohammed Alaioud carefully articulates what might constitute a "bakery," identifying the oven, the millstone, and the mixer. He identifies the various spaces that contain one or more of such features. Excavations revealed the presence of 14 millstones at Banasa, many small and in houses, which leads Alaioud to conclude that most households of Banasa milled their own grain and baked their own bread. Only three of the millstones at Banasa are basalt, like those of Volubilis.[81] Alaioud identifies the stone used to make most the mills as a fine sandstone, suggesting that a difference in the baking traditions of the two cities or possibly in their access or ability to afford the basalt millstones transported from greater distances. At the very least, the typology for millstones set out for Volubilis by Akerraz and Lenoir does not seem to graft onto the millstones of Banasa.

Ovens were found in only two of the possible bakeries at Banasa.[82] The bakery in the northeast quarter contains a fixed meta millstone resting directly on the ground without a base, with fragments of a *catillus* nearby. Alaioud reports that all of the millstones in bakeries are made of sandstone rather than basalt. In another room there are two limestone kneaders. Raymond Thouvenot describes an area of terracotta tiles measuring 3.50 × 2.50 m, which he interprets as an oven. The bakery in the southwestern quarter consists of one large room, linked to the house of Venus. Part of the room is paved with brick tiles, which Alaioud identifies as a platform for an oven. In the same room, a mixer was found, as well as a small rectangular stoneware container. There are also a number of possible bakeries at Banasa that do not contain ovens or a full complement of diagnostic bakery features. Thouvenot describes a circular brick base in the possible bakery in the *macellum* which he interprets as a platform for a rotary millstone; nearby mills corroborate this to him, but the platform was integrated into a later building.[83] A possible bakery on the south side of Insula A contains a fixed basalt millstone and two kneaders in sandstone.

Volubilis and Banasa, in many ways, form a single cultural unit that have bakeries with modest investment in equipment, scale of production comparable to Pompeii's bakeries. They are among the few places in the Mediterranean to have their particular type of annular millstone. It is unclear the extent to which Banasa's bakeries had a relationship with elite domestic space. We also see that Banasa's pattern of networks of supply mirror that of other sites, that is to say that millstones were of a type that suggest they were imported, but that some technologies were seemingly of a more local stone. The use of sandstone for mills, as identified by Alaioud, is an interesting departure from the exclusive use of basalt millstones in bakeries at Volubilis. Much more material analysis is needed in Morocco to corroborate this reconstructed pattern of material acquisition.

The Iberian Peninsula

The Iberian Peninsula, much like Sicily and Sardinia, was a place where several different cultures came into contact, giving the later Roman commercial baking a number of existing traditions from which to grow. The *tannūr*, which was always relegated to the coasts, disappears from the Romanized city centers and none of them are evident in bakeries. One of the existing pre-Roman traditions was earthen or clay hearths; and in fact at least one oven at Augusta Emerita was made of adobe or *pisé*. Two others are built directly on *cocciopesto* surfaces, but these were apparently made of bricks, the domes for which are no longer extant. Another oven in the House of the Planetarium at Italica has two chambers, side by side, and is built on a platform of brick masonry with a dome of the same material, more akin to the masonry ovens of central Italy.

A small rotary quern is located in the kitchen/bakery of the House of the Amphitheater and a platform for a millstone was found in the other bakery at Augusta Emerita. At Italica, no millstones were found in bakeries, but millstones found throughout the region suggest that there were rotary querns in many contexts, but also that there were larger hour-glass millstones and also annular millstones, particularly in the Bas-Guadalquivir basin, identical to those found in Mauretania Tingitana like at Volubilis or Banasa, suggesting a connection between the two regions.[84] But no millstones have been found in any of the bakeries and one bakery found at Emerita Augusta had a masonry platform made of reused tiles and bricks upon which a rotary millstone was once located, but it remains unclear what type of millstone it supported.

Italica

The two bakeries in Italica are both located in the Nova Urbs, or 'New City', the portion of Italica expanded in the first century CE (Fig. 2.15). Both are in small shops that are on insulae with large elite houses, but neither workshop communicates directly with the house. The first bakery is associated with—and on the same insula as—the so-called House of the Birds.[85] It consists of one room with a masonry oven placed directly on the floor. There are no indications of millstones, mixers, tables, or shelves. The oven itself is masonry, but the dome is only preserved to its first few courses and appears to have been bedded directly on the *cacciopesto* floor. If there were other technologies in the bakery during antiquity, such as millstones or mixers, they may have been moved.

The bakery on the insula with the House of the Planetarium (2) consists of two rooms, both paved with large tiles.[86] No millstones or mixers were found in this bakery, but the southern of the two rooms contains two ovens, both now significantly reconstructed. Both comprise part of a single masonry construction inserted into the southeast corner of the room. The bakery is almost entirely reconstructed. The walls separating the bakery from the House of the Birds are reconstructed, but there is no indication in the actual remains of a door between the house and the workshop. Antonio Caballos Rufino says that the only parts of the oven that are original are the base plate, which is directly on the floor, and the first few courses of the dome. The oven itself is oval-shaped, with a length of 2.1 m and a width of 1.9 m.

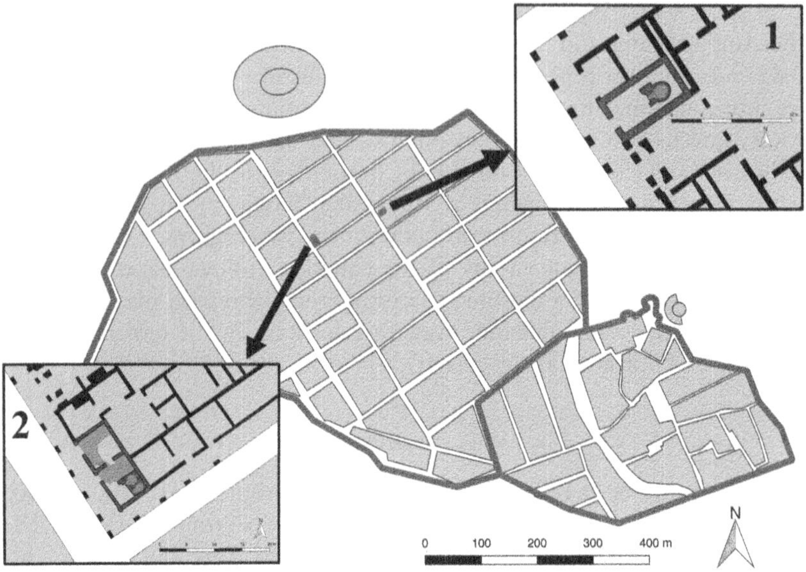

Fig. 2.15 Plan of Italica with Details of the Bakery near the House of the Birds (1) and the One near the House of the Planetarium (2)

Augusta Emerita

There are two bakeries at Emerita Augusta, both of which resided outside the city's fortification walls, surely a product of where excavations have occurred and not representative of the actual distribution of bakeries in the ancient city (Fig. 2.16). One bakery resides to the north at a small excavation on Calle Almendralejo, part of what seems to have been a commercial area because the space found next door to the bakery is also a workshop containing a large number of dolia.[87] The bakery itself consists of an adobe oven and a raised brick platform for a millstone, now gone. The oven itself closely resembles reconstructions of the adobe ovens evident at Volubilis, but the raised platform has no parallel in Mauretania. The workshop is small and consists of only three spaces: the mill room to the front, the oven to the back, and a small room to the south of the oven.

The second bakery, to the south, is part of the Villa of the Amphitheater and accessed from the main courtyard of the house.[88] Excavators identified the space as a kitchen, which may well be true, but the single room

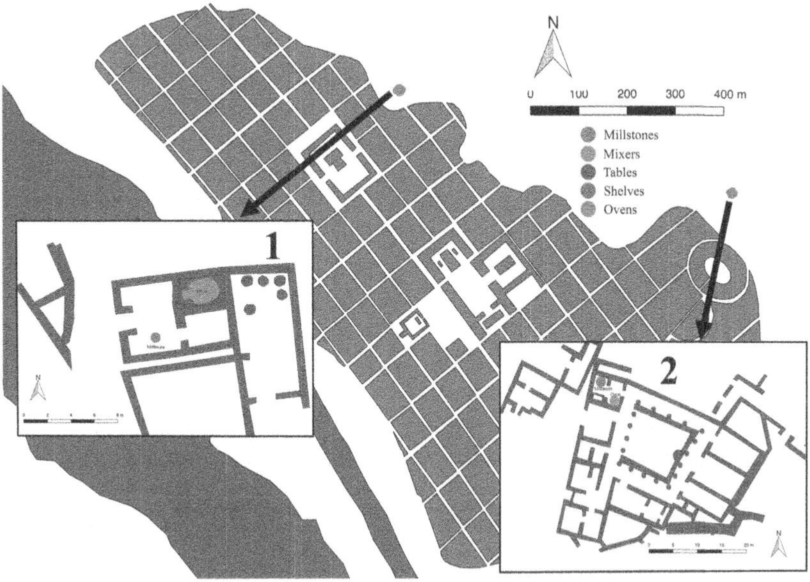

Fig. 2.16 Plan of Augusta Emerita with Details of the Bakery on Calle Almendralejo (1) and Another in the Villa of the Amphitheater (2)

contained a masonry oven bedded directly on the floor, much like the oven in the bakery on the insula with the House of the Birds in Italica. The room also contained a rotary millstone. Extra-urban villas such as the Villa of the Amphitheater in Augusta Emerita are not uncommon, known also from Compania and Gaul. The elaborate ovens and workshop format might reflect the size of household that needed to be fed, but we should not exclude the possibility that such villa bakeries in suburban contexts did not also sell their surplus.

Gaul and Britannia

The emergence of specialized commercial bakers in Gaul probably did not occur until Roman occupation, or at least that is when the ovens begin to be built out of masonry rather than mud and soil. In a feat of remarkably careful excavation and analysis, a first century CE bakery has been identified at Saint-Bézard à Aspiran from ash deposits, four carbonized fragments of bread, and residual elements of the ovens in the later walls.[89] A

'Pompeian'-type millstone was also found in the building. This evidence, combined with the lack of attachment to a large elite house, leads excavators to conclude the space served as a modest bakery with the ability to bake up to 30 loaves at a time, based on the reconstruction of the oven.

A similar bakery was discovered at Springhead in Kent and shows a possible hybridization of local traditions and Mediterranean influences. The bakery, excavated in 1951 and published in 1958, consisted of three rooms comprising a long structure.[90] Material from strata below the ovens dated them to the late first or early second century CE. Two of the rooms contained an oven. The first oven was oblong, but poorly preserved. On its long axis it measured about 1 m. The second oven was better preserved and more circular. It measured about 0.75 m and consisted of a clay bedding serving as the refractory surface and supporting a ring of stones. Excavators identified rubble inside the oven as the remnants of the superstructure. They also identified two apertures to the oven, one of which had a clay ramp leading up to it and another to the side, which may be damage to the oven rather than an actual opening. The clay is baked hard and excavators saw indications of the tools used to apply the clay or possibly brushes used to clean it out. A millstone was found in the area in the eighteenth century, but is now lost. The ovens are unique. They are both earthen, incorporating not only the soil of the rooms' floors, but also using clays to help build the oven floor. On the other hand, stone blocks (albeit not brick-and-mortar masonry) comprise the superstructure, recalling influences from the Mediterranean.

Another bakery at Bourton dates to the third century CE and appears to have been part of the nearby Leadenwell Villa.[91] Much like the first oven at Springhead, the Bourton oven is oblong (0.6 × 1 m). Also like the ovens at Springhead, the Bourton oven is carved into the ground and uses the natural clay as a refractory surface and bedding for a stone superstructure, suggesting that pre-Roman traditions could persist well into the later periods of Roman occupation. Inside the oven excavators found layers of ash, presumed to be debitage from the baking process. The bakery almost certainly served the household, which is not to say the bread produced in it was not sold or traded, but that it was not, strictly speaking, a workshop. In general, most of the masonry ovens and large millstones in Britain and Gaul come from houses, and frequently from villas, not from proper workshops.[92] Such a phenomenon is also well attested in the elite houses and villas of Italy during the same time period. Early ovens in such houses vary in size, but not unlike those in Pompeii, range from 0.75 m to 2 m.[93]

The question is: do the ovens and kitchens in these elite households bear any resemblance to the bakeries that must have existed in Roman-period cities throughout Gaul and central Europe. The bakeries of other cities seem to suggest that they would. The bakeries in the rural villas of Campania, such as the one in the Villa of P. Fannius Synistor at Boscoreale, strongly resemble the bakeries of Pompeii and Herculaneum and the bakeries in elite houses, such as the one in the House of the Labyrinth in Pompeii, are nearly identical to workshop bakeries. Similarly, the bakery near the House of the Birds in Italica has a nearly identical oven to the one found in the Villa of the Amphitheater at Augusta Emerita. Even if we cannot assume that workshop bakeries in urban contexts matched precisely in form and equipment the bakeries in villas, it stands to reason that the form and technologies of workshop bakers would follow many of the same trends evident in bakeries in elite households, which were beginning to shift away from certain pre-Roman traditions, such as the earthen oven, to the use of masonry resembling in form and construction those found in contemporary Spain and Italy with masonry ovens sometimes bedded on the ground, and other times raised on platforms.

A Mediterraneanization of central-European baking is corroborated by the presence of 'Pompeian' millstones from around the region. Such millstones, we have seen, exist throughout the empire. A long-standing discussion of the trade of such millstones, grounded in petrology and sourcing, has led scholars to believe many come from a central Italian quarry near Orvieto.[94] More recent work in France has corroborated Orvieto as a source of millstones of the Pompeian type, but has also shown that many mills of that type are made from local, porous volcanic stones.[95] We can make several inferences from the sourcing of the millstones. First, the millstone trade that spread the hopper-rubber and then the 'Morgantina'-type millstone around the western Mediterranean also contributed to the diffusion of the 'Pompeian' type. Second, we can infer that local suppliers were seeing and emulating technological innovations from other places. But it would be a mistake to infer that the producers of a technology were also its innovators; in other words, the quarry at Orvieto may have been one of the primary suppliers, but it may not have been the place of origin for the type. Indeed, the rotary millstones of the hour-glass type are found everywhere, traded all about, in a wide variety of shapes dating back to the fourth-century BCE 'Morgantina' type. Innovation in such an environment should be considered coeval: growing generally from an integrated whole comprised of many local market economies rather than a singular innovation from one region.

Germania and Other Provinces on the Limes

The tension between—or hybridization of—pre-Roman traditions and pan-Mediterranean forces is evident in Germania and the other provinces on the *limes*; the ovens at Trier are in a Roman-style house for Roman legions, made from bricks, and take a bee-hive dome form, but also incorporate clays and adobe, a possible example of continuity from pre-Roman habits. Three ovens, dating from the first half of the second century CE to the third century CE, were found at Trier in a peristyle house.[96] No more than two of the ovens were in operation at a time because one is built atop another. They have tile refractory surfaces with a large number of legionary brickstamps and their domes were identified as clay or adobe. Similar phenomena are evident at the Roman villa at Reinheim.[97] The villa consisted of a main house and a number of annex buildings on the same grounds. Ovens were found in multiple phases from the villa, both in the building and outside of it, often on clay floors. In the last phase of the villa, dating to the late third to the middle of the fourth century CE, a bakery was installed into one of the annex buildings.[98]

Augusta Raurica

One of the best-preserved ovens—and possibly bakeries—north of the Alps was found in the 1960s at Augusta Raurica and was part of a strip of ovens (Backofengürtel) near the theater.[99] Investigations at the site began as early as 1590, with the unearthing of the theater. Excavation of the rest of the city began in 1966 when a suburban developer began building in the area.[100] A number of ovens were found just west of the theater, including a remarkably intact baking oven (Fig. 2.17). The clustering of the ovens near the city's theater (insula 5, 9, and 5/9), including a number of stones that might have been presses or slaughter floors for a butcher, has drawn speculation that the theater, as a place of public gathering, attracted commercial activity.[101]

The best preserved oven was found in a small, two-story workshops. The ground floor of the shop was subdivided by thatched walls. The very back of the space offered access to the second floor. The rubble from the collapse of the second story contained some prestige goods, including bronze figurines of a religious nature and militaria of various metals. There were also high concentrations of chicken bones and tools of a functional or domestic character.

Fig. 2.17 Adobe and Masonry Oven in the Inn/Shop/Squater Bakery at Augusta Raurica

The structure of the bakery dates to the late second century CE, but the oven was not added until the third quarter of the third century CE. Excavations below the floor of the workshop revealed the remnants of a hypocaust system, suggesting that the space may have previously been part of a bath complex. Just west of the main oven, there is a smaller oven. Sandra Ammann and Peter-Andrew Schwarz, however, question the interpretation of the space as either a bakery or some type of *taberna*. The assemblages on the floor when the building collapsed at the end of the third century suggest to them that, in the structure's final phase, the space was not exclusively engaged in bread production but may in fact have been consistent with repurposing of the space by squatters who may have used it for commercial purposes.[102] After the collapse at end of the third century CE, the structure was not rebuilt.

Baking and the Roman Army on the Limes

The liminal provinces in the north also present something of a unique case. In some ways commercial baking appears driven by many of the same forces that define the habits of bakers in other parts of the western empire: a tension between local traditions and the pan-Mediterranean forces incurred with the advent of the Roman Empire. But there are some factors specific to the region, none more important than the presence of the army. The idea that the presence of the Roman army dictated the nature of the local economy in liminal provinces is an old one, best expressed by Keith Hopkins.[103] The presence of the army not only served as an infusion of capital and resources, it also dictated the nature of production and distribution. A number of ovens and baking installations have been found in places where the army was stationed. These installations share some traits; they all consist of multiple ovens in close proximity. Such installations are evident at Gelduba in Germania Inferior, Saalberg, Housesteads, Chesters, and Birdoswald (among other forts). The techniques and materials employed to build the ovens varied widely. In some places, such as Sallberg or Housesteads, the ovens were masonry. At Gelduba or the impermanent ovens in Scotland, the ovens tended to be earthen. Although not commercial in nature, the military ovens of Roman forts suggest they too were grounded in local traditions and, because most of the legions in the western Empire were stationed in the north along the *limes*, they mirror the earthworks of the pre-Roman traditions or the somewhat Romanized mix of masonry and local materials.

The presence of the army on along the limes had another effect on baking in the area by also attracting the attention and eventually the permanent presence of emperors. Even if some workshops were small, high levels of production were possible in cities with large populations where imperial governance or regional administration might be centered, particularly Cologne or Trier. In the fourth-century palace of Trier, of which Constantine's basilica was a part, there are some indications of baking, albeit fragmentary.[104] More indicative are several funerary inscriptions from Gaul that attest bakers with unique titles and indicate greater levels of complexity in the systems of bread production. In one case, Marcus Liberius Victor is described as a *negotiator frumentarius* (a grain merchant).[105] A similar inscription is found at Narbonne commemorates a certain Tertinius Secundus Nervius and describes him as a *negotiator pistoricius* (a bread/milling merchant).[106] The meaning of *negotiator* is not self-evident, but Koenrad Verboven has argued that, in the case of crafts-people and commercial activity, it is probably not the production in itself that gives such men the title, but rather their investment in the production as a commercial enterprise for social or financial capital.[107] Such complexity and indirect participation are evident only in densely populated areas with large cities, a topic discussed at greater length in Chap. 3. Moreover, Cologne, Narbonne, and Rome/Ostia served as administrative centers and, presumably as a result, commercial or public baking was closely intertwined with the administration of those cities.

Conclusion

Traditionally, when one says 'Roman' bakeries, what is frequently meant is really Pompeian bakeries. These well-known workshops are familiar not only because they comprise one of the most famous archaeological sites in the world, but also because they are well equipped with technologies familiar to modern and early modern peoples: the masonry pizza oven, the millstones, and the mixers. The bakeries of central Italy are not, however, the source from which every bakery in the Roman world descended or the template to which every Roman bakery aspired. Similarities between bakeries around the Mediterranean and those of central Italy is a production of convergent, rather than divergent, traditions (to borrow concepts from the study of evolution). That is to say, there was no single source or historical tradition from which the many bakeries descended, thus accounting for their similarities. Instead, baking began from a place of diversity, grounded in regional and familial traditions, and converged in method and practice to an identifiable type with domed ovens, hourglass millstones, and mixers. But even in a period of general homogeny in bakery form, the diversity of the early periods persisted, giving the bakeries of various regions their own unique flavor, metaphorically speaking.

Three broad phases can be delineated in the changing habits of bakers in the western Mediterranean, as defined by the various technologies employed by bakers. Baking in the first phase (700–100 BCE) was grounded in the traditions of individual families or kinship groups, creating much variation from community to community, but also with regional commonalities grafting onto historically distinct populations of central Indo-European, eastern Indo-European, and Afro-Asiatic peoples. The second phase (100 BCE–250 CE) is defined by increasing homogenization and commercialization fostered by contact between the different peoples of the western Mediterranean, at first in the Hellenistic world, but subsequently under the Roman Empire. The third and final phase (250–700 CE) is redefined by regional variation as the unifying forces of the empire gave way to more regional forces, and as the ancient world succumbed to the medieval one.

There are three broad categories of ancient baking assemblages in the western Mediterranean prior to the first century BCE: terracotta baking devices used with lava-stone hopper-rubbers in southern Italy and Sicily, earthen ovens with rotary querns in Germania, Hispania, Gaul, and possibly eastern North Africa, and vertical baking *tannūr*-style ovens with rotary querns in central North Africa, Sardinia, Sicily, and possibly Mauretania Tingitana. To some extent, these regions generally graft onto historically and culturally distinct populations as defined by linguistics and other attributes. The vertical *tannūr*-style ovens prevail in areas that were traditionally Afro-Asiatic, such as North Africa, but also in areas that were historically occupied or influenced by Phoenicians or Carthage, such as Sardinia or eastern Sicily. Earthen domed ovens, made of clay or adobe, with a horizontal aperture are the traditional baking technology for areas roughly aligning with the la Tène culture, evident in the later regions of Germania, Gaul, and parts of the Iberian Peninsula. In central and southern Italy, with Italic, Greek, and Etruscan populations, terracotta baking vessels were the primary means of baking.

These regions of common baking practices paint a picture of homogeny that somewhat betrays the remarkable amount of variation in the different types of ovens and millstones even within a single culture or even community. The cultural unit upon which baking should be understood in this early period, at least for most communities, was the family or kinship group. In fact, most bread consumed, even in urban contexts, was probably baked by the household for the household, with surplus possibly sold. The commercialization of baking in the western Mediterranean was only beginning in the third century CE and culminated in the first century CE. We tend to conceive of the ancient Mediterranean dichotomously, in terms of pre-Roman and Roman, but homogenization was clearly part of a longer-term trend of increasing contact between different peoples that only accelerated with the advent of Roman dominion. There is no doubt that the political unification under the Roman empire had some homogenizing effects, opening more long-distance trade and exchange, which were likely coeval with other phenomena such as specialization and commercialization. The mechanisms for the homogenization of baking in the western Roman Empire, from the third century BCE forward, remain unclear, but the millstone trade—and trade in general—surely played an important role. But that would really only account for technological similarities. The military, human trafficking of slaves, and general human mobility almost surely played a role as well. The elite household played some role, where clear bakeries are found they are often have proximity to large houses, such as at Pompeii, Volubilis, or Italica. We might have to imagine that these cities had a local population and a Roman or Romanized elite grafted onto them that brought with them certain tastes and preferences that dictated the form of Roman bakeries and bread. Centering production on elite households helped to create a convergent development in supply and investment, thus furthering homogenization.

100 BCE to 250 CE, while variation between cities could be quite high, even between neighbors such as Pompeii and Herculaneum or Volubilis and Banasa, within a single city there was some consistency grounded in common traditions, available resources, and shared infrastructure. But even between cities and regions, a notion of a Roman bakery emerges that is both pan-Mediterranean and heavily grounded in local traditions. The typical Roman bakery had hourglass millstones, mixers, and domed ovens. The operational sequence largely moved from exterior to interior, with millstones near doors and ovens in interior spaces. It was small and produced on a workshop level, only dabbling in high levels of production in urban centers with complex economies and large populations, such as Ostia and Rome.

In the later periods, what little homogeny in bakery existed evaporated as the unity of the Roman period ebbed. Some regions maintained high levels of production in cities that hosted regional and imperial authorities, such as Trier, Cologne, or Rome. In other places, such as Cosa or Djemila, monasteries and churches become contexts for baking, be it commercial or communal. But most bakers probably remained small-scale producers, similar to those evident in earlier times, at cities such as Pompeii, Italica, or Volubilis.

Notes

1. Bustamante et al. (2014, 14–17) and Maune, Monteix, and Poux (2013, 9–26).
2. Woolf (2004), Oltean (2008), Sinner (2015) and Haeussler (2016).
3. Delgado and Ferrer (2007).

4. Hoyos (2010, 110).
5. Sparkes (1981, pl. 4).
6. Khanoussi et al. (2004, 55).
7. Samuel (1999).
8. Hodgson et al. (2014) and Amorós Ruiz and Fili (2019, 285).
9. Pasqualone (2018, 15–17).
10. Khanoussi et al. (2004, 55) and Fantar (1985, 155–156).
11. Sparkes (1981, 175–76), Bartoloni (1987, 243–244, fig. 12) and Bartoloni (1990, 62, 78, fig. 11) and Campanella (2009, 469–98).
12. Helas et al. (2011, 98–102), Russenberger (2016, 235–36) and Docter (2019, 447).
13. Gener Basallote et al. (2014: 30–31) and Docter (2019, 446–447).
14. Wefers (2011, 70).
15. Morel (2001).
16. Williams-Thorpe and Thorpe (1990).
17. Woolf (2004, 191).
18. Pliny *Nat. Hist.* XVIII.12.
19. Maune, Monteix and Poux (2013).
20. This reconstruction of a Bronze-Age clay oven, from what is referred to as the Ottomány culture, was in a small house in a fortified settt near NižnÁ Myšla in eastern Slovakia. Similar morphologies are evident throughout central and western Europe. Olexa (2003).
21. Währen (1996, 11).
22. Währen (1996, 12).
23. Währen (2002, 392).
24. Almeida et al. (1981, Est. III, p. 4), Almeida (1982), Sørensen (1999, 161–65) and Währen (2002, 393–97).
25. González-Ruibal (2006, 15). Two deliberate deposits of animal remains were found under an oven at Ulm, including an entire calf directly below the oven deposit, further indicating that baking and ovens probably had some ritual connotations. Pressmar (1979, 21–23).
26. Dedet (1990, 41). "Dans toute cette partie de la salle, les grains de céréales carbonisés sont nombreux, dispersés mais avec une densité maximale dans la moitié ouest de la zone absidiale, qui est aussi la plus riche en fragments de contenants en matière légère et en poterie. Prend place également dans cette région de l'habitation une concentration de grains et de charbons de bois d'une vingtaine de centimètres de diamètre sur 2 ou 3 cm d'épaisseur (fig. 3, n° 6)."
27. Chabot (1978): L. Chabot, Découverte de fours à pain en pisé dans les oppida de la Tène III de la périphérie de l'étang de Berre, B.-du-Rh., CCSAP, 6, 1978, 1–17.Py (1990, 668). "Rappelons enfin que les structures de cuisson comprennent aussi, au IIe Age du Fer, des fours à usage

très probablement culinaire (fours à pain, à galette ou autre). Un type particulier est constitué par des fosses arrondies tapissées d'argile, dan s lesquelles la braise était déposée, et qui étaient parfois sans doute recouvertes d'un dôme de torchis. Un deuxième type correspond aux fours à sole mobile percée, attestés du BFIIIb au IVe s., et pour lesquels une utilisation culinaire est envisa geable170. Les fours à base plane (sole d'argile à même le sol recouverte d'une calotte en dôme) sont attestés en place aux IVe-IIe s." Sa Caleta: Ramon Torres (2007: 132, 165, 176, 187, 205–206).

28. Py (1990, 436).
29. Wefers (2011, 70).
30. Wefers (2011).
31. Curtis (2001, 282).
32. Frankel (2003).
33. Bouloumié (1972) and Potter (1976).
34. Sparkes (1962, 127) and Tsoukala (2009, 388).
35. Cahill (2002, 248) and Bonias and Perreault (2002, 110–111, fig. 1, pl. 2).
36. Bouloumié (1978).
37. Cubberly et al. (1988, 101).
38. Walthall et al. (2018, 8).
39. Lucore 2015, 93.
40. Riediker-Liechti (2016, 9–10).
41. Tsakirgis (1984, 51).
42. Tréziny and Mège (2018, 264–266) (*Megara Hyblaea* 7).
43. Rossetto (1973), Brandt (1993, 14–15), Curtis (2001, 358–60); Petersen (2006, 87–88).
44. Pliny the Elder *Nat. Hist.* XVIII, 107–8.
45. Plautus, *Asinaria*, I.200.
46. *CIL* X 3779, dated to 106 BC by Boak (1916, 28).
47. Fujisawa (1995, 175); "*in pistrino pisetur*", Varro, *De Re Rustica*, 1.63.
48. Pliny the Elder *Nat. Hist.* XVIII.28.
49. Mayeske (1972, 82–136).
50. Mayeske attempts to address commercial versus domestic production by dividing bakeries according to their relationship with domestic spaces, bakeries linked with large houses or bakeries with no domestic space. The critique of this sort of analysis (Wallace-Hadrill 1994) has been that any space could be considered domestic and that it emphasizes elite particaption in commercial activity over the contributions of the entire workgroup.
51. Monteix (2016, 154–69).
52. Peacock (1989).
53. Monteix (2016, 234 fig. 7.7).

54. Monteix (2016, 161–64).
55. Maiuri (1958, 451–61), Deiss (1989, 122–24); Wallace-Hadrill (2011, 275–77) and Guidobaldi et al. (2012, 183–9).
56. Monteix (2010, 255–288).
57. Maiuri (1958, fig. 410).
58. Coates-Stephens (2006).
59. Gaius, *Institutiones*, 1.34; *FV* 233; *Dig*. 3.4.1–3.4.1.3 (Gaius); *FV* 235; *HA Aurelianus* 35.1.
60. Kirschenbaum (1987, 99).
61. There is sporadic evidence, such as millstones found in a building below the Capitoline near the Teatro Marcello southwest of via delle Tre Pile (Muñoz and Colini 1930, 53–4; Lugli 1940, 7; Muñoz 1943, 10; Colini 1998, 130–3, 143–4) and millstone floor found on slopes of the Palatine, which might suggest a water mill was present (Wilson 2003). Coates-Stephens identified millstones outside the Porta Maggiore dating to the first century BCE.
62. Bakker (1999, 60).
63. Marquardt (1886, 423), Tengström (1974, 76–77), Sirks (1991, 307), Wacke (1992, 648) and Erdkamp (2005, 253–54).
64. Fentress and Bodel (2003, 72–78).
65. Amraoui (2017).
66. Antonelli (2010) and De Vos et al. (2011, 142–44).
67. Leschi (1953, 260).
68. Allais (1954, 352).
69. Ballu (1909, 77) and Amraoui (2017, 113–114).
70. Gsell (1918, 90).
71. Amraoui (2017, 200–201).
72. 120 CIL VIII, 16921 = ILAlg, l, 579.

    121 C/L VIII, 24678 = AE 1896, 83 L(ucius) Atilius L(uci) l(ibertus) Hiero furnari(us) / Valeria |(mulieris) l(iberta) Euterpefurnaria / vivit / C(aius) Valerius C(ai) l(ibertus) Dionisius(!) triari(us) / vivit

    CIL VIII, 22944 = AE 1903, 238 = AE

    1903, 258. D(is) M(anibus) s(acrum) / L(ucius) Calpurnius / Furnarius vixit / annis LX et bene / vixit et ad funus / eius erogati |(denarii) C
73. Wilson (2002, 15) and Lepelley (1981, 499–500).
74. Amraoui (2017, 201).
75. Leduc (2008, 2011).
76. Leduc (2008, 488–94).
77. Benton (2020).
78. Es-Sadra (2010, 598).
79. Zehnacker and Halier (1964, 392).

80. Alaioud (2010, 577–81).
81. Alaioud (2010, 577).
82. Alaioud (2010, 580–81); THOUVENOT, Une colonie romaine, cit., p. 21–23; R. THOUVENOT, A. LUQUET, Le quartier sud-ouest, «PSAM», XI, 1954, p. 71–72.
83. Thouvenot (1954, 72).
84. Ponsich (1974, 1979: 70 Pl. XVI). Bigi (2019); Similar connections have been isolated by Hassini (2008, 431).
85. Bustamante et al. (2014, 39–41 fig. 24).
86. Caballos Rufino et al. (1999, 70), Caballos Rufino (2010, 90 fig. 7.7) and Bustamante et al. (2014, 39–41 fig. 23).
87. Bustamante et al. (2014, 38–39 fig. 22).
88. Bustamante et al. (2014, 43–44 fig. 27).
89. Mauné et al. (2013).
90. Penn (1958).
91. Adams (2005).
92. Mauné et al. (2013, 147 fig. 154).
93. In Narbonne, the oven of the Vautubiere at Codoux (Bouchesdu- Rhone) has a diameter of 1.70 m (Bouet 1992, 252) and that of the villa of Labassan (Gard) is 1.80 m in diameter (Buffat 2011, 140). An early second-century oven at Toulon with 2 m (fragment) (Brun 1999, 794).
94. Peacock (1980, 1986), Thorpe (1988), Thorpe and Thorpe (1990, 1993), Antonelli et al. (2000, 2001), Renzulli et al. (2002) and Antonelli and Lazzarini (2010).
95. Jaccottey and Longepierre (2011).
96. Reusch (1970, 49–51).
97. Sărăţeanu-Müller (2011).
98. Sărăţeanu-Müller (2011, 312).
99. Ammann and Schwarz (2011, 317).
100. Berger (1977, 29).
101. Ammann and Schwarz (2011, 275–318).
102. Ammann and Schwarz (2011, 394–396).
103. The idea that the presence of the Roman army dictated the nature of the local economy in liminal provinces is an old one, best expressed by Keith Hopkins (1980) who argued that areas in which legions were stationed relied heavily on soldiers' pay to fuel their economy.
104. Reusch (1970) identifies a cavity found in the palace as a tannūr-style oven of the sort found Tunisia, which is possible in a multicultural, large urban center such as Trier, especially in an Imperial court. But this identification is grounded in only partially preserved remains and has no parallel in Trier or in other Imperial palaces more generally.
105. M. Liberius Victor CIL XIII 8725 NEGOTIATOR FRVMENTARIVS.

106. Tertinius Secundus CIL XIII 8338 NEG PISTORICIVS.
107. Verboeven (2007, 10). "Pourtant, dans le cas de negotiatores producteurs, ce n'est sans doute pas la production en soi qui leur confère la qualité de negotiator, mais le fait qu'ils ont investi leur argent dans une entreprise dont ils commercialisaient ensuite les produits."

References

Adams, Geoff W. 2005. *Romano-Celtic élites and their Religion: A Study of Archaeological Sites in Gloucestershire.* Armidale: Caeros Publishing.

Alaioud, Sidi Mohammed. 2010. Les activités artisanales à Banasa: témoignages archéologiques. In *L'Africa romana: i luoghi e le forme dei mestieri e della produzione nelle province africane: atti del XVIII convegno di studio, Olbia, 11–14 dicembre 2008*, ed. Marco Milanese, Paola Ruggieri, and Cinzia Vismara, 51–68. Roma: Carocci.

Allais, Y. 1954. Les fouilles de 1950–1952 dans le quartier Est de Djemila. *LIBYCA* 11 (2e): 343–361.

Almeida, C.A.B. 1982. Castelo de Faria. Campanha de Escavações de 1981. *Barcellos-Revista* 1 (1): 79–88.

Almeida, C.A.F., C.A.B. Almeida, T. de Soeiro, and A.J. Baptista. 1981. *Escavações arqueológicas em Santo Estêvão da Facha.* Ponte de Lima: Câmara Municipal de Ponte de Lima.

Ammann, S., and P.A. Schwarz. 2011. *Eine Taberna in Augusta Raurica: ein Verkaufsladen, Werk- und Wohnraum in Insula 5/9: Ergebnisse der Grabungen 1965–1967 und 2002.* Augst: Museum Augusta Raurica.

Amraoui, Touatia. 2017. *L'artisanat dans les cités antiques de l'Algérie: 1. siècle avant notre ère – 7. siècle après notre ère.* Oxford: Archaeopress.

Antonelli, Fabrizio, and Lorenzo Lazzarini. 2010. Mediterranean Trade of the Most Widespread Roman Volcanic Millstones from Italy and Petrochemical Markers of Their Raw Materials. *Journal of Archaeological Science* 37: 2081–2092.

Antonelli, F., G. Nappi, and L. Lazzarini. 2000. Sulla "pietra da mole" della regione di Orvieto: Caratterizzazione petrografica e studio archeometrico di macine storiche e protostoriche dall'Italia centrale. In *Proceedings of I Congresso Nazionale di Archeometria*, ed. M. Martini et al., 195–207. Patron Editore: Verona.

———. 2001. Roman Millstones from Orvieto (Italy): Petrographic and Geochemical Data for a New Archaeometric Contribution. *Archaeometry* 43 (2): 167–189.

Bakker, Jan Theo. 1999. *The Mills-Bakeries of Ostia: Description and Interpretation.* Amsterdam: J.C. Gieben.

Ballu, A. 1909. Rapport sur les fouilles executes en 1908 par le Service des Monuments historiques de l'Algerie. *BCTH*: 75–111.

Bartoloni, P. 1987. Cuccureddus. La ceramica fenicia. *RendLinc* 42: 237–244.

———. 1990. S. Antioco: area del Cronicario (campagne di scavo 1983–86). I recipienti chiusi d'us domestico e commerciale. *RStFen* 18: 37–80.

Benton, J.T. (2020). "The Bakeries of Volubilis: Process, Space, and Interconnectivity." *Mouseion* 17; 2.

Berger, Ludwig. 1977. Ein gut erhaltener Backofen in Augusta Raurica. *Regio Basiliensis* 18: 28–40.

Bigi, Leonardo. 2019. *Gli oleifici di Volubilis e della Mauretania Tingitana*. Roma: Edizioni Quasar.

Boak, A.E.R. 1916. The Magistri of Campania and Delos. *Classical Philology* 11 (1): 25–45.

Bonias, Z., and J. Perreault. 2002. Ἄργιλος, Ανασκαφή 1998–1999. *To Archaiologiko Ergo sti Makedonia kai Thraki* 14: 109–115.

Bouet, A. 1992. Balnéaire et cuisine: une unité domestique sur une villa de la basse vallée de l'Arc, la Vautubière à Coudoux (Bouches-du-Rhône). *Revue Archéologique de Narbonnaise* 25: 241–264.

Boulomié, B. 1972. Murlo (Poggio Civitate, Sienne): céramique grossière locale, L'instrumentum culinaire. *Mélanges de l'École française de Rome, Antiquité* 84: 61–110.

———. 1978. Nouveaux instruments culinaires en céramique de Murlo (Poggio Civitate). *Mélanges de l'École française de Rome, Antiquité* 90: 113–131.

Brandt, Olle. 1993. Recent Research on the Tomb of Eurysaces. *Opuscula Romana* 19 (2): 13–17.

Brun, J.-P. 1999. *Carte archéologique de la Gaule 83, Le Var 2*. Paris: Académie des inscriptions et belles-lettres.

Buffat, Loïc. 2011. *L'économie domaniale en Gaule narbonnaise*. Lattes: Archéologie des Sociétés méditerranéennes.

Bustamante, Álvarez, Javier Salido Domínguez Macarena, Eulalia Gijón Gabriel, and Jean-Pierre Brun. 2014. *Pistrina Hispaniae panaderías, molinerías y el artesanado alimentario en la Hispania romana*. Montagnac: M. Mergoil.

Caballos Rufino, A. 2010. *ItÁlica-Santiponce: Municipium y Colonia Aelia Augusta Italicensium*. Roma: L'Erma di Bretschneider.

Caballos Rufino, A., J.M. Marín Fatuarte, and J.M. Rodríguez Hidalgo. 1999. *Itálica arqueológica*. Sevilla: Universidad de Sevilla.

Cahill, Nicholas. 2002. *Household and City Organization at Olynthus*. New Haven: Yale University Press.

Campanella, L. 2009. I forni, i fornelli e i bracieri fenici e punici. In *Nora: il foro romano: storia di un'area urbana dall'età fenicia alla tarda antichità, 1997–2006, Volume II.1*, a cura di Jacopo Bonetto, Andrea Raffaele Ghiotto,

Marta Novello, and Giovanna Falezza, 469–597. Padova: Università degli Studi di Padova – Dipartimento di Archeologia.
Chabot, L. 1978. Découverte de fours à pain en pisé dans les oppida de la Tène III de la périphérie de l'étang de Berre, B.-du-Rh. *Centre de coordination des Sociétés Archéologiques de Provence* 6: 1–17.
Coates-Stephens, R. 2006. Un Pistrinum Tardo Repubblicano a Porta Maggiore. *Atti Della Pontificia Accademia Romana Di Archeologia* LXXVIII: 473–498.
Colini, A.M. 1998. In *Appunti degli scavi di Roma*, ed. C. Buzzetti, G. Ioppolo, and G. Pisani Sartorio. Roma: Quasar.
Cubberley, A.L., J.A. Lloyd, and P.C. Roberts. 1988. Testa and Clibani: The Baking Covers of Classical Italy. *Papers of the British School at Rome* 56: 98–119.
Curtis, Robert I. 2001. *Ancient Food Technology*. Leiden: Brill.
de Vos, M., R. Attoui, and M. Andreoli. 2011. Hand and 'Donkey' Mills in North African Farms. In *Bread for the People: The Archaeology of Mills and Milling: Proceedings of a Colloquium Held in the British School at Rome*, ed. David Franklyn Williams and David P.S. Peacock, 131–150. Oxford: Archaeopress.
Dedet, B. 1990. Une maison à absides sur l'oppidum de Gailhan (Gard) au milieu du V s. avant J.-C. La question du plan absidial en Gaule du Sud. *Gallia* 47: 29–55.
Deiss, Joseph Jay. 1989. *Herculaneum: Italy's Buried Treasure*. Malibu: J. Paul Getty Museum.
Delgado, A., and M. Ferrer. 2007. Cultural Contacts in Colonial Setting: The Construction of New Identities in the Phoenician Settlements in the Western Mediterranean. *Stanford Journal of Archaeology* 5: 18–42.
Docter, Roald. 2019. Residential Architecture. In *The Oxford Handbook of the Phoenician and Punic Mediterranean*, ed. Brian R. Doak and Carolina López-Ruiz, 435–452. New York: Oxford University Press.
Erdkamp, Paul. 2005. *The Grain Market in the Roman Empire: A Social, Political and Economic Study*. Cambridge: Cambridge University Press.
Es-Sadra, L. 2010. Les espaces économiques dans les maisons de Volubilis. *L'Africa Romana* XVIII: 593–604.
Fantar, Muhammad. 1985. *Kerkouane: cité Punique du Cap Bon (Tunisie)*. Tunis: Institut National d'Archéologie et d'Art de Tunisie.
Fentress, Elizabeth, and John P. Bodel. 2003. *Cosa V: An Intertmittent Town, Excavations 1991–1997*. Ann Arbor: Published for the American Academy in Rome by the University of Michigan Press.
Frankel, Rafael. 2003. The Olynthus Mill, Its Origin, and Diffusion: Typology and Distribution. *American Journal of Archaeology* 107 (1): 1–21.
Fujisawa, A. 1995. I 'Pistores' nel Primo Impero. *Acme* 48 (2): 169–181.
Gener Basallote, J.-M., M.Á. Navarro García, J.-M. Pajuelo Sáez, M. Torres Ortiz, and E. López Rosendo. 2014. Arquitectura y urbanismo de la Gadir fenicia: El yacimiento del 'Teatro Cómico' de Cádiz. In *Los Fenicios en la Bahía de Cádiz. Nuevas investigaciones*, ed. M. Botto, 14–50. Pisa/Rome: Fabrizio Serra editore.

González-Ruibal, Alfredo. 2006. House Societies vs. Kinship-Based Societies: An Archaeological Case from Iron Age Europe. *Journal of Anthropological Archaeology* 25: 144–173.

Gsell, Stéphane. 1918. *Khamissa, Mdaourouch, Announa, fouilles exécutées par le Service des monuments historiques de l'Algérie. Troisième partie. Announa. Texte explicatif par Stéphane Gsell, plans et vues par Charles-Albert Joly.* Alger: A. Jourdan.

Guidobaldi, Maria Paola, Domenico Esposito, and Luciano Pedicini. 2012. *Ercolano: colori di una città sepolta.* San Giovanni Lupatoto, Verona: Arsenale Editrice.

Haeussler, R. 2016. *Becoming Roman? Diverging Identities and Experiences in Ancient Northwest Italy.* London: Routledge.

Hassini, H. 2008. Réflexions économiques et chronologiques sur le site de *Cotta*. *Africa Romana XVII*: 425–440.

Helas, S., O. Hofmeister, A. Werner, J. Schumann, G. Zuchtriegel, and G. Mammina. 2011. *Selinus II. Die punische Stadt auf der Akropolis.* Wiesbaden: Reichert.

Hodgson, J.A., C.J. Mulligan, A. Al-Meeri, and R.L. Raaum. 2014. Early Back-to-Africa Migration into the Horn of Africa. *PLoS Genetics* 10 (6): e1004393. https://doi.org/10.1371/journal.pgen.1004393.

Hopkins, Keith. 1980. Taxes and Trade in the Roman Empire (200 B.C.-A.D. 400). *The Journal of Roman Studies* 70: 101–125.

Hoyos, B.D. 2010. *The Carthaginians.* Milton Park: Routledge.

Jaccottey, L., and S. Longepierre. 2011. Pompeian Millstones in France. In *Bread for the People: The Archaeology of Mills and Milling: Proceedings of a Colloquium Held in the British School at Rome, 2009*, ed. D.F. Williams and David Peacock, 97–116. Oxford: Archaeopress.

Khanoussi, M., S. Ritter, and P. von Rummel. 2004. The German-Tunisian Project at Dougga: First Results of the Excavations South of the Maison du Trifolium. *Antiquités Africaines* 40–41: 43–66.

Kirschenbaum, Aaron. 1987. *Sons, Slaves, and Freedmen in Roman Commerce.* Jerusalem: Magnes Press, Hebrew University.

Leduc, M. 2008. Les Pistrina Volubilitains, Temoins Majeurs du Dynamisme Economique Municipal. In *L'Africa Romana. Le Ricchezze dell'Africa Risorse, Produzioni, Scambi. Atti del XVII Convegno di Studio. Sevilla, 14–17 Dicembre 2006*, 475–505. Rome: Carocci.

———. 2011. L'artisanat au Coeur de la ville: l'exemple des pistrina de Volubilis. In *La ville au quotidien: regards croisés sur l'habitat et l'artisanat antiques: Afrique du Nord, Gaule et Italie: actes du colloque international, Maison méditerranéenne des sciences de l'homme, Aix-en-Provence, 23 et 24 novembre*, ed. Souen Fontaine, Stéphanie Satre, and Amel Tekki, vol. 2007, 181–189. Aix-en-Provence: Publications de l'Université de Provence.

Lepelley, C. 1981. *Les cités de l'Afrique romaine au Bas-Empire: Étude d'histoire municipal.* Vol. 2. Paris: Études Augustiniennes.

Leschi, Louis. 1953. *Djemila, antique Cvicvl.* Algiers: Gouvernement Général de l'Algérie.

Lucore, S.K. 2015. Le Terme Sud di Morgantina . impianti idrico e di riscaldamento. In *Morgantina Duemilaequindici. La ricerca archeologica a sessant'anni dall'avvio degli scavi*, ed. L. Maniscalco, 92–101. Palermo: Assessorato dei Beni Culturali.

Lugli, G. 1940. *I monumenti antichi di Roma e suburbia, supplemento: un decennio di scoperte archeologiche.* Roma: G. Bardi.

Maiuri, Amadeo. 1958. *Ercolano: i nuovi scavi (1927–1958) Vol. 1.* Roma: Istituto Poligrafico dello Stato.

Marquardt, Joachim. 1886. *Das Privatleben der Römer, T. 1.* Leipzig: Hirzel.

Mauné, S., N. Monteix, and M. Poux. 2013. Cuisines et boulangeries en Gaule romaine. Gallia. In *Paris.* CNRS Editions: Revue Gallia.

Mauné, S., Charlotte Carrato, Núria Rovira, Julie Le Fur, Samuel Longepierre, et al. 2013. La boulangerie de Saint-Bézard à Aspiran (Hérault), du I er s. au IV e s. apr. J.-C.: Un exemple d'espace culinaire domanial en Narbonnaise centrale. *Cuisines et boulangeries en Gaule romaine* 70 (1): 165–190.

Mayeske, Betty Jo B. 1972. Bakeries, Bakers, and Bread at Pompeii: A Study in Social and Economic History. Ph.D. dissertation, Ann Arbor.

Monteix, N. 2010. *Les lieux de métier: boutiques et ateliers d'Herculanum. Collection du Centre Jean Bérard, 34.* Rome: École française de Rome.

———. 2016. Contextualizing the Operational Sequence: Pompeian Bakeries as a Case Study. In *Urban Craftsmen and Traders in the Roman World*, ed. Miko Flohr and Andrew Wilson, 153–182. Oxford: Oxford University Press.

Morel, J.P. 2001. Aux origines du moulin rotatif? Une meule circulaire de la fin du VIe siècle avant notre ère à Carthage. In *Techniques et sociétés en Méditerranée. Collection Atelier Méditerranéen*, ed. J.-P. Brun and Ph. Jockey, 241–249. Paris: Maison méditerranéenne des sciences de l'homme.

Muñoz, A. 1943. *L'isolamento del Colle Capitolino.* Roma: M. Bretschneider.

Muñoz, A., and A.M. Colini. 1930. *Campidoglio.* Roma: Biblioteca d'Arte.

Olexa, Ladislav. 2003. *NižnÁ Myšla: osada a pohrebisko z doby bronzovej.* Košice: SlovenskÁ Akadémia Vied, Archeologický ústav Nitra.

Oltean, I.A. 2008. *Dacia: Landscape, colonisation, and Romanisation.* New York: Routledge.

Pasqualone, A. 2018. Traditional Flat Breads Spread from the Fertile Crescent: Production Process and History of Baking Systems. *Journal of Ethnic Foods* 5 (1): 10–19.

Peacock, D.P.S. 1980. The Roman Millstone Trade: A Petrological Sketch. *World Archaeology* 12 (1): 43–53.

———. 1989. The Mills of Pompeii. *Antiquity* 63: 205–214.

Peacock, D.P.S., and D.F. Williams. 1986. *Amphorae and the Roman Economy: An Introductory Guide*. London: Longman.
Penn, W.S. 1958. The Romano-British Settlement at Springhead. Excavation of the Bakery, Site A. *Archaeol Cantiana* 71: 53–105.
Petersen, L.H. 2006. *The Freedman in Roman Art and Art History*. New York: Cambridge University Press.
Ponsich, M. 1974. *Implantation rurale antique sur la Bas-Guadalquivir I*. Madrid: Casa De Velázquez.
———. 1979. *Implantation rurale antique sur la Bas-Guadalquivir II*. Parigi: Casa De Velázquez.
Potter, T.W. 1976. *A Faliscan Town in South Etruria*. London: British School at Rome.
Pressmar, E. 1979. *Elchinger Kreuz, Ldkr. Neu-Ulm, Siedlungsgrabung mit urnenfelderzeitlichem Töpferofen*. Kallmünz, Opf: Lassleben.
Py, M. 1990. *Culture, économie et société protohistoriques dans la région nimoise Vol. 1 & 2*. Rome: École Française de Rome.
Ramón Torres, J. 2007. *Excavaciones arqueológicas en el asentamiento fenicio de Sa Caleta (Ibiza)*. Barcelona: Edicions Bellaterra.
Renzulli, A., P. Santi, G. Nappi, M. Luni, and D. Vitali. 2002. Provenance and Trade of Volcanic Rock Millstones from Etruscan-Celtic and Roman Archaeological Sites in Central Italy. *European Journal of Mineralogy* 14: 175–183.
Reusch, W. 1970. Backöfen orientalischer Form im römischen Trier. *TZ* 33: 49–56.
Riediker-Liechti, E. 2016. *Takeaway in Antiquity—A Roman Tavern on Monte Iato (PA)*. Paper presented at the 14th Annual International Conference on History & Archaeology, Athens, June 27–30.
Rossetto, P.C. 1973. *Il sepolcro del fornaio Marco Virgilio Eurisace a Porta Maggiore*. Rome: Istituto di studi romani.
Ruiz, Victoria Amorós, and Abdallah Fili. 2019. Le Ceramique. In *Volubilis après Rome: les fouilles UCL/INSAP, 2000–2005*, ed. Elizabeth Fentress, Ali Aït Kaci, and Vincent Jolivet, 215–292. Leiden: Brill.
Russenberger, C. 2016. Punier am Berg. Archäologische Szenarien punischer Präsenz im Binnenland des frühhellenistischen Westsizilien am Beispiel des Monte Iato. In *Karthago Dialoge. Karthago und der punische Mittelmeerraum–Kulturkontakte und Kulturtransfers im 1. Jahrtausend vor Christus*, ed. F. Schön and H. Töpfer, 227–251. Tübingen: Eberhard Karls Universität Tübingen.
Samuel, D. 1999. Bread Making and Social Interactions at the Amarna Workmen's Village, Egypt. *World Archaeology* 31 (1): 121–144.
Sărăţeanu-Müller, F. 2011. The Roman villa Complex of Reinheim, Germany. In *Villa Landscapes in the Roman North: Economy, Culture, Lifestyles*, ed. Nico Roymans and Ton Derks, 301–315. Amsterdam: Amsterdam University Press.

Sinner, A. 2015. Cultural Contacts and Identity Construction: A Colonial Context in NE Spain (2nd – Early 1st c. B.C.). *Journal of Roman Archaeology* 28: 7–37.
Sirks, A.J.B. 1991. *Food for Rome: The Legal Structure of the Transportation and Processing of Supplies for the Imperial Distributions in Rome and Constantinople.* Amsterdam: J.C. Gieben.
Sørensen, M.L. 1999. *Gender Archaeology.* Cambridge/Oxford/Malden: Polity Press.
Sparkes, B.A. 1962. The Greek Kitchen. *The Journal of Hellenic Studies* 82: 121–137.
———. 1981. Not Cooking, but Baking. *Greece & Rome* 28: 172–178.
Tengström, E. 1974. *Bread for the People. Studies of the Corn-Supply of Rome During the Late Empire.* Stockholm: Skrifter utg. av Svenska institutet i Rom.
Thorpe, O.W. 1988. Provenancing and Archaeology of Roman Millstones from the Mediterranean Area. *Journal of Archaeological Science* 15: 253–305.
Thorpe, O.W., and R.S. Thorpe. 1990. Millstone Provenancing Used in Tracing the Route of a Fourth-Century BC Greek Merchant Ship. *Archaeometry* 32: 115–137.
———. 1993. Geochemistry and Trade of Eastern Mediterranean Millstones from the Neolithic to Roman Periods. *Journal of Archaeological Science* 20: 263–320.
Thouvenot, R., and A. Luquet. 1954. Le quartier sud-ouest. *PSAM* XI: 71–72.
Tréziny, H., and F. Mège. 2018. *Mégara Hyblaea. 7, 7.* Rome: École française de Rome.
Tsakirgis, B. 1984. The Domestic Architecture of Morgantina in the Hellenistic and Roman Periods. PhD diss., Princeton University.
Tsoukala, V. 2009. Cereal Processing and the Performance of Gender in Archaic and Classical Greece: Iconography and Function of A Group of Terracotta Vases and Statuettes. Presented at the Proceedings of the XI Symposium on Mediterranean Archaeology, Istanbul Technical University, 24–29 April 2007, BAR International Series 1900: 387–395.
Verboven, K. 2007. Good for Business. The Roman Army and the Emergence of a "Business Class" in the Northwestern Provinces of the Roman Empire. In *The Impact of the Roman Army (200 BC–AD 476): Economic, Social, Political, Religious and Cultural Aspects*, Proceeding of the 6th Workshop of the Network Impact of Empire. Capri 2005, ed. L. de Blois and E. Lo Cascio, 295–313. Leiden/Boston: Brill.
Wacke, A. 1992. Mühlen und Müllerbäcker im römischen Reich und Recht. In *Europarecht, Energierecht, Wirtschaftsrecht*, ed. Jürgen Baur, Peter-Christian Müller-Graff, and Manfred Zuleeg, 641–670. Köln: C. Heymann.
Währen, M. 1996. Vorgeschichtliche Brotreste aus der nördlichen Lüneburger Heide. *Harburger Jahrbuch* 19: 11–38.
———. 2002. Pain, pâtisserie et religion en Europe Pré- et Protohistorique Origines et attestationscultuelles du pain. *Civilisations* 49 (1/2): 381–400.

Wallace-Hadrill, A. 1994. *Houses and Society in Pompeii and Herculaneum*. Princeton: Princeton University Press.

———. 2011. *Herculaneum: Past and Future*. London: Frances Lincoln Limited.

Walthall, A., T. Souza, J. Benton, E. Wueste, and A. Tharler. 2018. Preliminary Report on the 2015 Field Season of the American Excavations at Morgantina: Contrada Agnese Project (CAP). *FastiOnLine Documents & Research* 408: 1–23.

Wefers, S. 2011. Still Using Your Saddle Quern? A Compilation of the Oldest Known Rotary Querns in Western Europe. In *Bread for the People: The Archaeology of Mills and Milling: Proceedings of a Colloquium Held in the British School at Rome, 4th–7th November 2009*, ed. D.F. Williams and David Peacock, 67–76. Oxford: Archaeopress.

Wilson A. 2002. *Urban production in the Roman world, the view from North Africa*. Papers of the British School at Rome LXX, 231–274.

———. 2003. Late Antique Water-Mills on the Palatine. *Papers of the British School at Rome* 71: 85–109.

Woolf, G. 2004. *Becoming Roman: The Origins of Provincial Civilization in Gaul*. Cambridge: Cambridge University Press.

Zehnacker, H., and G. Hallier. 1964. Les premiers thermes de Volubilis et la Maison a la citerne. *Mélanges d'archéologie et d'histoire* 76: 343–418.

CHAPTER 3

Modes of Production: Bakeries as Factories and Workshops

Commercial baking, as we saw in the last chapter, was defined by variation not only because it grew out of family, kinship, and cultural habits, but also because different communities were tapped into different networks of supply and had different levels of economic complexity. When baking is considered as cultural heritage, as it was in the last chapter, one tends to highlight the differences between workshops even within a single city.[1] But there is also value in considering the commonalities—those traits that comprise a universal 'Roman bakery'—particularly in considering the different sorts that existed. Roman bakeries were small workshops that relied upon small workgroups. But we also saw that there were some notable exceptions to this generalization. At Ostia, bakeries were massive structures completely divorced from domestic space with as many as six millstones and massive ovens with average diameters over 5 m. This chapter will accomplish two things. First, it establishes the dichotomous nature of the evidence for commercial baking in the Roman world and provides a parallel to that evidence in the bakeries of Newark, New Jersey, during the Industrial Revolution. Second, the chapter adopts 'modes of production,' as per Marx's conceptualization of commercial activity, as a framework for the evidence for ancient commercial baking, but also as a way to tie all the disparate evidence together into a coherent model. Using the different modes of production as a point of departure, the chapter establishes that there were also complementary shifts in conceptualizations of work and home, families and workforces, and the strategies of their leaders. Such a

J. T. Benton, *The Bread Makers*,
https://doi.org/10.1007/978-3-030-46604-6_3

coherent model of bread production allows the exploration, in successive chapters, of topics for which we have little or no material evidence, such as exploitation, training, shared risk management, and collective identity.

That the economies of larger cities differed from those of smaller towns is not a new observation. Cameron Hawkins, for instance, observes that the size of demand in large cities created thicker markets with more opportunity to generate thin profit margins, but substantial wealth. Smaller towns lacked that same demand and mass-produced bread at cheap prices was not the economic strategy.[2] Thus the size of the market effected the strategy of economic actors. This divide is also very evident in the data derived from bakeries, such as oven size, bakery size, and millstone or mixer quantities. Some bakeries fit the general model proposed in the last chapter—small workshops grounded in a family unit—but another bakery type existed that was much larger and capable of much greater production levels. When we examine the scale of production in bakeries, two broad categories emerge from the data. First, examining oven diameter of bakeries across the western Mediterranean from 200 BCE to 700 CE, most ovens fall within a range of 1.5–3 meters, with a median at about 2.6 meters (Fig. 3.1). There is another category of ovens, found mostly in Ostia and North Africa in the third century and later, which ranges from four to six meters in average diameter. The area of workspace, that is the space within the workshop or house where production took place, displays a similar pattern and, again, Ostia emerges as a unique case. Bakeries in general fall neatly into two categories, with workspaces either under 100m^2 or over 200m^2; all of the latter are at Ostia (Fig. 3.2). The average number of millstones in those bakeries where millstones are in fact evident is 2.4, but at Ostia some bakeries have as many as ten.

The epigraphic evidence reveals a similar dichotomy in the commercial baking industry. Most bakers throughout the Roman empire have simple epitaphs referring to them as *pistores*, but in certain cities some participants in the commercial baking industry have titles such as *pistor* and *redemptor*, *negotiator pistoricius*, or *quinquennalis* of the *collegium pistorum*, which imply some greater degree of economic complexity.[3] That is to say, some participants in the baking industry had activities that were somehow more than the traditional repertoire of the Roman miller-baker.

The unique character of commercial baking in large urban centers, especially in the bakeries of Ostia, has been noted before.[4] But what has largely been absent in such analyses is a framework, through which to understand the binary nature of our evidence. 'Modes of production'

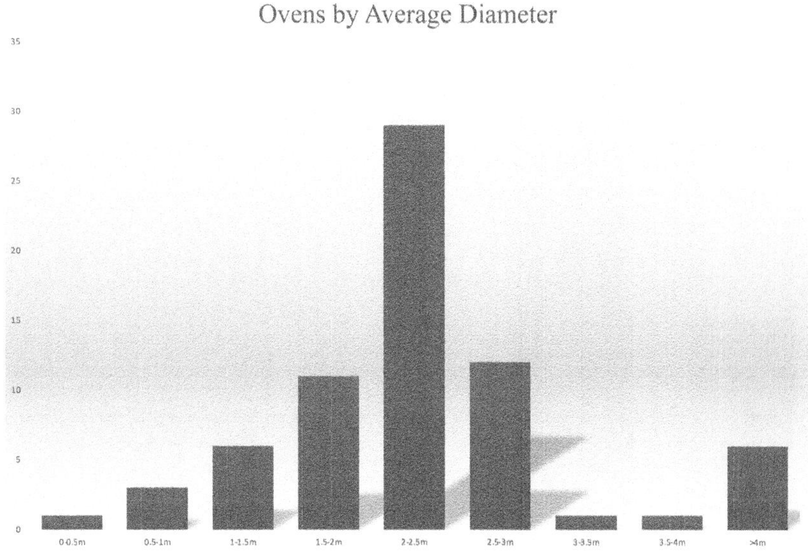

Fig. 3.1 Roman-Period Ovens in Bakeries by Average Diameter

offer just such a model. They were not, however, original to archaeology; they were products of the economic philosophers of the eighteenth and nineteenth centuries, who were trying to understand the nature of human history and its progress since the Upper Paleolithic. Adam Smith, for example, viewed different methods of production as a means of periodizing history, moving in a linear trajectory of progress with hunting giving way to the domestication of plants and animals and ultimately commerce. But modes of production, at least as a tradition in archaeological thought, were distilled through social historical materialism and a legacy of Marxist thought.[5] For Marx and Engels, modes of production were always more than the scale or means of production; modes were the social relations, political institutions, and economic systems that facilitated the use of available technologies to produce goods and services, which were in turn used to perpetuate or change such systems.[6]

Archaeologists and anthropologists, at least those influenced by Marxist traditions, have long deployed ‘modes of production’ as a way to periodize human history based on technologies and systems of production or to provide coherent models of production that acknowledge that economic

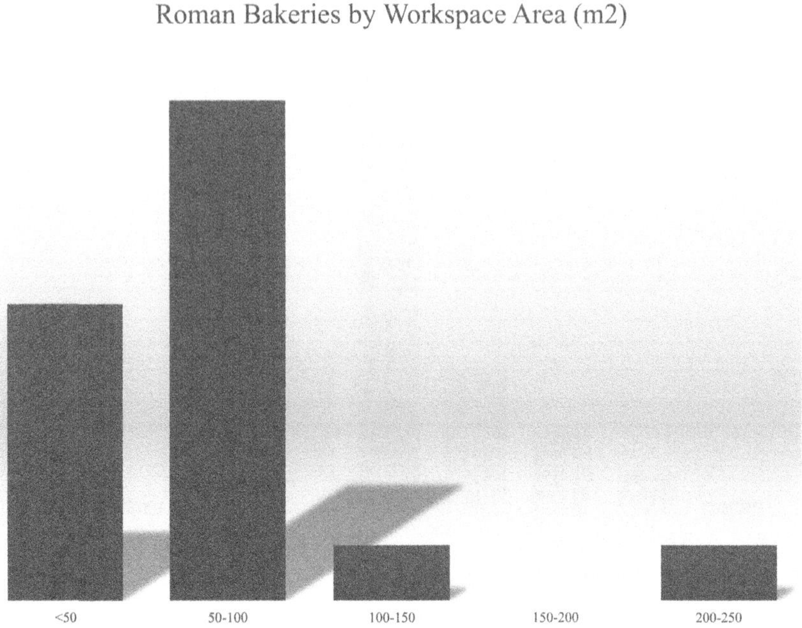

Fig. 3.2 Roman-Period Bakeries by Workspace Area

activity was embedded in – and reproduced – social constructs and institutions of power.[7] The literature that deploys 'modes of production' has often focused on categorizing production into universal types of production, but it is worth examining how Roman bakeries might align with these types. Eric Wolf describes three types of production: kin-ordered, tributary, and capitalist modes. Kin-ordered mode of production is the same as domestic or household production, which we saw was common if not dominant throughout the urban centers of the western Roman world in the last chapter. Wolf summarizes the tributary mode of product as one "in which the primary producer, whether cultivator or herdsman, is allowed access to the means of production, while tribute is exacted from him by political or military means." Wolf clearly placed the urban craftsmen of the Roman empire in the category of 'tributary,' which seems an accurate description of how local elites would have indirectly accessed the wealth generated by craft activity through social relationships and rents. In fact, we have two leases of bakeries, both from first-century CE Tebtynis and the other from seventh-century CE Oxyrhynchus.[8]

On the other hand, we saw that there was another type of bakery demonstrating large-scale production and technological innovation, which certainly evokes the third mode of production identified by Wolf: capitalist modes of production. For Wolf, three main attributes delineated capitalist from tributary modes.[9] First, capitalists detain the means of production; that is to say entrepreneurs control how goods are made and services provided.[10] Second, laborers are prevented from controlling the means of production; the craftsmen of the tributary mode of production were now employees rather than business owners in their own right. Third, production is maximized by increasing productivity through technological innovation and keeping labor costs down through low wages. It would be a mistake to push Wolf's description of capitalist modes of production onto Roman commercial baking, and labelling Roman baking as a certain mode will in general accomplish little. In fact, more recent work has moved away from "typological quibbling" and universalist approaches to the way production intersects with power structures and social habits.[11] But Wolf's analysis does point us in the direction of what phenomena might signal that fundamentally different sorts of production (and the way they intersect with power and wealth) existed in the Roman world, specifically businessmen (what Wolf would call capitalists or entrepreneurs), a growing shift from craftsmanship toward labor, and increased production and productivity through technological innovation. Moreover, Wolf's modes suggest where we might look to find a comparandum to serve as an appropriate sounding board: the shift from craft production to factory production.

The Industrial Revolution exemplifies a major shift in modes of production and has a number of interesting parallels with the dichotomous nature of the ancient baking industry. From 1889 to 1902, the authorities of New Jersey inspected workshops and factories around the state and published their findings in an *Annual Report of the Inspector of Factories and Workshops*.[12] During those 14 years, officials reviewed 371 different bakeries in the city of Newark alone. They were inspecting for cleanliness and to control for child labor laws. As such, they recorded the number of employees, their gender, and whether they were under-age. The reports refer to two types of spaces, bakeshops and bakehouses, but the definitions of these terms are never clarified. Despite imprecision in terminology, a dichotomy similar to that found among the Roman-period bakeries is also evident in the bakeries of Newark. The vast majority of Newark's bakeries,

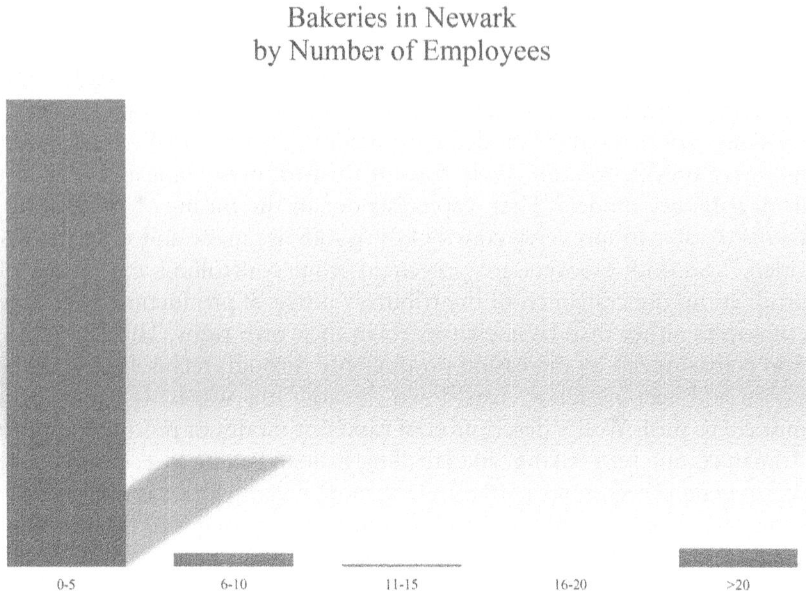

Fig. 3.3 Bakeries of Newark by Number of Employees Reported in the Annual Report of the Inspector of Factories and Workshops

355 or 96%, employ under ten people, with most of these employing two or fewer employees (Fig. 3.3). The other 4 percent of bakeries employed over 20 employees and on average employed 46 people. The addresses of the smaller bakeshops are not recorded, but the addresses of some of the larger bakeries are sometimes provided. Many of the original buildings are gone, but they can sometimes be identified on the Sanborn Insurance Maps and again the dichotomy of small and large bakeries emerges (Fig. 3.4).[13] The smaller bakeries range from 50 to 100m^2 in area, but the larger ones, such as the Mengels and Schmidt bakery, range from 500 to 1000m^2.

The parallels between the bakeries of the Roman world and those of late nineteenth-century Newark are significant. Some bakeries are small and produced on a modest scale with few employees. The larger bake-houses of Newark, on the other hand, had dozens and in some cases hundreds of employees. Richard Sennett characterized the different between the production of the workshop and that of the factory: "the workshop, as well as a home for families, was small in scale, each containing at most a

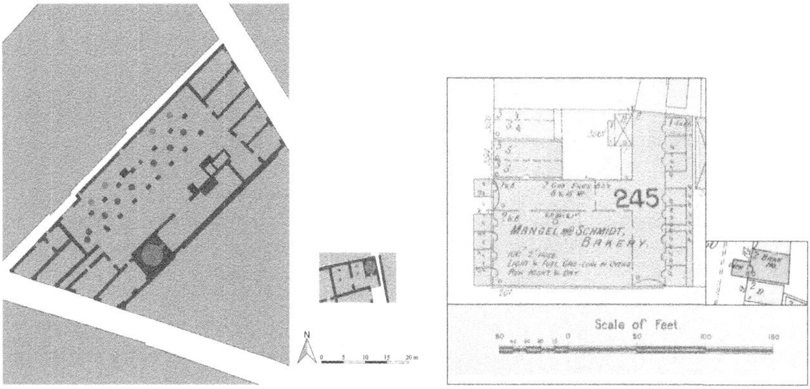

Fig. 3.4 The Molino at Ostia (I.XIII.4) the Forum Bakery at Volubilis on the same scale with 19th-Century Bakeries from Sanborn Insurance Maps, including the Mengels and Schmidt bakehouse

few dozen people; the medieval workshop looked nothing like the modern factory containing hundreds or thousands of people."[14] In terms of production, Sennett's quotation points to some obvious distinctions between the pre-industrial and the industrial: small scale vs. large scale in levels of production, size of workspace, and size of workforce. But as modes of production, the industrial and the pre-industrial have other differences that move beyond production (Table 3.1).

Work and Home

There is almost universal acceptance that the small workshops that were responsible for the bulk of production in Roman cities around the empire were places where people both lived and worked. Andrew Wallace-Hadrill once wrote, "postindustrial society has become accustomed to a divorce between home and place of work. Status is generated at work not home, so the home became endowed with a 'privacy' alien to the Roman."[15] The history of thought on the relationship between work and home in Roman studies is extensive and often fraught with methodological problems. Early efforts focused on whether workshops were located in—or shared accessibility with—large elite houses.[16] Other scholars, such as Felix Pirson, recast built space as properties that could be owned and rented, which allowed other scholars to suggest that elites could profit from commercial

Table 3.1 Describing the Two Modes of Roman-Period Bakeries: the Workshop and the Factory

Workshop Mode	*Factory Mode*
Small-scale production	Large-scale production
Small workspace	Large workspace
Home and work integrated	Home and work delineated
Small workgroup grounded in kinship	Large workforce not grounded in kinship
Success predicated on skill and charisma of master craftsman	Success predicated on the business and political savy of owner

activity even when the workshop did not communicate directly with elite housing. Still others questioned the wisdom of framing all housing questions around elite domesticity, pushing for a fluid understanding in which space could serve as both workspace and house. Jennifer Baird, for example, casts doubt on the distinction between commercial and domestic production in general.[17] Even if it is hard for us to quantify or even qualify the extent to which any given workshop also served domestic functions, the growing consensus is that most workshops were small spaces where the workgroup, for the most part, both lived and worked.

The bakeries at Ostia, and the city's workshops in general, do not conform to this model. Miko Flohr, for example, suggests that workers in Ostian workshops probably did not live where they worked.[18] As noted above, most bakeries in Ostia are much larger than those around the rest of the Roman empire, but they also lack the indications of domesticity that existed in the shops and workshops of Pompeii and Herculaneum. Even in the more modest Pompeian houses in which bakeries are found there were indications of domestic life. Wallace-Hadrill notes the regular use of fourth-style wall painting even in small spaces traditionally thought of as shops and a number of Pompeian bakeries have lararia or indications of domestic worship.[19] Not one bakery in Ostia had these sorts of traits. Moreover, if someone did live or sleep in the massive bakeries of Ostia, the quality of such a life would be very low.

There will probably never be a way to demonstrate, beyond any doubt, that no one ever called one of Ostia's bakeries 'home.' Perhaps more compelling evidence that the relationship between work and home had shifted in Ostia are the massive *insulae* of the city. The *insulae*, here meaning the large housing complexes found throughout Ostia but not elsewhere, indicate a massive shift in the nature of domestic space not seen in most urban centers around the Mediterranean.[20] The urban fabric of Pompeii, and that of other similar cities such as Volubilis or Italica, is dominated by large elite houses with smaller spaces and buildings filling out the rest of the city. From Ostia's insulae, it is safe to infer that a portion of the population was not living in elite houses or in the same place where they worked.[21]

To return to comparanda of the bakeshops and bakehouses of Newark: in that city, people were forbidden by law from living where the bread was produced. This policy was intended to protect sanitation and hygiene: "that the sleeping-places for workmen and others employed in bakehouses shall be separate and distinct from the places used for the making of bread."[22] It is unclear the extent to which the rule reflected reality, but its very existence suggests that some bakeries were housing workers and in fact a number of the larger bakehouses were cited for improperly dividing workspace and sleep space or for providing group housing that did not meet the basic requirements of human decency. A relatively large number of people working in the larger bakehouses and other factories were clearly not living where they worked, since modest housing complexes grew up around Newark.[23] These tenement housing complexes have been the subject of much scholarly attention, mostly within the context of urban decline and the suburbanization of America. Many of the tenement housing complexes of Newark, which were once intended to provide a middle-class lifestyle for an urban working class, eventually became dens of poverty, crime, and iniquity.

We should be cautious about how far we push the comparison of Ostian *insulae* and the tenement housing of Newark. Slaves, within the broadly defined Roman *familia*, could be leased to a bakery only to return to their master's home each night. Such a possibility would never have existed in nineteenth-century Newark, since slavery was no longer a part of the American economy in the late nineteenth century and never had been in New Jersey, not to say there was no exploitation. Moreover, whatever type of life the tenement housing was intended to foster in Newark, there can be little doubt that, for the most part, the quality of life in them was poor. At Ostia, there are definite indications of wealth in some apartments, even mosaics and wall painting.[24] We should probably not paint insulae or modern apartments with a broad brush; even today some are high-end lofts while others are slums and the two can often be side by side. Despite very real differences between Newark and Ostia, the parallels are also striking. There are large-scale bakeries that seem either not to have had people living in them or were prohibited from doing so. Contemporaneous with the advent of such bakeries, among other industries, we see the rise of housing complexes evidently intended for sub-elites, completely devoid of overlapping commercial and domestic spaces.

Families and Workforces

Participation in craft activities has been a topic of regular scholarly debate, focused primarily on the participation of elites. During the second half of the twentieth century, most scholars of the ancient economy were in agreement: Roman elites did not engage in—or they were socially incentivized to eschew—participation in economic activity.[25] In the post-Finleyan era, this issue has been repeatedly revisited, but often within the context of the "social status of agents in the Roman economy."[26] Exploration of the intersections of social status and participation in craft and trade activities has been significantly aided by a shift away from a focus on the social status of master craftsmen to a broad view of social stratification in the work place. Elizabeth Murphy, drawing inspiration from studies of the Roman house and household, cleverly distinguishes between the workshop and the workgroup, which allows her to begin addressing the social organization of the workshop.[27] This method works well for the small workshops in the smaller urban centers, which were operated by craftsmen with modest levels of production. It works less well for the large urban centers for which there is growing evidence that commercial activity was integrated into society vertically and that there were, at the top of what Murphy might call the workgroup, people who were not directly experienced with and engaged in the actual production or services or were involved in multiple businesses through investment rather than labor.[28]

The same scholarship that characterized the nature of workshops around the Roman world has also begun addressing the question of who lived and worked in these spaces. Pirson speculates that the small *tabernae* in Pompeii were operated and inhabited by small families.[29] Flohr agrees, suggesting that "the probable size of the households occupying Pompeian *tabernae* nicely fits in with the size of an average nuclear family consisting of a man, a woman, some children, one or two surviving parents and perhaps one or two servants."[30] These Pompeian conclusions, at least, seem corroborated by the bakeries from elsewhere in the Roman world, with small workshops that are largely integrated into households pervading the urban centers of the western Mediterranean. One might only add to Flohr's statement that some bakeries seem to have been integrated into the elite family because some of the small bakeries found in the Roman world are integrated in back spaces of large, elite houses.

One of the unintended outcomes of monolithically studying the "social status" of craftsmen was that it gendered craftsmanship as male. Tiinde Kaszab-Olschewski, for instance, argues without evidence that "the traditional daily work to be done for a woman of antiquity included heating the furnaces, grinding the grain and baking bread (Columella, Rust. 12. 4. 7). In commercial bakeries, which made the hard work of baking bread at home dispensable, only male workers were employed."[31] If a family was the core labor unit for the bakery workshop, then women certainly participated in the production of bread as part of the family unit that produced – and relied on the profits produced from – bread. We saw that Pliny, at least, believed early Roman women were responsible for the production of a household's bread. But there is also good reason to think that some of the master bakers were women through the use of the word *pistrix*, the female form of *pistor*. Lucilius and Varro both allude to *pistrices* in their respective works. This would seem corroborated by our epigraphic evidence; several inscriptions from Numidia refer to a woman as a *pistrix*, the female form of baker. *Pistrix* also means sea-monster, complicating the issue, and some have interpreted the use of the word in these inscriptions as a cognomen.[32] There is also at least one example of a woman depicted managing a mill from a mosaic in Saint Romain-en-Gal, but the mosaic is not a bakery scene; it is from a calendar with activities appropriate to the season shown for each month. The data from Newark, on the other hand, clearly indicates that women could be master bakers in the late nineteenth century. The censuses of the smaller workshops in the *Annual Report of the Inspector of Factories and Workshops* often titles the bakeshops with the name of the master baker or owner; of those in which the gender of the owner is indicated, about seven percent bear the name of a woman. One might infer that the number of women who identified as *pistores* constituted a small portion of the overall number of bakers, and that is paralleled by the data from Newark, but it is unclear how well the epigraphic evidence can serve as proxy data for the social and gender makeup of the corpus of Roman bakers. Female bakers may well have felt less incentivized to self-present in epigraphy than their male counterparts, whose social aspirations were less circumscribed and restricted by society's laws and cultural mores. In fact, women may well have been incentivized to downplay their profession in their funerary iconography or self-presentation in general. Surviving friends and family, whose were responsible for commemorating the dead, may have chosen to highlight more socially acceptable components of women's lives.

Whatever the number of master bakers who were women, they were, as family members, surely very involved in bread production even in those bakeries that were run by men, possibly their husbands or other male relatives. Children were almost assuredly also a part of this process, possibly as apprentices or just as the sons and daughters of the craftsman learning their parents' trade. Men, women, and children were also probably involved in a way that was not evident in nineteenth-century Newark: as slaves. Much scholarship has shown that the Roman *familia* not only consisted of the core family unit, but also of its slaves and freedmen.[33] Modest households, such as those that might operate a small workshop, likely owned only a few slaves. The small bakeshops of Newark also relied on people outside the nuclear family, in the form of employees. On average, they employed—or at least reported—only 2.5 employees. This same phenomenon also existed in Roman world, as evidenced by people working in small bakeries. Plautus famously worked in a bakery turning the mills.[34] However apocryphal the story, it suggests that employment of free poor existed. Indeed, an inscription in Pompeii, CIL IV 6877, records the price of a workman at a *denarius* a day (16 *asses*), plus one loaf of bread.[35] The extent to which any given bakery relied on slaves or hired workers probably varied from baker to baker and city to city, as we saw in the last chapter.

If small bakeries around the Roman empire benefited from a few slaves or employees but relied primarily on the family unit to operate it, the larger bakeries in Ostia had different needs and therefore a different profile. For one, an Ostian bakery would require more workers. Flohr notes a difference in what he calls 'staff networks' between 'industrial' *fullonicae* and smaller workshops, suggesting that small workgroups fostered cohesion and familiarity, whereas large workgroups of the 'industrial' *fullonicae* resulted individual familiarity with fewer members of the workgroup.[36] Flohr uses intervisibility as a way of proving this, looking at the proximity of the vats used in the *fullonica*. The same must have been true in the large bakeries of Ostia. The *fornax* (worker tending the oven) may regularly see the people forming loaves out of dough, but he might be less well acquainted with the people watching the donkeys turn the millstones. In his case, Flohr is interested in the horizontal bonds of those in the workshop versus the industrial *fullonica*. The lack of familiarity worked vertically as well. While a master baker might have a close and even familial relationship with the people operating his bakery, the owner of the industrial bakery would have little or nothing do with the people working for him. Not only were they not his wife and children, but they also were not his household slaves, whom he knew and trusted, or employees he knew by face or counted as friends.

The cause of this growing distance between those in charge and those working was sheer numbers, but the result of it was the social stratification of the large-bakery workforce. We cannot know the numbers of workers employed in a bakery from the material remains, but we do have some indication that the large bakeries of Ostia were manned by large numbers of people. We can also make some inferences about the hierarchy within the workforce of the bakeries. The frieze from the tomb of the baker represents large-scale production on par with the obvious wealth needed to produce such a monument. The frieze is most frequently used as evidence for how bread was made, but that is not what it is. It is an idealized depiction of the workshop that served the social needs of the deceased.[37] Despite such idealization, there are a large number of figures depicted on the frieze and there is a striking amount of stratification among the figures. The frieze itself is incomplete, but even in its fragmentary form no fewer than 42 figures are depicted. Does this mean that Eurysaces employed no fewer than 42 people? Certainly not, nor should we assume he owned only one bakery. But we can say that the frieze does not depict a family at work, rather a different enterprise altogether consisting of many figures, all male, and dressed in a variety of ways. Lauren Hackworth Petersen identifies two types of people in the frieze, "workers in short tunics and official-looking togate figures."[38] But not all of the workers are in tunics or togas; some are entirely bare-chested with only a modest loincloth to clothe them. Similarly, all the men working on the Romolo relief are clothed in a tunic or a simple girdle, while many are bare-chested. Andrew Wilson and Katia Schorle interpret the lack of shirts as a product of both the heat in the bakery and the status of the individuals as slaves.[39] The modest depiction of the workforce only serves to highlight the togate owner, who is highlighted as above labor.

Large workforces are also evident among the large bakehouses of nineteenth-century Newark – as noted above, as many as 100 employees, but on average employing about 43 people. There can be no doubt that the 100 employees reported by the large bakehouses did not graft onto some kinship group. Again, however, we should be careful how to compare this data to the situation in third-century Ostia. There were institutions in the Roman world, but not the nineteenth century, that were capable of integrating such a workforce into an elite family, namely *institoria* and slavery. It is hard to imagine that the power and potential profits garnered by the commercial production of bread did not attract the attention of elite Romans in large urban centers, even if they refrained from direct participation. Elite families could use *institores* (individuals serving as economic proxies) to ensure production and make their money, or they could employ familial relationships with freedmen to fill out a workforce.[40] Even so, we are talking about workforce of dozens, not two. The incorporation of such a large workforce into the broadly defined Roman *familia* would compromise the closeness, familiarity, and kinship that existed both vertically and horizontally in smaller workgroups.

The Master Baker and the Businessman

The workshop had always been organized hierarchically, with a master craftsman or -woman at the helm who directly participated in production. The *Annual Report of the Inspector of Factories and Workshops* rarely records the names of small bakeshops that employ on average 2.5 people, preferring instead to record the names of the person in charge, such as Fanny Leibhauser, Gustav Kraeutler, or Francesco Chiaravallo. Over the fourteen years from 1889 to 1902, the same names appear repeatedly year after year, but turnover could also be very fast for such enterprises. On average, a bakeshop owner remains in the inspector's annual reports for 3.7 years, always consecutively. Occasionally, when one baker's name disappeared, another would appear with the same last name the next year, such as Otto Daeneke from 1897 to 1900, who was succeeded by Minnie Daencke from 1901 to 1902.

We can make two inferences from these patterns: first, the inheritance of the bakeshop operation by a relative further corroborates the foundation of workshop organization on the family unit. But the short tenures of bakery operations also suggest that bakeshops could be high-risk operations with regular turnover. The success of individual bakers was probably predicated on a number of factors, including location, quality of the product, and the ingenuity and charisma of individual bakers, but also on the ethnic, racial, and gender biases of the clientele. For the small bakeshops around the western Roman empire, this data from Newark suggests that, even if an ancient bakery was an architectural entity for a generation or more, it might see a number of different owners, operators, occupants, or lessees through the course of its existence. Furthermore, individual craftspeople were most likely the foundation of the bakery's production, its continued existence, and its intergenerational transmission.

The larger bakeries, employing over 20 employees and on average 43 people, tell a very different story. Their names are less personal such as Fritsche Baking Co., but in other cases in even more impersonal ways, such as Goodrich Health Bread Co. The owner is presented as a central figure, but the size of their reported workforces indicates a group larger than the plausible size of a family. Moreover, the institutions also persist for on average 6.8 years, nearly double the tenure of the craftsman-run bakery. This ability to sustain business suggests that the larger bakery's success was founded on factors other than the skill of the individual baker. Its impersonal nature may have mitigated the impact of customer biases. But larger bakeries, with their more socially stratified workforce, had another advantage: investment from businessmen who were unlikely to be directly involved in production. Such resources could sustain an enterprise during periods of adversity that might claim smaller institutions.

That there were people who owned bakeries but did not work in them is very clearly evident in Roman law. In the opinions of the jurists concerning inheritances, they frequently address whether slaves who work in a bakery are part of its *instrumenta*. In the *Digest of Justinian*, the jurists Paulus and Vitellius explain that "when *instrumentum* is legated, it is sometimes also necessary to consider the person of the testator, as, when the *instrumentum* of a *pistrinum* is legated, the *pistores* themselves can be regarded as included only if the head of the household ran the *pistrinum*. For it makes a very great difference whether the *instrumentum* was intended for the *pistores* or for the *pistrinum*."[41] One can infer from this passage that there were two types of bakeries: those that were owned and operated by the head of the household and those that were owned by a head of household who did not operate (*exercuit*) the bakery himself.

Julien Shoevaert refers to these men, because they seem to have been exclusively male, as *hommes d'affaires*.[42] The evidence for the existence of such men largely overlaps with where we find the large baking facilities or factory mode bread production. Moreover, their epigraphic activity also expands the extent of the second model, that of large-scale commercial baking, into some areas where no archaeological evidence for it has been found. One example of our earliest evidence for such men again comes from Eurysaces' tomb in Rome. The inscription does not refer to the man as *pistor*, but as *pistor* and *redemptor* (contractor, maybe?).[43] This fact has attracted much attention and has spurred the suggestion the Eurysaces was some sort of contract baker, perhaps supplying the army or providing for imperial distributions of free bread.[44] We will probably never know exactly what exactly Eurysaces did to earn the wealth that allowed him to build such an opulent tomb, but we infer that it was somehow different from what his counterparts were doing in the small workshop bakeries scattered around the smaller urban centers of the Roman empire.

Similar participants, however, do appear in other inscriptions, using titles like *negotiator frumentarius* or *negotiator pistoricius*.[45] The meaning of *negotiator* is not self-evident, but Koenrad Verboeven has argued that, in the case of craftspeople and commercial activity, it is probably not the production in itself that gives such men the title, but rather their investment in the production as a commercial enterprise to increase their social or financial capital.[46] Only in central Italy is such complexity also evident, at least in the western Roman empire, a topic discussed at greater length in Chap. 4. Both Cologne and Rome/Ostia served as administrative centers and, presumably as a result, commercial or public baking was closely intertwined with the administration of those cities. In at least one case at Ostia, there is potential evidence for investment in commercial baking. Marcus Licinius Privatus was originally a member of the *collegium fabrorum tignuarium*, the builders' association, and then joined the *collegium pistorum* as a *quaestor* and *quinquennalis*.[47] Nicolas Tran argues that the additional membership signals Privatus' acquisition of several bakeries.[48] We know that he was also a man of wealth and power from other inscriptions, including one that recorded his donation of 50,000 HS to the city and his subsequent induction into the order of the local decurions.

There is other evidence for businessmen who owned bakeries, but also integrated their business interests. Eve D'Ambra suggests that Tiberius Claudius Eutychus may have been just such a man; on his tomb (Tomb 78 at Isola Sacra) both a boat and a scene of milling were depicted, which suggests Eutychus was invested in both shipping and commercial baking (Fig. 6.8).[49] Tran, for example, singles out a man named Caerellius Iazemis who was *quinquennalis* of the *collegium pistorum* (bakers' association) of Ostia, but also *codicarius* (shipper) and *mercator frumentarius* (grain merchant).[50] Shoevaert argues that such complementary activities suggest that Iazemis was more than a simple baker who was confined to the practice of his profession.[51] Schoevaert further argues that the man's cognomen, Iazemis, is neither Latin nor Greek, and R. Valjus identifies the name as Cappadocian, a region reputed for the quality of its bread.[52] Wim Broekaert identifies the case of Iazemis, on the other hand, as an example of backward vertical integration, when one economic actor participates in multiple stages of production normally conducted by multiple actors.[53] For instance, Iazemis not only secured his own supply of grain as *mercator frumentarius*, he also invested in bakeries. With the existence of businessmen, different sectors of the production of bread could comprise part of a coherent economic system consisting of assets belonging to the same owner or owners, whose interest lay in enacting a production strategy that might be integrated from the main activity forward in the supply chain or backward to the primary-sector production, or both. It is easy to imagine someone such as Iazemis forming a backward integration strategy that would include securing grain, milling it at one location, and finally baking the bread at an altogether separate location.

Horizontal and Vertical Specialization

Businessmen who pursued vertical integration strategies may have led to vertical specialization within the Roman baking industry. Although specialization in the late-antique baking industry is often alluded to, it has not been the subject of intensive study. Nevertheless, there is a coherent narrative about how millers and bakers became separate occupations that deserves revisiting and critiquing. Boudewijn Sirks uses shifts in legal vocabulary and the etymology of the words for 'bakery' to suggest a shift in the practices of commercial bakers.[54] He notes that the word for bakery in juridical evidence had been, since at least 200 BCE, *pistrinum*, literally the 'milling' or 'grinding place'. But around 350 CE the legal texts began using the term *paneficium*, literally the 'bread making place' or 'the duty of baking bread.' From this, Sirks infers that bakeries, at least some of those in Rome, were baking but not milling. Scholars who date the separation of the miller and the baker to the later fourth century parallel this shift with the adoption of the watermill, which they say removed milling from bakeries to places with water. Indeed, the watermills found in Rome on the Janiculum date to the third century CE, which is consistent with the shift in juridical terminology a century later, and Procopius singles out water mills as playing an important role in provisioning Rome.[55]

A similar phenomenon is evident in North Africa. At Timgad, a large number of ovens were found around the site. All of the ovens are of the domed sort, but it is not always clear that they had a defined relationship with workshops and commercial bakers, often being found in public spaces or on the grounds of a basilica. Not one oven was found in a workshop with millstones or other technologies, but millstones are found in great numbers at the site, which raises the question for Touatia Amraoui of whether vertical specialization may be happening, with milling and baking separating into separate professions.[56] She bases this interpretation on the use of *furnarius* for baker, derived from *furnus* (oven), rather than the more traditional *pistor*, a body of evidence more fully discussed in the last chapter. The shift in terminology might reflect a shift in operational practices; a *furnarius* might have made bread, but might not have performed some of the other tasks involved in turning grain into bread, such as milling. The shift from *pistor* to *furnarius* in the North-African epigraphy mirrors the shift from *pistrinum* to *paneficium* in the central Italian legal evidence and both changes occurred in the second half of the fourth century CE, suggesting a moment when such specialization may well have occurred, if etymologies can be used as evidence for workshop realities, of which I have my doubts.

What drove any specialization is not entirely clear. The hypothesis that innovation, namely the watermill, drove specialization in the commercial baking industry is probably an oversimplification. Örjan Wikander, for instance, notes that watermills had been around for centuries before the fourth century CE and the mills on the Janiculum could not have provided flour for more than 5 or 6 percent of the city's population, meaning most flour for Rome's bread was not being milled by hydraulic power.[57] Moreover, Roman miller-bakers in small urban centers around the Mediterranean clearly continued to mill in their bakeries after the fourth century CE and the first reference to millers as a separate group dates to the second half of the fifth century in the edict of Dynamius, the city prefect.[58] Part of the problem is that the evidence has not been understood within an economic framework or couched in an economic understanding of specialization. The economic division of labor, wherein certain producers or service people focus on specific tasks and not others, is often framed in terms of *vertical* or *horizontal* specialization.[59] Kai Ruffing elegantly summarizes the distinction:

> Horizontal specialization describes the diversity of goods and services produced in a society by using different professional formations or work roles. Thus, for example, the demand for skills for the production of amphorae is different from that for the production of shoes or textiles, and so on. The number of goods and services produced in an economy in this way is proportional to the number of specializations. Vertical specialization, on the

> other hand, describes the number of separate work roles and skills used in manufacturing a single product. A good example is the building of an ancient ship, which requires a set of different skills: carpentry, ironwork (for nails), rope-making, as well as textile production (for the sails). Moreover, both the building process itself and the supply of building materials and finished products need to be coordinated.[60]

The traditional narrative about specialization in the ancient baking industry could then be recast in these terms: horizontal specialization existed in the ancient baking industry with *pistores* focused on the final product, bread, but vertical specialization did not occur until the Middle Ages. Ruffing notes that specialization in general has traditionally been thought, since the work of Adam Smith, to have been incentivized by market competition. That is to say, having competitors drove producers to increase their productivity through the adoption and implementation of new, more advanced technologies and methods. But Ruffing and others have also noted that there is a close correlation between population size and levels of specialization; greater levels of specialization and vertical specialization exist in communities with larger populations.[61]

The hydraulic mechanization of milling, the specialization of millers and bakers, and their association in a vertical relationship in the fourth century CE might be symptoms of the same cause: a shift in the mode of production, in certain cities, necessitated by increasing population size and driven by a sort of businessman. Returning to the case of Iazemis: he secured his own shipping rather than using others.' Second, he secured his own supply of grain as *mercator frumentarius.* With a vertically integrated strategy, bakeries without millstones and mills without ovens could still be integrated, albeit dislocated from another. Such bakeshops and millhouses could comprise part of a coherent economic system consisting of assets belonging to the same owner or owners, whose interest lay in enacting an integrated production strategy. It is easy to imagine someone such as Iazemis developing an integration strategy that included securing grain, milling it at one location, and finally baking the bread at an altogether separate location. For indirect participants, such as Iazemis, the financial benefits of compartmentalized production and implementation of innovative technologies may have trumped the symbolic capital of milling and millstones, which was so important to the miller-baker workshop.

Conclusion

The dichotomy of the small bakeshop and the large bakehouse, known from Newark, are also evident in the Roman world. The small bakeries occupying, on average, less than 150 m^2, pervade the cities around the western Mediterranean. In certain cities, a larger bakery capable of greater production existed. This second category of commercial baking is demonstrated by larger bakeries (over 200 m2 in area) and by possible tenement housing, but such architectural remains are largely confined to Rome, Ostia, and further east in the Mediterranean.[62] But Ulrich, among others, observes that our evidence for insulae is evident only in urban centers with large populations, which must also be true of the large baking operations.[63] As such, population size may be a guide as to where to begin documenting industrial-scale commercial baking, especially when accompanied either by mechanized water mills (at least those away from military installations) or epigraphy attesting investment and vertical-integration strategies. The population estimates adopted here are from J.W. Hanson and S.G. Ortman whose recent study is the most convincing effort to use the nature of the urban fabric of cities to infer their likely population density and then apply that to their extent or area, arriving at a population estimate.[64] For the cities they do not address, other bibliography was used. Rome, Ostia, Cologne, Trier, Timgad, and Nimes are all cities that demonstrate factory-production or businessman bakers, clustering in central Italy, along the Rhine river valley, and in Mediterranean Gaul. Excluding Rome, these cities have an average population estimate of ca. 42,000 people (Table 3.2). The smaller workshop bakeries are attested instead at a much smaller type of city, with an average population of ca.7500.

The type of bakery prevalent in a city largely correlates with its population size. There can be little doubt that urban centers with large population sizes had needs that smaller ones did not and there should be no surprise that a growing population would induce change in a city's means of production. This is especially true about bread production; as a staple and a necessity its production would be particularly impacted by changes in population. The relationship between population size and economic complexity is a well-studied phenomena in the field of economics, but assuming a simple causal relationship would neglect reflexive relationships between production and population size: more people necessitates new means of production, but new means of production also allow for larger populations. Moreover, it is very clear that the ancient economy and

Table 3.2 Population Estimates and Bakery Types

Bakery Type	*City*	*Population Estimates*	*Size (ha)*	*Density*	*Bibliography*
Factory-like	Rome	400–500,000	1400	321/ha	Carcopino (2003, 14) and Storey (1997)
Factory-like	Ostia	69,366	154	450/ha	Nibby (1829, 61), Packer (1971, 71), Meiggs (1973, 532–5), Storey (1997, 974–75) and Schoevaert (2018, 78)
Factory-like	Cologne	20–25,000	96.8	232/ha	Russell (1958, tb. 89) and Tchernia (2016, 112)
Factory-like	Trier	20–80,000	280	178/ha	Goudineau (1980, 309–10), Pelletier (1982, 226) and Woolf (1998, 137)
Factory-like	Nimes	ca. 50,000	220	227/ha	Lot (1996, 71)
Factory-like	Timgad	17,846	50	357/ha	Bowman and Wilson (2009, 58) and Hopkins and Kelly (2018, 198)
Workshop	Pompeii	7791	60	130/ha	Jongman (1988, 110–12), Wallace-Hadrill (1991: 199–200) and Bowman and Wilson (2009, 58)
Workshop	Italica	3178	49	65/ha	Carreras Monfort (1996, tb. 1) and Bowman and Wilson (2009, 57)
Workshop	Augusta Emerita	9720	81	120/ha	Carreras Monfort (1996, tb. 1)
Workshop	Volubilis	9058	43	211/ha	MacKendrick (1980, 300)
Workshop	Djemila	699	12	58/ha	

commercial activity were integrated into Roman social and political institutions. Over-emphasis on population reduces Roman craftsmanship and large-scale production of bread to epiphenomena.

Conceiving of bread production in terms of modes of production allows for one to approach all types of commercial baking and bread production synthetically, viewing the system as a whole in all its nuance, incorporating social institutions or political factors. The small bakeries in the smaller urban centers, often integrated into domestic space, relied on the nuclear family unit for their operation, as was the case with medieval and early-modern craftsmanship. There are also small bakeries integrated into large homes, which suggests that, unlike later bakeshops, small Roman bakeries could also be founded inside the elite household and probably relied on slavery to complete the workgroup. For the most part, the fortunes of the small Roman bakery relied on the charisma and skill of the master baker. Newark's small-scale bakers appearance for only a few years, on average, suggests that such an enterprise might have been high-risk, with relatively quick turnover within the industry.

The larger bakeries show no traces of domesticity, neither elite or sub-elite; this does not mean that no one slept there, but the disappearance of markers of domesticity from the bakeries was complemented by the appearance of insulae at Ostia and probably other large cities. Moreover, the evidence from nineteenth-century cities corroborates this association of larger bakeries with the development of tenement housing. That separation of work and home is mirrored by a growing divorce of those who were the owners from their workforce. Moreover, those in charge of large bakeries were not directly engaged with the work and the success of the enterprise was not predicated on their personal skill or charisma. Instead their strategy hinged on their business acumen and their ability to integrate their interests vertically, such as investing in grain shipping, to secure supply and reduce costs and increase profits.

But looking at bakeries and bakers synthetically, within the framework of modes of production, also allows for the inclusion of other factors that more directly address the living and working conditions within the bakeries. Using comparanda from other time periods as a foundation, one can deploy the evidence to start exploring processes that leave little or no material record, such as exploitation of labor, training, or shared risk management. The following chapters address these issues in greater detail.

Notes

1. Workshops, even in one city, rarely display remarkable uniformity. In Pompeii, for example: Flohr (2013, 183) and Monteix (2016, 149).
2. Hawkins (2016, 12 and 125).
3. *CIL* VI, 01958a; *CIL* XIII, 8725; *CIL* XIV, 4234.
4. Flohr (2007, 143–144) and Broekaert and Zuiderhoek (2013, 323).
5. Rosenswig and Cunningham (2017, 1–20).
6. Marx (2011, 14).

7. Sahlins (1972) and Wolf (1982).
8. *P.Mich.* X 586; *P.Oxy.* 1890.
9. Wolf (1982, 78).
10. Wolf (1982, 122): "from court-based power holders who still relied on the arrangements of a tributary mode to coalitions of provincial entrepreneurs."
11. Rosenswig and Cunningham (2017, 20).
12. New Jersey, Inspector of Factories and Workshops, 1889–1902.
13. https://library.princeton.edu/libraries/firestone/rbsc/aids/sanborn/essex/newark.html
14. Sennett (2009, 53).
15. Wallace-Hadrill (1994, 12), Ellis (2000, 78–80), Robinson (2005), Baird (2007, 431), Pirson (2007, 468–469), Flohr (2016, 149–150) and Ellis (2018, 9).
16. Mayeske (1972) and Robinson (2005).
17. Baird (2007, 431); Ellis (2018, 9).
18. Flohr (2007, 143–144) and Broekaert and Zuiderhoek (2013, 323).
19. Wallace-Hadrill (1994, 110) and Joshel and Hackworth Petersen (2014, 146–152 and especially n.68).
20. Rome: Gros and Torelli (2014) and Storey (2001, 2002). Ostia: Packer (1971) and Ulrich (1996).
21. Packer (1971) and Gering (1999).
22. *General Factory Act of 1885*, Sec. 14. *ARIFW* 1893, 142.
23. Addenda to the General Factory Act of 1885 indicate that housing could be available in bakehouses, provided the spaces were separated, but most of the employees likely lived in tenement housing. Later companies would provide their employees with housing in apartment complexes, such as the Prudential Apartments that still stand in Newark today.
24. Hermansen (1970, 1981), Frier (1977), Gering (2001) and Stevens (2005, 117).
25. Finley (1999) and Moeller (1976), whose work on the fullers of Pompeii suffered from a number of theoretical and evidentiary missteps, offers a notable exception.
26. Andreau (2002, 209).
27. Murphy (2016, 135).
28. Rickman (1980, 124–127), Potter and Mattingly (1999, 182–186) and Tran (2006, 106).
29. Pirson (1999, 165).
30. Flohr (2013, 267). Flohr, however, cautions that the nature of the evidence might not, at least given current methods, allow us to confirm these hypotheses about small family-based workshops.
31. Kaszab-Olschewski (2019, 205).

32. *ILAlg* 2.1.3181; *CIL* VIII, 2889. Schafer (1998, 194).
33. Gardner and Wiedemann (1991: esp. 3), Ellis (2000: 174–79) and Allison (2001, 63–64).
34. Aulus Gellius *Noct. Att.* III.3.
35. OPERARI(s) PANE(m) DENARIV(m).
36. Flohr (2013, 265).
37. Joshel and Hackworth Petersen (2014, 126).
38. Hackworth Petersen (2006, 106).
39. Wilson and Schorle (2009, 104).
40. Kirschenbaum (1987, 93), Verboven (2002, 25 and 285) and Holleran (2012, 203 and 230).
41. *Dig.* XXXIII.7.18.1 (Paulus, Vitellius), trans. Watson et al. (1985, 129).
42. Schoevaert (2018, 192–194).
43. *CIL* VI, 01958a.
44. Hackworth Petersen (2006, 117), Tran (2006, 127–30), Silver (2009, 176–77), Mayer (2012, n. 36), Erdkamp (2013, 276) and Bernard (2016, 69–70). Mayer (2012, 88) notes that the municipal law of Urso prevented *duumviri* from taking gifts from *redemptores.*
45. Tertinius Secundus *CIL* XIII, 8338 NEG PISTORICIVS; M. Liberius Victor *CIL* XIII, 8725 NEGOTIATOR FRVMENTARIVS.
46. Verboven (2007, 99). "Pourtant, dans le cas de negotiatores producteurs, ce n'est sans doute pas la production en soi qui leur confère la qualité de negotiator, mais le fait qu'ils ont investi leur argent dans une entreprise dont ils commercialisaient ensuite les produits."
47. *CIL* XIV 374.
48. Tran (2006, 105).
49. D'Ambra (1988, 98–99).
50. Tran (2006, 223–229). *CIL* XIV 4234.
51. Schoevaert (2018, 192). "Ces activites complementaires (negoce, batellerie et boulangerie) indiquent probablement qu'Iazemis etait plus qu'un simple boulanger qui se cantonnait a la pratique de son metier."
52. Valjus (1998, 259–264).
53. Broekaert (2012).
54. Sirks (1991, 307).
55. Procop. *Goth.* 5.19.8–19; Wikander (1979, 13–36), Bell (1992, 1994, 73–89) and Wilson (2000, 219–46).
56. Amraoui (2017, 200–201).
57. Wikander (2002, 130).
58. Tengström (1974, 77), Sirks (1991, 349) and *CIL* 6.1711.
59. Bowman and Wilson (2009, 27) and Bernard (2016, 73–75).
60. Ruffing (2016, 117).

61. North (1992, 141), Loomis (1998, 251–254), Temin (2001), Wilson (2008) and Ruffing (2016, 118–119).
62. McKay (1975, 214) and Ulrich (2014, 334).
63. Ulrich (2014, 334).
64. Hanson and Ortman (2017, table 4).

References

Allison, P.M. 2001. Placing Individuals: Pompeian Epigraphy in Context. *Journal of Mediterranean Archaeology* 14 (1): 53–74.

Amraoui, Touatia. 2017. *L'artisanat dans les cités antiques de l'Algérie: 1. siècle avant notre ère - 7. siècle après notre ère*. Oxford: Archaeopress.

Andreau, J. 2002. Twenty Years after Moses I. Finley's *The Ancient Economy*. In *The Ancient Economy*, ed. W. Scheidel and S. von Reden, 33–49. Edinburgh: Edinburgh University Press.

Baird, J.A. 2007. Shopping, Eating and Drinking at Dura-Europos: Reconstructing Contexts. In *Objects in Context, Objects in Use: Material Spatiality in Late Antiquity*, ed. L. Lavan, E. Swift, and T. Putzeys, 413–437. Boston: Brill.

Bell, M. 1992. Mulini ad acqua sul Gianicolo. *Archeologia Laziale* 11: 67–74.

———. 1994. An Imperial Flour Mill on the Janiculum. In *Le Ravitaillement en blé de Rome et des centres urbains des débuts de la République jusqu'au Haut-Empire. Actes du colloque international de Naples, 14–16 Février 1991*, 73–89. Rome: École Française de Rome.

Bernard, S.G. 2016. Workers in the Roman Imperial Building Industry. In *Work, Labour, and Professions in the Roman World*, ed. K. Verboven and Christian Laes, 62–86. Boston: Brill.

Bowman, A., and A. Wilson. 2009. *Quantifying the Roman Economy: Methods and Problems*. Oxford: Oxford University Press.

Broekaert, W. 2012. Vertical Integration in the Roman Economy. *Ancient Society* 42: 109–125.

Broekaert, W., and A. Zuiderhoek. 2013. Industries and services. In *P. Erdkamp ed. the Cambridge companion to ancient Rome. Cambridge companions to the ancient world*, 317–335. Cambridge: Cambridge University Press.

Carcopino, J. 2003. *Daily life in ancient Rome: The people and the City at the height of the empire*. New Haven: Yale University Press.

Carreras Monfort, C. 1996. A New Perspective for the Demographic Study of Roman Spain. *Revista de Historia da Arte e Arqueologia* 2: 59–82.

D'Ambra, E. 1988. A myth for a smith: A Meleager sarcophagus from a tomb in Ostia. *American Journal of Archaeology* 92 (1): 85–99.

Ellis, S. 2000. *Roman Housing*. London: Duckworth.

Ellis, S.J.R. 2018. *The Roman Retail Revolution: The Socio-Economic World of the Taberna*. Oxford: Oxford University Press.

Erdkamp, P. 2013. The food supply of the capital. In *The Cambridge companion to ancient Rome*, ed. P. Erdkamp, 262–277. Cambridge: Cambridge University Press.
Finley, M.I. 1999. *The Ancient Economy*. 2nd ed. Berkeley: University of California Press.
Flohr, M. 2007. Nec quicquam ingenuum habere potest officina? Spatial contexts of urban production at Pompeii, AD 79. *Bulletin Antieke Beschaving: Annual Papers on Classical Archaeology* 82: 129–148.
———. 2013. *The World of the Fullo*. Oxford: Oxford University Press.
———. 2016. Constructing Occupational Identities in the Roman World. In *Work, Labour, and Professions in the Roman World*, ed. K. Verboven and Christian Laes, 147–172. Boston: Brill.
Frier, B. 1977. The Rental Market in Early Imperial Rome. *Journal of Roman Studies* 67: 27–37.
Gardner, J.F., and T. Wiedemann. 1991. *The Roman Household: A Sourcebook*. London: Routledge.
Gering, A. 1999. 'Medianum-apartments': Konzepte von Wohnen in der insula im 2. Jh. n.Chr. *Mededelingen van het Nederlands Instituut te Rome* 58: 103–115.
———. 2001. Habiter á Ostie: La fonction et l'histoire de l'espace 'privé.'. In *Ostia: Port et porte de la Rome antique*, ed. J.-P. Descoeudres, 199–211. Georg: Geneva.
Goudineau, C. 1980. *"Les Villes de la Paix Romaine." Histoire de la France Urbaine v. 1, 155–391.* Paris: Seuil.
Gros, P., and M. Torelli. 2014. *Storia dell'urbanistica: il mondo romano*. Roma: Laterza.
Gsell, Stéphane. 1918. Khamissa, Mdaourouch, Announa, fouilles exécutées par le Service.
Hanson, J., and S. Ortman. 2017. A Systematic Method for Estimating the Populations of Greek and Roman Settlements. *Journal of Roman Archaeology* 30: 301–324.
Hawkins, C. 2016. *Roman artisans and the urban economy*. Cambridge: Cambridge University Press.
Hermansen, G. 1970. The Medianum and the Roman Apartment. *Phoenix* 24: 342–347.
———. 1981. *Ostia. Aspects of Roman City Life*. Edmonton: University of Alberta Press.
Holleran, C. 2012. *Shopping in Ancient Rome: The Retail Trade in the Late Republic and the Principate*. Oxford: Oxford University Press.
Hopkins, K., and C. Kelly. 2018. *Sociological studies in Roman history*. Cambridge: Cambridge University press.
Jongman, W. 1988. *The economy and Society of Pompeii*. Amsterdam: Gieben.

Joshel, Sandra R., and Lauren Hackworth Petersen. 2014. *The Material Life of Roman Slaves*. Cambridge: Cambridge University Press.

Kaszab-Olschewski, T. 2019. Central and Northern Europe. In *The Routledge Handbook of Diet and Nutrition in the Roman World*, ed. Paul Erdkamp and Claire Holleran, 189–207. London: Routledge, Taylor & Francis Group.

Kirschenbaum, Aaron. 1987. *Sons, Slaves, and Freedmen in Roman Commerce*. Jerusalem: Magnes Press, Hebrew University.

Lepelley, C. 1981. *Les cités de l'Afrique romaine au Bas-Empire: Étude d'histoire municipal*. Vol. 2. Paris: Études Augustiniennes.

Loomis, W.T. 1998. *Wages, Welfare Costs and Inflation in Classical Athens*. Ann Arbor: University of Michigan Press.

Lot, F. 1996. *The End of the Ancient World and the Beginnings of the Middle Ages*. London: Routledge.

MacKendrick, P.L. 1980. *The North African Stones Speak*. Chapel Hill: University of North Carolina Press.

Marx, K. 2011. *A Contribution to the Critique of Political Economy*. New York: Barnes & Noble Digital Library.

Mayer, E. 2012. *The Ancient Middle Classes: Urban Life and Aesthetics in the Roman Empire, 100 BCE–250 CE*. Cambridge, MA: Harvard University Press.

Mayeske, Betty Jo B. 1972. Bakeries, Bakers, and Bread at Pompeii: A Study in Social and Economic History. Ph.D. dissertation, Ann Arbor.

McKay, A.G. 1975. *Houses, Villas and Palaces in the Roman World*. Ithaca: Cornell University.

Meiggs, R. 1973. *Roman Ostia*. 2nd ed. Oxford: Clarendon Press.

Moeller, W.O. 1976. *The Wool Trade of Ancient Pompeii*. Leiden: Brill.

Monteix, N. 2016. Contextualizing the Operational Sequence: Pompeian Bakeries as a Case Study. In *Urban Craftsmen and Traders in the Roman World*, ed. Miko Flohr and Andrew Wilson, 153–182. Oxford: Oxford University Press.

Murphy, E.A. 2016. Roman Workers and Their Workplaces: Some Archaeological Thoughts on the Organization of Workshop Labour in Ceramic Production. In *Work, Labour, and Professions in the Roman World*, ed. K. Verboven and C. Laes, 133–146. Boston: Brill.

New Jersey Inspector of Factories and Workshops. 1889–1902. *Annual Report of the Inspector of Factories and Workshops of the State of New Jersey*. Trenton: Inspector of Factories and Workshops.

Nibby, A. 1829. *Viaggio antiquario ad Ostia*. Roma: Nella Società tipografica.

North, D. 1992. *Institutionen, institutioneller Wandel und Wirtschaftsleistung. Die Einheit der Gesellschaftswissenschaften, 76*. Tübingen: Mohr Siebeck.

Packer, J.E. 1971. *The Insulae of Imperial Ostia*, Memoirs of the American Academy in Rome, 31. Roma: American Academy in Rome.

Pelletier, A. 1982. *Vienne Antique: de la Conquête Romaine aux Invasions Alamanniques, (IIe siècle avant - IIIe siècle après J.-C.)*. Roanne: Horvath.

Petersen, L.H. 2006. *The Freedman in Roman Art and Art History*. New York: Cambridge University Press.
Pirson, F. 1999. *Mietwohnungen in Pompeji und Herculaneum*. Munich: Pfeil.
———. 2007. Shops and Industries. In *The World of Pompeii*, ed. J.J. Dobbins and P.W. Foss, 457–473. London/New York: Taylor and Francis.
Potter, D.S., and D.J. Mattingly. 1999. *Life, Death, and Entertainment in the Roman Empire*. Ann Arbor: The University of Michigan Press.
Rickman, G. 1980. *The Corn Supply of Ancient Rome*. Oxford: Oxford University Press.
Robinson, D. 2005. Re-thinking the Social Organisation of Trade and Industry in First Century A.D. Pompeii. In *Roman Working Lives and Urban Living*, ed. A. MacMahon and J. Price, 88–105. Oxford: Oxbow Books.
Rosenswig, R.M., and J.J. Cunningham. 2017. *Modes of Production and Archaeology*. Gainesville: University Press of Florida.
Ruffing, K. 2016. Driving Forces for Specialization: Market, Location Factors, Productivity Improvements. In *Urban Craftsmen and Traders in the Roman World*, ed. A. Wilson and M. Flohr, 115–131. Oxford: Oxford University Press.
Russell, J.C. 1958. Late ancient and medieval population. *Transactions of the American Philosophical Society* 48 (3): 1–152.
Sahlins, Marshall. 1972. *Stone Age Economics*. Hawthorne: Aldine de Gruyter.
Schäfer, Ch. 1998. *Spitzenmanagement in Republik und Kaiserzeit: die Prokuratoren von Privatpersonen im Imperium Romanum vom 2. Jh. v.Chr. bis zum 3. Jh. n.Chr.* St. Katharinen: Scripta Mercaturae.
Schoevaert, J. 2018. *Les boutiques d'Ostie: L'économie urbaine au quotidien. Ier s. av. J.-C.–Ve s. ap. J.-C.* Rome: École française de Rome.
Sennett, R. 2009. *The Craftsman*. New Haven: Yale University Press.
Silver, M. 2009. Glimpses of Vertical Integration/Disintegration in Ancient Rome. *Ancient Society* 39: 171–184.
Sirks, A.J.B. 1991. *Food for Rome: The Legal Structure of the Transportation and Processing of Supplies for the Imperial Distributions in Rome and Constantinople*. Amsterdam: J.C. Gieben.
Stevens, S. 2005. Reconstructing the Garden Houses at Ostia: Exploring Water Supply and Building Height. *BABesch* 80: 113–123.
Storey, G. 1997. The population of ancient Rome. *Antiquity*, 71, 274: 966–978.
———. 2001. Regionaries-Type Insulae 1: Architectural/Residential Units at Ostia. *American Journal of Archaeology* 105 (3): 389–401.
———. 2002. Regionaries-Type Insulae 2: Architectural/Residential Units at Rome. *American Journal of Archaeology* 106 (3): 411–434.
Tchernia, A. 2016. *The romans and trade*. Oxford: Oxford University Press.
Temin, P. 2001. A Market Economy in the Early Roman Empire. *Journal of Roman Studies* 91: 169–181.

Tengström, E. 1974. *Bread for the People. Studies of the Corn-Supply of Rome During the Late Empire*. Stockholm: Skrifter utg. av Svenska institutet i Rom.

Tran, N. 2006. *Les membres des associations romaines: le rang social des collegiati en Italie et en Gaules, sous le Haut-Empire*. Rome: École Française de Rome.

Ulrich, R.B. 1996. Contignatio, Vitruvius, and the Campanian Builder. *American Journal of Archaeology* 100 (1): 137–151.

———. 2014. Courtyard Architecture in the Insulae of Ostia Antica. In *A Companion to Roman Architectur*, ed. R.B. Ulrich and C.K. Quenemoen, 324–341. Malden: Wiley-Blackwell.

Valjus, R. 1998. An Oriental Baker at Ostia. *Arctos: Acta Philologica Fennica* 32: 259–264.

Verboven, K. 2002. *The Economy of Friends: Economic Aspects of Amicitia and Patronage in the Late Republic*. Brussels: Editions Latomus.

———. 2007. Ce que negotiari et ses dérivés veulent dire. In *Vocabulaire et expression de l'économie dans le monde antique*, ed. J. Andreau and V. Chankowski, 89–118. Bordeaux: Ausonius.

Wallace-Hadrill, A. 1991. Houses and households: Sampling Pompeii and Herculaneum. In *Marriage, divorce and children in ancient Rome*, ed. Beryl Rawson, 191–227. Oxford: Oxford University Press.

———. 1994. *Houses and Society in Pompeii and Herculaneum*. Princeton: Princeton University Press.

Watson, A., T. Mommsen, and P. Krueger. 1985. *The Digest of Justinian. V. 1–4*. Philadelphia: University of Pennsylvania.

Wikander, Ö. 1979. Water-Mills in Ancient Rome. *Opuscula Romana* 12: 13–36.

———. 1984. *Exploitation of Water-Power or Technological Stagnation? A Reappraisal of the Productive Forces in the Roman Empire*. Lund: CWK Gleerup.

———. 1985. Archaeological Evidence for Early Water-Mills – An Interim Report. *History of Technology* 10: 151–179.

———. 2000. The Water-Mill. In *Handbook of Ancient Water Technology, Technology and Change in History*, ed. Ö. Wikander, vol. 2, 371–400. Leiden: Brill.

———. 2002. 'Where of Old All the Mills of the City Have Been Constructed': The Capacity of the Janiculum Mills in Rome. In *Ancient History Matters: Studies Presented to J. E. Skydsgaard on His Seventieth Birthday*, Analecta Romana Instituti Danici Suppl. 30, 127–133. Rome: Danish Institute.

Wilson, A. 2000. The Water-Mills on the Janiculum. *Memoirs of the American Academy in Rome* 45: 219–246.

———. 2002. Machines, Power and the Ancient Economy. *The Journal of Roman Studies* 92: 1–32.

———. 2008. Large-Scale Manufacturing, Standardization, and Trade. In *The Oxford Handbook of Engineering and Technology in the Classical World*, ed. J.P. Oleson, 393–417. Oxford: Oxford University Press.

Wilson, A., and K. Schorle. 2009. A Baker's Funerary Relief from Rome. *Papers of the British School at Rome* 77: 101–123.

Wolf, E.R. 1982. *Europe and the People Without History*. Berkeley: University of California Press.

Woolf, G. 1998. *Becoming Roman: The origins of provincial civilization in Gaul*. Cambridge: Cambridge University Press.

CHAPTER 4

Experiencing the Bakery: Training, Status, Labor, and Exploitation

Workshops and other places of commerce and production in general are often treated in one of two ways. On the one hand, they are characterized as nice places, idealized workshops filled with "familiar faces" and a closely-knit workgroup.[1] On the other hand, there is a sense that workshops were unpleasant, disgusting places addled by injustice and mistreatment of slaves and other vulnerable populations.[2] In the last chapter we saw that there were two modes of production among Roman bakeries, the small workshop bakery and the large industrial bread factory, and one is tempted to simply graft the two characterizations onto the different modes of production: comfortable family run workshops and exploitative factories run by insidious businessmen who had no relationship with their workers. The purpose of this chapter is threefold. First, the chapter confronts flaws in how social relations and hierarchy in Roman bakeries have been inferred largely from literary and iconographic evidence. Second, a fuller body of evidence is presented, framed by the lessons learned about modes of production in the last chapter. Finally, the inequalities of the factory-like bakeries are compared with those of the workshop bakery, the former being more impersonal and grounded in decreasing costs while the workshop bakery's inequalities were more grounded in the typical asymmetries of the Roman *familia*.

The argument for the iniquitous bakery hinges largely on textual evidence, collected and summarized most succinctly by Boudewijn Sirks. The

J. T. Benton, *The Bread Makers*,
https://doi.org/10.1007/978-3-030-46604-6_4

most expansive example of such evidence, and the one most commonly cited, is from Apuleius' *Metamorphoses.* His protagonist, Lucius, describes the poor wretches he sees while working in a bakery.

> Dii boni, quales illic homunculi vibicibus lividis totam cutem depicti dorsumque plagosum scissili centunculo magis inumbrati quam obtecti, nonnulli exiguo tegili tantum modo pubem iniecti, cuncti tamen sic tunicati ut essent per pannulos manifesti, frontes litterati et capillum semirasi et pedes anulati, tum lurore deformes et fumosis tenebris vaporosae caliginis palpebras adesi atque adeo male luminanti et in modum pugilum, qui pulvisculo perspersi dimicant, farinulenta cinere sordide candidati.[3]
>
> Good gods, what sorry excuses for human beings I saw. The pale welts from chains crossed every patch of their skin like brushstrokes. Their flogged-up backs under sparse patchwork were no better covered than stretches of ground that shade falls on. Some them had thrown on an exiguous vestiture, which extended only to the loins, yet all were clad so that their scraps of tatters kept no secrets. Their foreheads were inscribed with brands, their hair half-shaved, their ankles braceleted with fetters, their pallor hideous, their eyelids gnawed by the gloomy smoke of the murky fumes, which left them less able to access light at all. Like boxers, who fight bathed in find dust, these men were filthy white with floury ash.[4]

Such horrible working conditions evoke Sinclcairesque notions of an exploited labor in an Industrial-Revolution factory. The passage from Apuleius certainly suggests that hygienic conditions were a concern in bakeries. The slaves smokey and blurry eyed from the ovens and covered in flour and ash. One could argue that whatever satirical joke or social commentary is being expressed in the passage, it only works if it resonated with the actual situation in bakeries. Sarah Bond, citing this passage, describes bakeries as a "horrid environment still endured in the early empire by both the servile workers and the animals in mills."[5] It is unclear, however, what type of bakery is being described by Apuleius, whether a big factory-like bakery or a workshop bakery. Sandra Joshel and Lauren Hackworth Petersen observe that the slaves who worked in the bakery also lived in the baker's house.[6] Does this mean that Apuleius was thinking of a workshop mode bakery? It is almost surely not that simple. There is no reason to assume that Apuleius, or the ancient mind more generally, had a way to delineate one mode of production from another. Furthermore, Apuleius' work was fundamentally satirical; it is not clear that we should view his bakery as representative of a typical one. Lucius' time in the bakery is, by academic consensus, a critique of some component of Roman society, even if it is unclear what. Additionally, Apuleius uses the bakery passage as a vehicle for other inset tales within the Metamorphoses and so it may well be serving literary needs as well. In any event, there is good reason to suppose that Apuleius would have taken some poetic license in his portrayal of a bakery.

Iconographic depictions of bakeries have also provided a window into bakery operation for some scholars and such depictions stands in stark contrast to the conditions described by Apuleius. They are idealized depictions of bakeries from the tombs of bakers, the figures stand around togate and others are more modestly dressed, but they look fit, clean, and healthy. We saw in the last chapter that the iconography did support the conclusion that the workgroup in large bakeries were socially stratified and some were relegated to almost complete nudity within the workplace. The ability to be clothed while others are not is a well-studied marker of power differentials; the clothing serves to indicate that the person in the bakery is not a mere worker and, similarly, nudity of the slave or the powerless only serves as a point of contrast highlighting the clothedness of the person of higher social standing in the group. Just such a phenomenon might be at work here, the members of the workgroup in bakeries may have worked naked or nearly so for reasons of baking operation (maybe mistrust or cleanliness?), but it is equally possible that the nudity is a fabrication of the iconography intended only to emphasize that Eurysaces is togate.

Iconographic depictions of workshops and satirical descriptions of them make for bad evidence for the actual operation of bakeries because they are governed by the social needs of those who commissioned such works or by the literary intentions of the author. Archaeologically speaking, it is difficult to identify the sorts of phenomena that might affect how one might experience a bakery. Certain phenomena, such as sanitation might have material consequences that are discernable in workshops provided they were carefully excavated, which they were not for most of the history of archaeology. Other phenomena, such as malnutrition or abuse might have material consequences on the human body, but to my knowledge no pattern of physiological health, or lack thereof, in human remains has been linked to work in a Roman bakery. Furthermore, there are still other phenomena, such as humiliation or friendship, that would leave no material record whatsoever. Identifying inequality or the nature of labor conditions in the archaeological remains of Roman bakeries is probably impossible.

The framework offered by modes of production offers a way to disentangle and structure the nature of the evidence by offering a more comprehensive model of production. A "mode" is not merely the nature of production and the social complexity supporting it, a mode also encompasses the power dynamics that circumscribe production. Certainly the large bakeries at Ostia, as discussed in pervious chapters, evoke notions of Industrial Revolution factories and the inequity that accompanied them. Since the work of Karl Marx, many scholars have observed that the Industrial Revolution, the separation of work from home, a removal of those in charge from the workspace, and ultimately the growing unfamiliarity between workers and their bosses resulted in a deterioration of working conditions and general exploitation of labor. But the exploitation of labor in nineteenth century factories was systemic, a neglect of working conditions and a deliberate suppression of wages. This is not to say that there was violence in large Roman bakeries, only that we should be careful about how far we push such a modern construct on an ancient past.

A contrast with the industrial factory has led to a sort of fetishization of the ancient workshop as places run by master craftsmen whose families provide the labor and whose customers are friends. But we have good evidence to suggest that the bakery—and workshops in general—offered a work environment that was not so benign. Violence in such workshops was as personal as the relationship between the master craftsman and the friends and family who worked for him. Neglect and wage suppression may have occurred in such workshops, but the motivation for mistreatment is grounded more in personal concerns than systemic neglect or mistreatment. Moreover, the sorts of oppression that are evident in the workshop are endemic to the Roman family unit: slavery, child abuse, or lack of opportunity based on gender. The following analysis surveys the evidence for inequality in Roman bakeries and structures the discussion around the two modes of production described in the previous chapter: industrial mode bakeries and workshop mode bakeries.

Apprenticeship and Workshops

One's experience in the bakery was almost surely predicated on their status within the workgroup. Age, gender, and social status, among other factors, surely played a part in determining where one found oneself in the hierarchy of the workshop. In a skilled craft, the experience and knowledge of an individual probably played a significant role in determining where someone fell within that hierarchy. As such, one's experience of a bakery was entangled with training and education in the workplace. Training, within the context of craftsmanship, usually evokes notions of apprenticeship. We have one possible instance in which the apprentice of a baker is referenced directly; a ***pistor candidarius*** (baker of fine white bread) is commemorated by his wife (*contubernalis*) and his apprentice (***discens***).

> L Aponio Celati
> l Eroti, pistori
> candidario
> Venusta contubern
> et Ospeus discens.[7]
> For Lucius Aponius Eros, freedman of Celatus, a baker who makes white bread, Venusta his companion and Ospeus, his apprentice (had this tomb made).[8]

We should be cautious about jumping to the conclusion that bakers were trained through formal apprenticeship. *Discens*, here, is fragmentary and could mean something as simple as student without the formal infrastructure and contractual obligations of apprenticeship and in some other cases it is read as *Ducieus*, part of a name. If the text does read ***discens***, the monument to a master baker by his student, suggests positive relationships between individuals of different social statuses within the hierarchy of the Roman workshop bakery. Such a conclusions corroborated by a number of funerary monuments for master craftsmen a variety of professions dedicated by their apprentices.[9] Conversely, the masters sometimes do the same for their apprentices.[10] The language used in such commemorations also speaks to the closeness of the relationship between a craftsman and his student; in one instance, CIL 10013, a master craftsman of an undisclosed profession claims to love his apprentice more than his own son (*quam si filium suum*).[11]

Despite closeness between masters and students, apprenticeship is a contractual relationship between a master craftsman and the father or master of the apprentice. Apprentices only had recourse against a craftsman insofar as their fathers or masters were willing to uphold the terms of the contract and even then mistreatment of children and apprentices could be seen as a necessary component of training. In fact, such training could have a violent component. Lucian describes how he was apprenticed to his uncle as a mason and, despite the familial relationship, was thrashed for breaking a stone slab that he was trying to polish. A similar situation is described by Ulpian in the *Digest*: a cobbler beats the eyeball out of an apprentice and the issue, for the jurist, resided in whether the mistreatment was excessive or part of the edification of the apprentice.

> Si magister in disciplina vulneraverit servum vel occiderit, an Aquilia teneatur, quasi damnum iniuria dederit Et Iulianus scribit Aquilia teneri eum, qui eluscaverat discipulum in disciplina: multo magis igitur in occiso idem erit dicendum. Proponitur autem apud eum species talis: sutor, inquit, puero discenti ingenuo filio familias, parum bene facienti quod demonstraverit, forma calcei cervicem percussit, ut oculus puero perfunderetur. Dicit igitur Iulianus iniuriarum quidem actionem non competere, quia non faciendae iniuriae causa percusserit, sed monendi et docendi causa: an ex locato, dubitat, quia levis dumtaxat castigatio concessa est docenti: sed lege Aquilia posse agi non dubito.[12]
>
> Julian writes that a man who had put out a pupil's eye in the course of instruction was held liable under the *lex Aquilia*. There is all the more reason for saying the same if he kills him. Julian also puts this case. A shoemaker, he says, struck with a last at the neck of a boy (a freeborn youngster) who was learning under him, because he had done badly what he had been teaching him with the result that the boy's eye was knocked out. On such facts, says Julian, the action for insult does not lie because he struck him not with intent to insult, but in order to correct and teach him; he wonders whether there is an action for breach of contract for his services as a teacher, since a teacher only has the right to administer reasonable chastisement, but I have no doubt that an action can be brought against him under the *lex Aguilia*.[13]

There is no way to know how common such abuse was in bakeries, but there is reason to think that it might have been quite common given that Ulpian entertains the possibility that such violence could be a natural part of education. Furthermore, Christian Laes notes that in apprenticeship systems of the early modern period such abuse was not only part of the training, but also a means of reinforcing the hierarchy of the workshop.[14] A hierarchy of apprentices might exist in a workshop informed by a number of factors, including social status, level of training, and gender. Violence was not only a tool used by master craftsmen and an expression of tension between different types of people, it was also a way of reinforcing the hierarchy or chain of command that sustained the workshop.

Girls surely faced the same adversities as the boys, but they also clearly faced some other challenges that the boys did not. Not one figure in all the iconographic depictions of baking is female. Such iconography depicts an idealized version of production that served the needs of the man who commissioned it and so we should not view this as. Girls, both freeborn and slave, appear as apprentices in contracts from Egypt, and as guardians and masters apprenticing a relative or slave, albeit not as apprentices to bakers.[15] They comprise about 25% percent of apprentices. Of the sixteen female apprentices known to us, five were freeborn females,[16] the others were slaves. Conversely, male apprentices were overwhelming freeborn. Some of these women surely practiced their craft as adults, but not one master from the Egyptian apprenticeship contracts is female.[17] Female producers probably faced obstacles at points of transition, such as from trainee to practicing professional or from practicing professional to a master with apprentices. It is hard to imagine, however, that practicing female producers played no role in training the next generation. The types of informal training or intra-familial training might have offered female producers an avenue to pass their knowledge to children, informal apprentices, or employees. But there are other less ideal ways in which women played a role in craft training. Most of the female apprentices from the contracts were slaves and few of them could probably expect manumission. Well trained slaves were valuable and accomplished female slave producers might be expected by their masters to train more slaves, even their own children.

Slavery as Institutional Training

Papyri from Egypt, at least, do attest that formal apprenticeship existed in the Roman world, but not one of those contracts belong to a baker despite bakers associations appearing regularly in the papyrological record (Fig. 4.1). Baking as a practice is not the same as weaving or metalworking, which were bodies of knowledge that were in many ways separate from the bodies of knowledge implement in domestic production. We saw in Chap. 2 that commercial baking was a natural outgrowth of household production; such a notion is harder to project onto some other crafts, such as weaving or metalworking. As such, perhaps we should not expect bakers to have maintained formal apprenticeship. Training could and did take other forms. Young bakers could also be trained within the family, with parents teaching the next generation of their kin. Moreover, bakers could train students outside the family without the formal infrastructure of apprenticeship. Such phenomena might be very hard to delineate from apprenticeship in our material and epigraphic record, using similar terminology and functioning in similar ways.

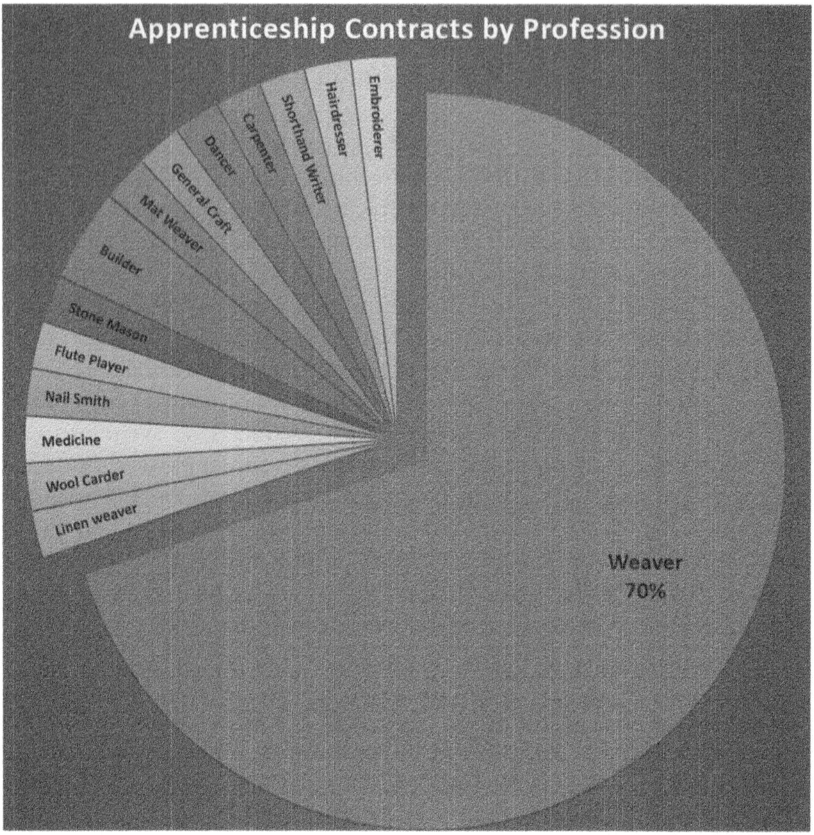

Fig. 4.1 Apprenticeship Contracts by Profession

That slavery was an integral part of the propagation of commercial baking as an industry is strongly suggested by funerary and commemorative epigraphy in which we have large number of slaves referred to as bakers and bakers who were once slaves. Three inscriptions, found in the *columbarium* of Livia Augusta, commemorate *pistores* who may have been free or freed, but who are grouped in with the *servi Caesaris* (slaves of the imperial household).[18] Another inscription, *CIL* VI 9000, seems to corroborate slave bakers having a close relationship to elite *familiae*. A certain Faustus is identified as the *pistor* of Marcella and Paullus (FAVSTUS / MARCELLAE PAVLLI / PISTOR).[19] The combination of one individual's name in the genitive with another in the nominative implies ownership. In each of these cases the slave bakers appear to be associated with a large household. The use of bakers in elite households is corroborated to an extent by the presence of bakeries in the backs of elite houses and villas throughout the Mediterranean west, such as that of the Casa del Labirinto at Pompeii or the Villa of the Amphitheater at Augusta Emerita.

There are also a large number of bakers identified in their funerary or commemorative epigraphy as freedmen. In an extraordinary example from outside Rome, an inscription records the name of sixteen bakers, ten names are recorded in full.[20] Of those ten, nine are identified as freedmen (*liberti*) and one is identified as freeborn. The inscription probably adorned a tomb outside Rome and it was found at Ulubrae (modern Latina). It has been taken as evidence of a collegium or association of bakers, a possibility explored further in the next chapter. The high incidence of freedmen among the baking profession is not a phenomenon isolated to the tomb at Ulubrae, there are freedmen bakers also evident in other parts of the western Mediterranean.[21]

Slavery was not only a social status but also an institution within Roman *familiae* that was itself diachronic, passed from one generation to the next and it provided means and incentive to train new craftspeople. Roman law regularly discusses the need to reevaluate the increased value of slaves if they received training at the behest of their master.[22] In other words, a master had financial incentive to have his or her slaves trained in a craft because it increased their worth and they were part of the *instrumentum* of the bakery, so they also increased the value of property.[23] Slaves could definitely be trained through apprenticeship, but they could also be trained by other slaves at the behest of their master withing the household. Furthermore, we should not discount the possibility that slaves were undertaking training secretly or at least of their own volition. By increasing their own value, slaves may have changed their living conditions within the household. Not all slaves were relegated to menial labor; some could act as proxies for their masters (*institores*), but one also imagines that a skilled slave was valued more than an unskilled slave and his or her quality of life might have increased significantly. As such, I think we can also imagine slaves actively searching to learn skills or crafts on their own as a means to improve their living conditions within the *familia* and possibly create future opportunity for manumission.

There was also a very dark side to slavery in the workshop bakery. Plautus occasional uses a motif of impertinent slaves threatened with dispatch to the bakeries as a punishment. Dating to the late third or early second centuries BCE, the *pistrina* that Plautus was thinking of are almost certainly workshops not factories. In his *Asinaria*, Plautus refers to the *pistrinum* as a place where the slave will be whipped as he runs.[24] At first glance this would seem to refer to a slave-driven rotary mill, but Moritz rightly notes that the young master is currently treating his slave as a four-legged creature.[25] The passage is clearly a joke paralleling slaves with chattel, but the use of the bakery as threat against slaves is also evident in other places in Plautus' plays, such as in his *Pseudolus*. The petulant slave, the play's eponymous character, frets that he will be sent to the *pistrinum* if his master is displeased.[26] The reaction of the slaves in Plautus' plays to the treat of labor in a bakery strongly suggests that working in one was not a pleasant experience, something to be feared.

Roman law is unsurprisingly silent on the treatment of slaves in bakeries, but there is concern about the responsibilities linked to *custodia* (safekeeping) of slaves in Roman law. Take, for example, a passage in the *Digest of Justinian*, in which the jurist Ulpian addresses the liability concerning breach of *custodia*. In one section, he addresses when legal action can be brought against someone charged with breaching a contract of safekeeping of property, in this case slaves. One of the examples he gives is that of labor in the bakery:

> Si quis servum custodiendum coniecerit forte in pistrinum, si quidem merces intervenit custodiae, puto esse actionem adversus pistrinarium ex conducto: si vero mercedem accipiebam ego pro hoc servo, quem in pistrinum accipiebat, ex locato me agere posse: quod si operae eius servi cum custodia pensabantur, quasi genus locati et conducti intervenit, sed quia pecunia non datur, praescriptis verbis datur actio: si vero nihil aliud quam cibaria praestabat nec de operis quicquam convenit, depositi actio est.[27]
>
> If anyone compels a slave held for safekeeping to work in a bakery, I think that there is an action on hire against him if he received payment for the safekeeping. However, if it was I who received payment for this slave whom he took into the bakery, I can bring the action on leasing. But if the work of the slave was payment for the safekeeping, this is as if it were a kind of leasing and hiring but, because money is not paid, an action *praescriptis verbis* is given. Indeed, if nothing other than food was supplied and nothing was agreed concerning the work, the action is on deposit.[28]

The issue is not that the bakery was deleterious to the health of the slave, although it may well have been. Ulpian's concern centers on the value of the slave labor and who was allowed to profit from that labor within the agreement of custodianship. Roman law offered little protection for slaves in workshops aside from their intrinsic value as chattel. Roman law does address child labor, particularly in the context of apprenticeship discussed further below, and there is clear concern for the wellbeing of children, but mostly in terms of the value of slaves or the level of force appropriate for a teacher to use. The jurists clearly have a concept of *infantia* (childhood) and Ulpian advises that the labor of children under five should not be calculated as part of their worth. This is an important point; for the jurists, children working is not illegal or immoral, but it is not to be valued equal to adult labor. There are several further inferences that we can make from Ulpian's opinion about slave labor, particularly in light of the characterization of bakeries in the plays of Plautus. First, Roman slave owners sometimes punished their slaves or merely lent them out to bakeries, potentially to turn a profit or simply for safekeeping. Second, the fear working in a bakery evident in Plautus' characters would only resonate if the experience of working one was bad.

On-the-Job Training

Training in the more factory-like environments was a different matter. Cameron Hawkins observes that "Fullers and bakers, for example, both broke down their production processes into relatively simple tasks that could be performed by workers who acquired the necessary skills quickly and on-the-job rather than via formal and intensive training."[29] The technological innovations of mixers, animal driven millstones, and elaborate ovens aided in this simplifying of bread production. In medieval and early modern Europe, state actors during the middles ages or early modern period, such as kings, local aristocrats, or religious leaders would leverage their power by monopolizing goods. For example, the local state actors, such as Bishop Philip de Poitou, used bakehouses in Durham as political tools, hiring—and paying wages to—master bakers to operate the bakehouse.[30] Within such contexts, large-scale producers often trained individuals to perform simple almost automated tasks without the eventual promise of a profession. They were even called apprentices on occasion, but they were apprentices in name only. They were hired as labor without the social components or contractual obligations of guild apprenticeship but were receiving on the job training nonetheless.[31] Modern economists and social scientists call this on-the-job employer-led training.[32] It relies more on wages and a form of training aimed at creating an efficient and specialized workforce; it tends to avoid teaching new professionals who might become competitors one day. We do, in fact, have some evidence for wage pay in bakeries. An inscription in Pompeii, CIL IV 6877, records the price of a workman at a *denarius*, plus one loaf of bread.[33] It is not clear if the inscription is advertising labor and this was the going rate of the worker or if this was a work-available sign. Walter Scheidel has cast some doubt on over reliance of anecdotal and uncontextualized data of this sort.[34] One has to imagine, however, that the vast majority of laborers working in large bakeries at specialized and simplified tasks were in facts slaves, but even for the free poor who might take such a job, there was no opportunity for advancement nor training sufficient to help launch a career.

Such a lack of opportunity was felt more acutely by certain vulnerable categories of people than by others. Women, for example, comprised about 7% of the master bakers operating workshops in 19th-century Newark but we have no evidence—and some serious doubts—that they had the opportunity to become the owner of one of the city's massive bakery factories. The same pattern is evident in the epigraphic evidence from antiquity, we saw some evidence for female bakers, but there is no evidence for businesswomen who were enacting integrated business strategies that incorporated baking, milling, or grain importation. Women were surely not the only vulnerable demographic that faced increased difficulty in a bakery hierarchy that probably did not facilitate vertical mobility within it. One could imagine that slaves, foreigners, or the disabled faced similar difficulties moving from kneader at the tables to master baker or businessman.

Exploitation and Forced Labor

In the last chapter, evidence was presented for large-scale production of bread that was accompanied by a separation of work and home and members of the industry who participated through investment and some of whom implemented vertically integrated economic strategies (at least in cities with large populations). Such phenomena in the industrial Revolution, at least for scholars operating in a Marxist tradition, were typically accompanied by an exploitation of labor that extended beyond training that might never lead to a better life. Karl Polanyi, for example, defines exploitation of labor as the "economic advantage of one partner at the cost of the other."[35] For Polanyi, at least in *The Great Transformation*, capital investors engineered systems that allowed them to maintain control the means of production while simultaneously maximizing their own profits by reducing costs via wage suppression. Such a notion is anachronistic in the Roman world in which labor was dominated by slavery, an intrinsically exploitative institution particularly where compensation is concerned. But exploitation during the Industrial Revolution took a number of forms, including deteriorating working conditions and child labor.[36] The data from Newark's nineteenth-century bakeries presented in the last chapter points to possible forms that exploitation could take. Two broad concerns drove the inspector's report: safety and exploitation of vulnerable groups for labor, in particular women and children. Such exploitation was not of a personal nature, but more of an impersonal neglect and self-interested indifference. In other words, in a workplace hierarchy where the person responsible for making decisions about working conditions and compensation has no personal or familial relationship with the laborers, they might not take the care to make sure working conditions were safe or that laborers were fairly treated. In fact, focus on investment and profit incentivized a deterioration of working conditions in an effort to keep costs low.

It is in the specifics of social relations within the operation of bakeries that the analogy from New Jersey breaks down and modes of operation forged for twentieth-century history; Standards concerning the employment and wage exploitation of vulnerable groups, particularly child labor, are not really a concern in a world defined by slavery and one in which children were probably very integrated into the workforce.[37] But even if there was no concern about exploitation of labor in the Roman world does not mean that it did not exist. Moreover, even if the nuances of social relations in the Roman world complicate any comparison from other periods, the motivations appear to have been the same. The exploitation of labor in capitalist or industrial modes of production was facilitated by the social separation of bosses from laborers and motivated by a desire to keep costs low and maximize profits. It was impersonal and opportunistic.

We have, in fact, extensive evidence for opportunistic and impersonal efforts to find workers in the form of the compulsory labor, particularly for escaped slaves and criminals. Returning to the passage from the Metamorphoses, Sirks notes Apuleius' placement of the bakery scene immediately after the capture of the bandits who held the donkey Lucius,[38] and identifies the association of the two passages as possible evidence for forced labor in Roman *pistrina* imposed as punishment on criminals.

Similarly, in the fifth century CE, Socrates Scholasticus describes massive underground bake-houses which were run by men referred to as *mancipes*, who purportedly used prostitutes to lure unsuspecting strangers into above-ground *tabernae* and then, by means of a trapdoor, enslaved the strangers to work in the mills.[39] The story forms part of a larger narrative about the purging of sin and iniquity from Rome by the Emperor Theodosius, including a banning of penal prostitution.[40] The enslavement of freepersons – and the story in general – is probably apocryphal, owed to the narrative of restoring order that Theodosius was pushing, but it is also part of a broader narrative of bakers actively seeking labor and opportunistically using escaped slaves or criminals. For example, Pliny the Younger writes to Trajan asking what to do with a man named Callidromos who had once been a slave of the emperor's general and co-consul, Laberius Maximus, but who had been captured in Moesia and sent to the king of Parthia as a slave.[41] Upon escape from Parthia, he had been captured in Nicomedia by two bakers, Maximus and Dionysius, and forced to work in their bakery. Pliny resolves to send the slave to Trajan, along with items corroborating his story. The forced labor in bakeries may have been part of a larger habit of privately giving slaves into the *custodia* of bakers in exchange for their labor. Cicero, in a letter to Quintus, asks his brother to help expedite the return of an escaped slave named Licinius, who had been living as a freeman in Athens, but had been caught and detained. Cicero notes that he was unable to learn whether the Licinius was held in a public prison (*publica*) or in a bakery (*pistrinum*). The contrast of the public incarceration with the *pistrinum* suggests that bakeries could be used as private prisons.

The habit of using bakeries as a place to hold criminals or punish slaves was not exclusively a private affair. It is hard to parse punishment, incarceration, and *custodia* of slaves in the evidence and it may well be that they are coeval phenomena. At least by the fourth century CE, the state was actively using bakeries as places of incarceration and punishment, condemning convicts to labor in the *pistrina* or *ergastula* as the jurists frequently refer to workshops. In 319, Constantine advises the governor of Sardinia to "let those who appear to deserve punishment for non-serious offences be consigned to the *pistrina* of Rome" administered by the Praefectus Annonae.[42]

Sirks infers from the juridical and literary references to forced labor in bakeries that such "*officinae* suffered from a shortage of manpower" and that "if there had been a sufficiently large supply of voluntary workers, this punishment would not have had to be imposed."[43] Sirks points to the two different points of view in the execution of forced labor in the bakery: that of the punishers (the state or the slave owners) and that of the bakers. The idea that there were labor shortages feels somewhat antiquated given more recent assessments of slave populations in late antiquity, but the bakery would have need for labor in any conditions. Moreover, the state's incentive for keeping criminals and slaves in the bakeries may have been punishment, but for the bakers it was almost assuredly the free labor for which there was no need to compensate an owner or pay a wage in the case of free workers. Viewed on its own, the forced labor in bakeries seems like an isolated incident of state-sponsored penal labor in which bakers participated, but when viewed from the producer side it appears more as a system (or mode) in which business-man like owners of bakeries opportunistically found a source of cheap labor outside their households and outside their responsibilities, reducing costs and padding profit margins.

Conclusion

The dichotomy presented here is that of impersonal exploitation and a lack of opportunity in factory like bakeries and very personal acts of violence and opportunity in the smaller workshop bakeries. The point of the analysis above was to characterize each mode of production by the defining interactions within them. None of this was to suggest that personal violence did not occur in large bakeries, in fact there can be little doubt that the exploitation of penal labor almost certainly necessitated violence. Moreover, the reliance on slavery and slaves for a labor force in large bakeries almost surely resulted in corporal punishment. On the other hand, small-scale bakers were also capable of exploiting labor like the businessmen of larger cities. It is worth delineating three broad phenomena concerning hierarchy, labor, and oppression in Roman bakeries: exploitation, violence, training, or opportunity.

Large, factory-like bakeries in large urban centers had close relationships with the state, explored further in the next chapter, and were often capable of using that relationship to reduce operating costs by exploiting penal labor. Smaller bakeries lacked that same relationship, but there are indications that the same habit existed among workshops through *custodia*. Slave owners could lend their slaves, maybe as a form of punishment, to bakeries. In other words, small-scale bakers could reduce their operating costs by using social relationships in the community to find slaves for cheap labor. So in some ways, the exploitation of labor between workshops and larger factory-like bakeries was a difference of degree, but the it was also one of kind. It is hard to imagine much legal protections for the criminals put to work in the *pistrina*. The treatment of lent-out slaves in small bakeries was probably predicated on—and constrained by—the nature of the relationship between the slave owner and the baker and the former's interest in maintaining the value of the slave. Moreover, laborers in workshops would have been exposed to the fully productive reality of the bakery giving them the opportunity to deploy that knowledge in the future for their own gain, whereas penal laborers were probably responsible for a very specialized task that prevented them from seeing the whole process and learning it.

Conversely, the is very clear evidence for violence in workshops, tied to the nature of training and grounded in familial asymmetries, such as parent and child or male and female. One inscription (CIL XII, 4502) suggests that at least some bakeries entered contractual relationships with apprentices to propagate the industry, but slavery within the elite household and simple familial, mother-to-daughter training were probably more common institutional vehicles for training the next generation of bakers. Tensions between groups of different status, training level, or gender were opportunities for violence, which itself could serve to reinforce hierarchy and was believed to be part of the training process, as evidenced by the incident with the cobbler and the apprentice's eyeball. There is no evidence for such violence in large bakeries at Ostia or in Rome, but such a lacuna more likely reflects a lack of concern for the wellbeing of workers than it does an actual absence of violence. It is hard to imagine that penal labor of the organization of large-scale slave labor was accompanied by no corporal punishment or tactical use of violence and, in fact, Roman law shows little concern for such working conditions.

Opportunity for advancement in bakeries or for changing one's quality of life was clearly predicated on the nature of training and hierarchy in the workplace, which itself was seemingly grounded in the scale of the production inside the bakery. Employer-led, process-focused training limited one's opportunity to advance or branch out on one's own. Just numerically, the likelihood that one could become the boss from a workforce of a hundred was much lower than in a workforce of five. Moreover, the labor in the bakery—of any scale—was very clearly gendered male. We have no evidence for businesswomen; in limited opportunity and in a profession gendered male, women surely faced unique obstacles that men did not.

Women likely fared better in workshop bakeries or in bakeries linked to elite households. Apprenticeship contracts indicate that girls, both free and slave, comprised a significant portion of trainees in such workshop systems. There were probably significant numbers of women working and learning in bakeries that were grounded in elite and sub-elite households. On the other hand, the number of female master craftsmen, even in the trades with large numbers of female apprentices such as weaving, is zero. The disparity between the number of female trainees, both slave and free, and the number of female master craftsmen is almost surely mirrored in the commercial baking industry. We do not have a clear picture of training in Roman workshop bakeries other than that it seems grounded in the family and in slavery as an institution within the elite household, but we have only a few female commercial bakers. Some women clearly chose to pursue a craft, but freeborn or freed women may have had social incentives to pursue other paths. Moreover, male craftsmen may have had advantages transitioning from trainee to workshop boss, such as networks of cooperation, collaboration, and shared risk management in the form of professional associations, the topic of the next chapter.

Notes

1. Flohr (2013, 264).
2. Bakker (1999, 7).
3. Apuleius, *Metamorphoses*, 9.12.
4. Trans. Ruden (2011, 194).
5. Bond (2016, 158).
6. Joshel and Hackworth Petersen (2014, 139).
7. *CIL* XII, 4502.
8. This translation based, in part, on the translation into French by Bonsangue (2010, n. 23).
9. RIT 447, 1–10; CIL XII.
10. *CIL* II 2243; *CIL* VI 33930; *CIL* VI 10013; 10,014; *CIL* IX 4437.
11. Laes (2011, 194) and *CIL* VI, 10013.
12. *Dig.* (Ulpian) 9.2.5.3.
13. Trans. Watson (1985, 278).
14. Laes (2011, 193).
15. Bradley (1991), Van Minnen (1998), Saller (2003) and Groen Vallinga (2013, 305).
16. *P. Heid.* 4. 326; *P. Ross. Georg.* 2. 18. 450; *P. Oxy.* 67. 4596; *P.Oxy.* LXVII 4596; *P. Aberdeen* 59.

17. Van Nijf (1997).
18. *CIL* VI 4010, 4011, 4012 and Hasegawa (2005, 45).
19. It is frequently assumed that this inscription refers to a well-known Roman noble couple of the first century BC, Claudia Marcella Minor and Paullus Aemilius Lepidus, who was consul in 34 BC (Fusco and Gregori 1996, 226–232).
20. De Nardis (2018, 220–234). *CIL* X 6494.
21. *CIL* VI 06338, *CIL* VI 9462a, *CIL* VI 9803, *CIL* VI 9805; *CIL* VI 13406 (Rome); *CIL* I 3034 (Ostia); CIL IX 3190 (Corfinum); *CIL* X 3779 (Capua); *CIL* X 5346 (Interamna Lirenas); *CIL* X 5933 (Anagni); *CIL* XII 4502 and 4503 (Narbo); *CIL* V 1036 and *CIL* V 1046 (Aquileia); *CartNova* 00134 and *CartNova* 00154 (Carthago Nova); *CIL* II 5975 (Gandia); *IRC-01*106 (Iluro); *AE* 1908 186 (Narbo).
22. Temin (2004, 535). *Dig.* 50.16.79.1(Paulus).
23. *Dig.* XXXIV.5.28 (Javolenus) *Dig.* XXXII.73.3; XXXIII.7.12.5; XXXIII.7.15; XXXIII.7.18.1; XXXIV.5.28.
24. Plautus, *Asinaria*, 709. "postidea ad pistores dabo, ut ibi cruciere currens" Afterwards I will give you to the bakers, so that they might whip you as you run.
25. Moritz (1958, 68). Plautus, *Asinaria*, 708. "nam iam calcari quadrupedo agitabo advorsum clivom" Now then I will drive you with spurs up that hill like a quadruped.
26. Plautus, *Pseudolus*, 1.5.80–86; and then again at 4.5.9.
27. *Dig.* (Ulpian) XVI.3.1.9.
28. Watson (1985, 11–12).
29. Hawkins (2016, 93).
30. Bonney (2005, 100–103).
31. Ogilvie (2011, 379).
32. Pigou (1932), Rosenstein-Rodan (1943, 204–205) and Becker (1964) (general vs specific skills); lots about this usually concerning why employers would train employees who would become more productive, but also more attractive to other firms increasing the competitiveness of the labor market, which is bad for employers.
33. OPERARI(s) PANE(m) DENARIV(m).
34. Scheidel (2010, 444).
35. Polanyi (2012, 301).
36. Edwards (1986), Nardinelli (1990) and Thompson and Smith (2010).
37. It is interesting, however, that among the depictions of commercial baking in iconography, there is only one depiction of a woman and her dress suggests she is an allegory. Work in the idealized bakery was gendered male, but we also saw that there is good reason to think that women were more involved in the commercial production of bread than text or image would suggest, even as the master craftsperson.

38. Sirks (1991, 414).
39. Socrates *HE* 5.18.
40. McGinn (2004, 28–29), also Bond (2016, 145), makes the case that mills were places impugned as places of prostitution because they were places where the sexes met. This is largely constructed from the sixth century passage from the *HE* and from Plautus' third-century use of the word *alicariae*, mill-girls, to refer to a specific group of prostitutes.
41. Pliny the Younger 10.74.
42. *C.Th.* IX.40.3.
43. Sirks (1991, 414).

References

Apuleius, and Sarah Ruden. 2011. *The Golden Ass*. New Haven: Yale University Press.

Bakker, Jan Theo. 1999. *The Mills-Bakeries of Ostia: Description and Interpretation*. Amsterdam: J.C. Gieben.

Becker, Gary S. 1964. *Human Capital: A Theoretical and Empirical Analysis, with Special Reference to Education*. New York: National Bureau of Economic Research.

Bond, Sarah. 2016. *Trade and Taboo Disreputable Professions in the Roman Mediterranean*. Ann Arbor: University of Michigan Press.

Bonney, Margaret. 2005. *Lordship and the Urban Community: Durham and Its Overlords, 1250–1540*. Cambridge: Cambridge University Press.

Bonsangue, M.L. 2010. "L'Apport de la Documentation Épigraphique à la Connaissane de l'artisanat à Narbonne (Fin ier siéc le av. J.-C. – ier siéc le ap. J.-C.)" In *Aspects de l'artisanat en milieu urbain: Gaule et Occident Romain*, (28e suppl. à la RAE), 183–194.

Bradley, Keith R. 1991. *Discovering the Roman Family: Studies in Roman Social History*. New York: Oxford University Press.

De Nardis, Mauro. 2018. CIL X, 6494: attestazione di un collegium di pistores nell'ager Pomptinus. In *Lavoro, lavoratori e dinamiche sociali a Roma antica: persistenze e trasformazioni: atti delle giornate di studio (Roma Tre, 25–26 maggio 2017)*, ed. Arnaldo Marcone and Elio Lo Cascio, 220–234. Roma: Castelvecchi.

Edwards, P.K. 1986. *Conflict at Work: A Materialist Analysis of Workplace Relations*. Oxford: Basil Blackwell.

Flohr, M. 2013. *The World of the Fullo*. Oxford: Oxford University Press.

Fusco, U., and G.L. Gregori. 1996. A proposito dei matrimoni di Marcella minore. *Zeitschrift für Papyrologie und Epigraphik* 111: 226–232.

Groen-Vallinga, M. 2013. Desperate Housewives? The Adaptive Family Economy and Female Participation in the Roman Urban Labour Market. In *Women and the Roman City in the Latin West*, ed. Emily Ann Hemelrijk and Greg Woolf, 295–312. Leiden: Brill.

Hasegawa, Kinuko. 2005. *The familia Urbana During the Early Empire: A Study of Columbaria Inscriptions*. Oxford: Archaeopress.
Hawkins, Cameron. 2016. *Roman artisans and the urban economy*. Cambridge: Cambridge University Press.
Joshel, Sandra R., and Lauren Hackworth Petersen. 2014. *The Material Life of Roman Slaves*. Cambridge: Cambridge University Press.
Laes, Christian. 2011. *Children in the Roman Empire: Outsiders within*. Cambridge: Cambridge University Press.
McGinn, Thomas A.J. 2004. *The Economy of Prostitution in the Roman World: A Study of Social History & the Brothel*. Ann Arbor: University of Michigan Press.
Moritz, L.A. 1958. *Grain-Mills and Flour in Classical Antiquity*. Oxford: Clarendon Press.
Nardinelli, C. 1990. *Child Labor and the Industrial Revolution*. Bloomington: Indiana University Press.
Ogilvie, S.C. 2011. *Merchant Guilds, Social Capital and the Commercial Revolution: Institutions and Economic Development in Medieval and Early Modern Europe*. Cambridge: Cambridge University Press.
Pigou, A.C. 1932. *The Economics of Welfare*. 4th ed. London: Macmillan.
Polanyi, Karl, Joseph E. Stiglitz, and Fred Block. 2012. *The Great Transformation: The Political and Economic Origins of Our Time*. Boston: Beacon Press.
Rosenstein-Rodan, P.N. 1943. Problems of Industrialisation of Eastern and South-Eastern Europe. *The Economic Journal* 53 (210–211): 202–211.
Saller, R. 2003. Women, Slaves, and the Economy of the Roman Household. In *Early Christian Families in Context: An Interdisciplinary Dialogue*, ed. D. Balch and C. Osiek, 185–204. Grand Rapids: William B. Eerdmans.
Scheidel, W. 2010. Real Wages in Early Economies: Evidence for Living Standards from 1800 BCE to 1300 CE. *Journal of the Economic and Social History of the Orient* 53 (3): 425–462.
Sirks, A.J.B. 1991. *Food for Rome: The Legal Structure of the Transportation and Processing of Supplies for the Imperial Distributions in Rome and Constantinople*. Amsterdam: J.C. Gieben.
Temin, P. 2004. The Labor Market of the Early Roman Empire. *The Journal of Interdisciplinary History* 34 (4): 513–538.
Thompson, P., and C. Smith. 2010. *Working Life: Renewing Labour Process Analysis*. Basingstoke: Palgrave Macmillan.
Van Minnen, P. 1998. Did Ancient Women Learn a Trade Outside the Home? A Note on *SB* XVIII 13305. *Zeitschrift für Papyrologie und Epigraphik* 123: 201–203.
Van Nijf, O. 1997. *The Civic World of Professional Associations in the Roman East*. Amsterdam: J.C. Gieben.
Watson, A., T. Mommsen, and P. Krueger. 1985. *The Digest of Justinian. V. 1–4*. Philadelphia: University of Pennsylvania.

CHAPTER 5

Voluntary Associations and Collectivity: A View from the East and the West

Professional associations in the western Roman Empire, which go by a variety of names including *collegia*, were far less common than they were in the Greek East. Our evidence for them is sporadic and inconsistent. This is no less true for bakers' associations, or *collegia pistorum*, for which we have ample evidence from Rome, Ostia, and throughout the eastern Mediterranean, but we have only hints that similar associations existed elsewhere, such as fines levied on bakers collectively or political programmata with which bakers seemingly advocated collectively for certain political candidates. This problem is not specific to voluntary associations of bakers; a dearth of evidence for intra-craft interactions has presented obstacles in understanding formal associations and the general evidence for collectivity among crafts- and tradespeople. Nevertheless, in the last 40 years our understanding of voluntary associations have grown considerably beyond the legal conceptualizations of them that dominated early studies, showing them to be integrated into the civic, social, and economic lives of their members. They facilitated collective funerary management, they served as personal and collective prestige generators, they allowed for collective bargaining with the state, and they probably lessened transactional costs for their members through access to networks of well-connected people. All of these observations, however, have been inferred almost entirely from juridical and epigraphic evidence, which not only privileges areas with intense epigraphic habits and state intervention, such as central Italy, it selectively focuses on associations that were wealthy

J. T. Benton, *The Bread Makers*,
https://doi.org/10.1007/978-3-030-46604-6_5

enough to have inscriptions or attract the attention of the state. Indeed, Jinyu Liu recently observed, the next push in our understanding of them will require studies with "more data input and micro-level realities" and those that "take full advantage of theoretical tools."[1] The purpose of this chapter is not to answer the many outstanding questions about voluntary associations in the Roman world, it is instead to provide context to the phenomena already observed about associations of bakers, pairing the epigraphic and juridical evidence with the material evidence for production within the framework of modes of production or intergenerational transmission of knowledge. Specifically, a heterogenous membership of the *collegium pistorum*, at least that of Ostia and Portus, is corroborated by the material remains of actual workshops in which we find both factory- and workshop-mode bakeries in a single city. Such heterogeneity in membership probably resulted in inequitable distribution of resources predicated on the social and economic capital of the member. Furthermore, the case is made here that voluntary associations were not limited to the eastern Mediterranean and Rome; they existed in other places and in lesser degrees wherever bakers lived and worked and they functioned in some similar ways, but probably lacked the stratification and asymmetrical exploitation so evident in the associations of larger cities.

Although this book concerns the western Mediterranean, the vast bulk of our evidence for voluntary associations of bakers comes from the eastern half of the Mediterranean. There are some very good reasons to treat what is happening in the east and west separately, as discussed in the introduction of the book, but the more extensive evidence means that we understand in much greater detail the voluntary associations of the east. We have remarkably little evidence for voluntary associations of bakers in general. We know of them at Rome,[2] Ostia and Portus,[3] Cologne,[4] Constantinople.[5] There are also a number of cities where there is evidence for bakers, collectively being the subject or object of some action, without clear evidence for a formal association. Some of these cities list bakers in the plural in a way that makes it hard to argue that some sort of association did not exist, like Ravenna,[6] Setifis,[7] Ephesus,[8] Antioch,[9] Miletus,[10] and Side,[11] and where bakers as a collective were given a communal space by authorities, punished collectively by imperial authorities, or use a type of nickname for a group of bakers. Finally, there are cities where bakers are referred to in the plural, but without the sorts of corporate capacity that implies an association: Pompeii,[12] Ulubrae,[13] Salpensa,[14] Akraiphia,[15] Arsinoë,[16] Oxyrhynchus,[17] and Thyatira.[18] These are important distinctions because it is often assumed that collective actions of craftspeople imply the existence of an association. In many such cases a formal association may well have existed, but it is a mistake to make such an inference because it precludes the possibilities that bakers could have taken collective action—or that state actors could have taken action upon bakers—without the existence of a formal association. There is also good reason to be cautious: the cities with formal and clearly stated *collegia* are all large urban centers with massive political importance, at some point serving as the seat of imperial authorities or a port for such a place. The cities where there is strong evidence for formal associations are also all large cities with populations well above the average. Finally, cities like Pompeii or Salpensa (probably Italica) were of a definitive category smaller. This neat grafting of the evidence for associations and collectivity of bakers onto population size should give us pause. As such, the evidence is not only divided into the eastern Mediterranean and the western, but also treated separately in small towns and larger cities.

Voluntary Associations of Bakers in the Greek East

We saw at Rome and some other larger cities that there were some participants in the commercial baking industry who contributed through investment in bakeries rather than direct participation in the production. There is some evidence for such men in the eastern Mediterranean, but they appear to have been more well integrated into the social fabric of cities, towns, and villages generally holding higher social status. A number of bakers throughout the eastern Mediterranean indicate their profession, but also their membership on local councils. A baker (*mankipos*) at Korykos describes himself as a *patrobolos* on his and his wife's sarcophagus.[19] Another baker (*artokopos*) at Ephesus describes himself as a member of the *gerousia*.[20] In other cases, some bakers clearly had achieved significant wealth; Aurelios Neikon identifies his sarcophagus and that of his wife, warning that it is forbidden to place anyone in it and anyone who does will be fined 1000 denarii, which should be paid to one of several gladiatorial clubs.[21] Integrated into the social fabric of cities such as they were, bakers had the same incentives to create social capital for themselves. One of the well-attested functions of voluntary associations of bakers was that they served as a means of generating prestige for their members. For example, the bakers at Akraiphia collectively help pay for the restoration of the cult of Apollo Ptoos in 42 CE.[22]

The function of associations was not limited to the generating social capital for their members; they also facilitated interactions between the state and the bakers collectively. Associations of bakers generated prestige (and maybe provided other benefits, economic or social) for important people and in return they likely expected favorable treatment. For example, two groups of bakers in the *nome* of Arsinoë, the *katharourgoi* (speciality bakers) and *plakountopoioi* (flat-bread makers) set up a portrait statue and honorific stele for Herakleides the *prostates* in 3 CE.[23] Similarly, the bakers (*artokopoi*) at Thyatira honored Gaius Julius Julianus Tatianus, who was distributor of grain (*triteutes*) and director of the market.[24] One of the ways that state actors repaid the honor – and probably organized – associations of bakers was by giving them a place (*topos*) presumably for meetings or for feasting. At Ephesus, a certain Marcus Fulvius Publicianus Neikephoros prolifically assigned *topoi* to a wide variety of crafts and trades.[25] The *topos* of the bakers at Miletus was marked by a column of blue marble which was found reused in a house, so the actual location is unknown.[26] Through acts of commemoration and monuments, important people and the associations acted as reflexive prestige generators.

But the relationship between associations and state actors extended beyond mutual commemoration. Associations of bakers offered a means to organize and implement policy on an industry that, for the most part, rested in private hands. Roman authorities, both local and imperial, were very concerned with the provisioning of large cities and associations of bakers offered a means to organize and regulate activities that were essential to the existence of the urban population. That concern may have increased during the second century CE into the third and state actors often engaged the commercial baking industry, which for the most part rested in private hands, collectively. A contract from Oxyrhynchus, *P.Oxy.* XII 1454, records an agreement of some bakers in the city in 116 CE to make bread from grain provided by the local *agoranomos*. By the end of the second century the authorities were taking more direct and extreme measures. In a remarkable example of this concern, *P.Oxy.* VI 908 records a contract between six Eutheniarchs of Oxyrhynchus that each will agree to outfit bakeries at their own expense.[27] Eventually, Oxyrhynchus moved to a dole[28] which is instructive, because it was not an effort to fight poverty, but rather a means of provisioning "the already privileged middle class of the cities, as in Rome."[29]

Authorities also found it useful to tax bakers collectively at points. A sixth century register of taxes from the *nome* of Arisonë assess bakers and specialty bakers collectively.[30] Taxing, however, was not the only way that the state could redress bakers collectively, they could also punish them collectively. Some authority, probably the proconsul of Asia, commemorated his punishment of the bakers of Ephesus for causing some sort of disturbance in an inscription dating to the second half of the second century CE[31]:

> And according to an agreement . . . thus it comes about at times that the people are plunged into disorder and tumults because of the meeting and insolence of the bakers in the marketplace, for which they ought to have been arrested and put on trial already. Since however it is necessary to consider the city's welfare more than the punishment of these men, I have resolved that it is necessary to bring them to their senses by an edict. I therefore order the bakers not to hold meetings as a faction nor to be leaders in recklessness, but strictly to obey the regulations made on behalf of the general welfare and to supply the city unfailingly with the labor essential for bread making. When from this time forward any one of them shall be caught in the act of attending a meeting contrary to orders, or of starting any tumult and *stasis*, he shall be arrested and shall be punished with the fitting penalty. And should anyone plot against the city dare to conceal himself, he shall in addition have *decuria* marked on his foot, and the receiver of such a man shall be liable to the same penalty.[32]

It is unclear what insolence (*athrasia*) of the bakers led to the disorder and tumult (*tarache kai thorybos*), but it was related to their assembly in the market (*syllogon*). In a remarkably transparent statement of the responsibility that Roman officials felt for provisioning the urban population of the empire, the proconsul resolved to stop short of arresting or otherwise punishing the bakers out of concern for the city's welfare (*polei sympheron*). It is never explicitly stated that the bakers had a formal association, but it is implied: part of their punishment is that they are prohibited from meeting as a faction or association (*hetairia*).

The prohibition on meeting and forming an association shows a different side of bakers associations; in some cases they were mutually beneficial and facilitated oversight of the commercial baking industry, but in other cases they could be nuisances when the interests of the state and that of the bakers association diverged. A similar example of bakers being involved in some form of unrest is evident in Libanius' *Orationes*. The fourth-century autobiographer describes his time at Antioch and tells of riot during which he arbitrated a disagreement with the mob and the governor.

> The countryside had experienced a bad winter, and the following summer was no better. Part of the grain had not even germinated, the rest was sparse, and even this was blighted. In consequence, the populace created disturbances against the city council, quite unreasonably since the council could not control the weather. Though the governors tried to get grain from every possible source, the price of bread rose higher and higher. The renowned Philagrius, having reached a higher office, though unable to improve the situations, was content if it got no worse. He kept urging the bakers' association (*sitopoion ethnos*) to be more reasonable, but was reluctant to enforce his demands, for he was afraid of the increasing desertion, which would have left the city ship-wrecked, abandoned by its crew.[33]

Not only is the same concern for provisioning evident in Libanius' description of the situation at Antioch, but so is a similar caution about how to handle the conflict between the state and associations of bakers. It is unlikely that he offers an unbiased assessment of the conflict, but Libanius provides some possible indication of what conditions might lead to a souring of the relationship between bakers and the state: exogenous factors causing shortages and higher prices. Grain shortages were a well-known cause of rioting in antiquity. The adverse conditions of drought decreased the supply of grain, meaning that primary-sector suppliers (probably landed gentry) needed to increase their prices to sustain their profitability. This increased grain prices for bakers, which meant higher prices of bread for the urban population or lower profits for the bakers. Grain shortages were a well-known cause of rioting in antiquity, but they also led to scenarios in which bakers' interests became contrary to those of the state and the landed gentry that comprise it.

Variation Among Associations in the Eastern Mediterranean

There are some basic assumptions that have somewhat plagued how we understand associations of crafts and trades, particularly for the eastern Mediterranean and it is necessary to confront them to disentangle the complexity of the evidence and arrive at clearer understanding of them. Associations are often treated as all-inclusive entities that represented all of the bakers in a city, but there is some indication that one city could have multiple associations of bakers. An inscription from Side, dating to the first half of the third century AD, commemorates the harmony between two different baker or baker-adjacent groups whose titles appear to be based on individual processes in the production of bread.[34] The first group mentioned, the ἀλευροκαθάρτες, is a combination of ἄλευρος (flour) and καθαρτής (cleanser). The second derives from ἀβάκιον (slab) and σταῖς (dough).[35] Despite the hopeful sentiments of the inscription, Onno van Nijf suggests that the emphasis placed on ὁμόνοια (harmony) might indicate "considerable tensions between different specialists" in the commercial baking industry.[36] It seems unlikely that the commercial bread industry had vertically specialized to the extent that sifters and kneaders operated different operations and workshops. Margaret Mitchell, on the other hand, posits that the two groups could represent two different bakers' associations.[37] Such names would be almost like nicknames and it might indicate the state might have some options and the ability to exploit divisions within an industry.

One of the other assumptions is that collectivity among bakers is often conflated with the existence of an association. For example, above I stated that that associations of bakers served as collective means of generating prestige for their members, citing the collective participation of the bakers in the restoration of the cult of Apollo Ptoos, but the inscription does not say that an association of bakers undertook the act, rather that the bakers did. The conclusion that one of the functions of such associations was that they generated prestige for their members is almost certainly correct, but assuming that all collective actions on the part of crafts- or tradespeople necessitated an association would be a mistake. Collective treatment of bakers by the state makes for better evidence. In tax reregisters, bakers—and other crafts and trades—are occasionally assessed collectively.[38] It is hard to imagine bakers could be taxed as a single unit if there was not some institution unifying them or some sort of collective treasury.

In fact, one of the other assumptions about associations of crafts and trades is that they served largely the same functions from Rome and Constantinople to groups of bakers in smaller communities. The reason that scholars, myself included, are prone to this assumption is that the evidence is disparate and incomplete; we can only create a full model of such associations if all that evidence is brought together. The risk in this method, however, is that we gloss past variation between cities. Philip Venticinque, whose work on craft and trade associations in the eastern Mediterranean will surely be a touchstone for future studies, notes that "a distinction should also be drawn between bakers' associations at Rome or Constantinople (and oversight of their activities) and bakers working elsewhere. Of the twenty-one laws related to bread making and the food supply that are preserved in book 14 of the Theodosian Code, more than half were addressed to the prefect of the city. Although the food supply remained a concern at all levels of the administration, bakers in Oxyrhynchus or Aphrodito operated under different levels of scrutiny."[39] We have seen that the Ephesian and Antiochan bakers probably also share this scrutiny, among other factors. In many ways the differences between the associations of bakers in large cities and those in smaller ones are ones of degree and scale that is predicated on population size.

But there were some fundamental differences between associations of bakers in large cities and the collectivity among bakers in smaller cities. For example, there seems to be greater homogeneity in wealth—and probably power—among groups of bakers in smaller cities. Some members of associations of bakers were wealthy and others were surely not. The bakers of smaller towns were uniformly of more modest means. A sixth-century tax list from Aphrodito in Egypt records the payment various craftspeople, among others, and the individual bakers (*katharourgoi*) comprise the largest single profession.[40] Their payments are either one third or one half of a solidus. Venticinque notes that, without a clear understanding of what was being taxed and how, one cannot be sure if the variation in the payments means that there was less income inequality in smaller towns than was evident in larger cities. On the other hand, a more homogenous population of bakers in smaller cities is consistent with our material evidence for workshops in the cities of the western Roman empire, which were consistently small in size and modest in scale of production in smaller towns and Ostia, our one large city with extensive remains of bakers, had workshop bakeries and factory-like bakeries. Bakers in smaller cities may have been more uniformly of modest means, but they shared the integration into the social and political fabric of their communities. For instance, a list of residents eligible for *sitologos*, official in charge of grain, in the small village of Karanis records the estimated wealth of Horos the flat-bread baker in 225 CE in the range of 700 drachma.[41] The value of the third-century denarius was certainly not what it had been in years prior and it would be hard to characterize that level of wealth within a relatively rural community, but Horos' eligibility strongly suggests that bakers in the eastern Mediterranean, at least at Karanis, could hold municipal offices.

Formal Associations in the West: The *Collegium* and the *Corpus Pistorum*

From its origins, scholarship on Roman craft or merchant associations in the western Mediterranean has focused primarily on their relationship with the state or the social functions they served, which is largely a result of the types of evidence deployed in their study. A great deal of our evidence comes from the Roman jurists in the *Digest of Justinian* or the *Codex Theodosianus* which naturally led to a focus on the relationship between craft and trade associations and the state or the legal status of associations. The other major body of evidence is Latin epigraphy, which is largely funerary or otherwise commemorative, which resulted in an emphasis on the communal funerary function of associations or as collective mechanisms that generated prestige for members and even normalized perceptions for professions deemed unseemly. Even more recently, scholars have been exploring what economic advantages might be conferred by membership in a craft or trade association. Wim Broekaert, for example, uses modern analyses of costs and profits to argue that craft associations could confer economic advantages to their members through communication and cooperation between professionals and the shared cost-burdens.[42] Similarly, Matt Gibbs observes that, while ostensibly voluntary in terms of membership, certain associations could wield enough influence to make membership the only viable option.[43]

It is not the purpose of this chapter review the vast and growing body of thought on the origins of Roman *collegia*, but given the advances in our understanding of Roman voluntary associations in both the eastern and western Mediterranean, a review of the evidence for associations of bakers helps provide context. Romans themselves canonically attributed the origin of *collegia* to the Rome's regal past. Plutarch (*Numa*, 17) writes that Numa Pompilius introduced *collegia* to Rome as a way of organizing the people that sooth the tensions between the Sabines and Romulus's original people. There was little, if any, specialization at such an early time and the few craftsmen that might have existed could hardly have constituted a trade association. Another possible origin for Roman *collegia* lies in the Twelve Tables, the legal compromise between the patricians and plebeians (ca. 450 BC). The jurist Gaius records a passage from the Twelve Tables in which members (*sodales*) of associations (*collegii*) are afforded the right to make contracts with whomever they want so long as they do not break the law.[44] Such origins are surely apocryphal; the Romans had a habit of retrojecting the invention of their institutions onto Numa Pompilius[45] and, although the Twelve Tables do appear to have been a very early form of Roman legislation, there is nothing in the quote from the tables about craft-based associations. It is in a separate quote of the law of Solon, not in Gaius' quote of the Twelve Tables, that association for profit (*praedam*) or enterprise (*netotiationem*) is addressed. Moreover, a fifth-century BCE date for the formation of a voluntary association of bakers in Rome is unlikely based on the evidence for specialization in central Italy outlined in Chap. 2, which dates to the third century BCE and possibly later in Rome. Craft-based associations of bakers could not exist without bakers, but specialization had occurred further east where larger populations and more complex urban economies supported institutions and infrastructure at an earlier time than in the west.

As commercially baked bread went from a prestige good intended for an elite customer to a staple of the urban diet, which we saw evidenced by the abandonment of home-baking devices in the first century BCE, pressure built on the state to make sure the urban population of Rome was fed. Although not explicitly a member of an association of bakers, the first century BCE baker Eurysaces referred to himself as a *pistor*, but also *redemptor* (contractor) and *apparetor* (public servant). Eurysaces' self-identification as a contractor and a public servant strongly suggests that the state was beginning to take an interest in the commercial baking industry as an important part of the provisioning of the city as early as the first century BCE. A first-century CE funerary inscription from the columbarium of the Statilii for a baker named Titus Statilius Anoptes, indicates that he was a *pistor de conlegio*.[46] The association (*conlegium*) is not referred to specifically as a *collegium pistorum* and a baker could belong to associations that were not craft based. Two other bakers in the columbarium also announce their profession, but neither identifies explicitly with a craft association.[47] In a more dramatic example, a first-century CE tomb at Ulubrae lists at least 20 individuals, all male, who are described as *pistores*.[48] Again, we cannot infer the presence of a *collegium pistorum* from the use of baker in the plural, but the complete absence of any non-*pistor* individuals strongly implies some sort of collectivity prior to the second century CE.

In any event, it is probably during the late first century BCE or the first century CE that associations of bakers began to develop in response to the needs of the state and, in fact, by the second century CE the state had begun to engage with commercial bakers.[49] At some point in the second century CE, a freedman of Augustus named Telesphorus commemorated his wife Calpurnia Soteria. Telesphorus identifies himself as in charge of the bakers (*qui praeest pistoribus*).[50] Another freedman, Publius Aelius Hermes, is described as *praepositus pistorum*, overseer of the bakers.[51] Similarly, a slave named Automatus, presumably owned by the emperor, is described as *contrascriptor pistorum*.[52] These three inscriptions, all second century CE, are also primarily dated to the principate of Trajan and, in fact, we have some good reason to think that Trajan took a particular interest in managing the commercial baking industry. Aurelius Victor, albeit writing in the mid fourth century CE, tells us that Trajan "showed admirable concern for the permanent grain supply by acknowledging (*reperto*) and strengthening (*firmato*) the guild of bakers."[53] Aurelius Victor's passage implies that a *collegium pistorum* existed before Trajan and that he somehow altered the conditions in which it existed. This may be a reference to certain concessions given by Trajan to the bakers. The emperor engaged with the commercial bakers of Rome in two ways: providing social incentives for those willing to operate large bakeries[54] and expanded rights and legal capabilities for associations of bakers, among other crafts and trades. We are told by Gaius in his *Institutiones* that Trajan "enacted that if a [Junian] Latin carry on the business of miller in Rome for three years, and grinds each day not less than a hundred measures of wheat, he shall attain Roman citizenship.[55] Furthermore, sometime before in 107 CE, the Emperor granted *excusatio tutelae* (exemption from the duty of guardianship) to other, any *pistor* who operated a *centenarium pistrinum* (a bakery processing 100 *modii* per day).[56] It is also during this time, probably in the principate of Trajan, that the *collegium pistorum* was granted the corporate capacities "to have common property, a common treasury, and an attorney or syndic through whom, as in a state, what should be transacted and done in common is transacted and done."[57] An intensifying relationship between associations of bakers which continued after Trajan's rule and well into the third century CE. *FV* 235 records that the bakers of the *corpus pistorum* were excused (*excusantur*) from guardianship (*tutela*), even from their duty to the children of their fellow bakers. Caracalla extended this *vacatio* to include obligations occurred prior to becoming a baker, but only to those *pistores* which he created himself (*ab ipso creatis pistoribus*). It is unclear the extent to which these corporate capacities extended into any interactions with the state or into any economic functions of the bakeries. In the early modern world, corporate capacity and collective resources expanded the scale of economic endeavors beyond the constrains of a single family. Koenraad Verboven acknowledges the corporate capacity of the *collegium pistorum*, but cautions that such rare examples should not be considered a first step "towards a generalization of incorporated *societates*."[58] The function of the corporate capacity of bakers existed, it seems, more for collective interaction with the state and the mutual creation of personal and collective prestige, even if it brought bakers into contact with one another and with people with resources, which might mitigate transactional costs.

The origins and nature of the voluntary associations of bakers is further complicated by the diverse terminology employed in the legal and epigraphic evidence.[59] For example, the first direct evidence for an association of bakers is found in an Ostian inscription dating to 140 CE and the association is called a *corpus*, not a *collegium*.[60] In Gaius' passage about corporate capacity, he listed three types of associations: the *societas*, the *collegium*, and other "*corpora* of this sort."[61] In the same passage Gaius writes that certain *collegia*, the *corpus* of which had been established by *senatus consulta* and imperial *constitutiones*, were allowed to exist including the *collegium pistorum*. For Waltzing *collegia* were associations that could be formed for any reason, and *corpora* held a privileged legal status, which is grounded in the interventions of Trajan and incentives he provided.[62] Cracco Ruggini, on the other hand, suggested that the *collegium* and the *corpus* were interchangeable.[63] Wim Broekaert agrees that "associations who didn't enjoy that special juridical position could easily call themselves a *corpus*, as the word also had the abstract meaning of an alliance 'tout court', as mentioned earlier. The main reason for the confusion of *collegium* and *corpus* in epigraphy can easily have been a matter of prestige: *corpus* was undoubtedly a much more respected designation."[64] But Broekaert also notes that the word could be both a general term of an association and in court jargon indicate a special legal standing: "the difference between *collegium* and a *corpus* must have been maintained. Otherwise, it would be pointless for the Roman state to bestow *corpus* upon certain *collegia*." For Broekaert, whose interest in these passages is the *corpus* and *collegium naviculariorum*, the *collegia* pre-dated the second century CE and *corpora* are entities born of their predecessors whose relationship with the state had now intensified. We have also seen that different associations based in the same craft may even exist in the same city, a possibility hinted at by the *excusatio* for some bakers, but not for those of other corpora (*qui in ceteris corporibus*) or for bakers not created by the emperor (*ab ipso creatis pistoribus*). There are also mention of a *corpus pistorum siliginiariorum*, *corpus* of fine, wheat-bread bakers, which may or may not be the same *corpus* as that of the *pistores* more generally.[65] It is possible that the *corpus* a legal framework for an engagement of all bakers, even those of different *collegia* or *societates.*

Whatever the origins and precise meaning of *collegium* and *corpus*, the legal and epigraphic evidence clearly indicate an increasingly intense relationship between associations of bakers at Rome and Ostia and the state, something we saw evident in the east as well. Part of this relationship was the mutual creation of prestige. The first mention of the *corpus pistorum* from Ostia, *CIL* XIV 4359, is a dedication by the *corpus* honoring the Emperor Antoninus Pius. Similarly, the bakers of Ostia, Portus, and Utrius honored Marcus Aurelius with a similar monument.[66] The state could also respond in kind. Aelius Vitalio, the grain measurer (*mensor perpetuus*), gifted and dedicated an altar to Annona the goddess on behalf of the *corpus pistorum siliginiariorum*.[67] At Rome, the corpus pistorum honoured Antoninus Pius with a monument.[68] In the east we saw that local officials might grant a *topos* (a place) for an association of bakers as an honor and a way to recognize them. This same habit is evident in Ostia: a fragmented marble slab found in the *località* Pianabella near the city records the gift of a public space (*locus*) to the *corpus pistorum* by Papirius Dionysus, then prefect of the annonae, and with permission of the *decuriones.*[69]

The work of Nicholas Tran has shown the extent to which the composition of associations based in crafts and trades at Ostia and Rome were defined by heterogeneity, with members from nearly every socioeconomic status, including slaves, freedmen, and free members. Archaeologically, we saw corroboration of that conclusion; both modes of production (factory-like and workshop) were evident at Ostia. That is to say, there were very large, high-production bakeries in the city, but there were also much smaller establishments with less productive capacity. This must also have been true of Rome and one can imagine that a *corpus pistorum* consisting of some wealthy businessmen such as Cerellius Iazemis, discussed at length in Chap. 3, but also some more modest members who operated smaller workshops and had more direct involvement in the production of bread. Members of the association, no matter their social status or wealth were integrated into the fabric of local society just like their eastern counterparts. At least at Ostia, members of the *corpus pistorum* may well have held certain offices, such as duovir, provided they were born free despite lacking any elite heritage.[70] But it is unlikely that such opportunities were available to all members of a *corpus* or *collegium* equally; wealthier members surely had the connections and the means to attain an office or Marcus Licinius Privatus, for example, was wealthy and gave 50,000 sestertii to the *res publica* of Ostia; in return a place was set aside for him in the Piazzale delle Corporazioni at Ostia by decree of the of the *decuriones* and the *collegium fabrum tignuariorum* of Ostia, of which he was president, erected a statue to him there. The base of the statue indicates that Privatus had been a slave who had been freed and worked as a clerk of the decurian library (*decuriali scriba librario*). He was also awarded honorary titles as *pater et avus decurionum* and *pater equitum Romanorum*. The monument was set up sometime before the end of the second century CE, but addenda in smaller letters were written in the margins of the text indicating that he was also *quinquennalis* of the *corpus pistorum* of Ostia and Portus. A freeborn man of Privatus' means might well have achieved even more, given the restrictions placed on him as a freed slave. Conversely, members of the *corpus pistorum* that lacked the wealth and success of Privatus were probably no less integrated into the social fabric of the city, but they probably did not attain the same honors or enjoy the same opportunities.

It is unclear what duties or responsibilities accompanied the titles of these important figures in the association of bakers, such as *quinquennalis*, but it has been observed that the hierarchical structure within an association mirrored municipal functions with *quinquennalis* correlating to *duumvir* or consul. To some extent, the titles are honorific, generating prestige for the office holder, but they almost surely served other functions. For one thing, they seem to have taken responsibility for the erection of honorific monuments to state actors or the emperor. The monument dedicated to Antoninus Pius was done at the care of Marcus Caerellius Zmaragdo and Lucius Salvius Epictetus both of whom are identified *quinquennales* of the association and demarcated by depictions of millstones (a fact returned to in the next chapter).[71] Two other figures indicated as involved in the construction of the monument, Gaius Pupius Firminus and Lucius Calpurnius Maximus, are listed as quaestors of the *corpus pistorum*. If the *quinquennalis* corresponded to the duumvir, the *quaestor corporis pistorum* might be a junior position as it formed the first step in the *cursus honorum*. But *quaestor* of the *collegium* might resemble the political office in its responsibilities and function as well. Political *quaestores* were bound to consuls and perhaps the *quinquennalis* played some role in the appointment of the *quaestor* of the bakers. The political *quaestor* managed the treasury of the *res publica* and saw to the organization needs of their superiors and so the *quaestor corporis pistorum* may have helped to manage events and coordinate logistics so the *quinquennalis* can pursue an agenda. In late antiquity, the *quaestor* also had a judicial function and Jinyu Liu has shown the need for further study of internal workings of *collegia* and *corpora*, particularly into the "brokers or bridgers" who created cohesion and efficiency in the systematic mechanisms of the association.[72] The responsibilities of the *quinquennalis* and *quaestor* of the *corpus pistorum* might have included mitigating conflict between members and serving as a representative for the interests of the *corpus*. In fact, FV 235 records Hadrian's granting of a *vacatio* to the *pistores* from a rescript to two bakers Verna and Montanus. How the two bakers came into contact with the state and the emperor is not specified, but the fact that the emperor responded to them suggests Hadrian cared very much about provisioning of the city but also that the two bakers had the social and economic capital to attract his attention. One suspects that Verna and Montanus may have been the *quinquennales* of their *corpus*.

It is here that economic advantages of membership in such associations emerge for some scholars; belonging to one is seen as a way of reducing operational and transactional costs via networks. A large body of scholarship has shown that ancient Roman craftspeople relied heavily on social relationships to mitigate risk, create opportunity, and normalize the perception of their profession.[73] Cameron Hawkins, for instance, argues that associations of crafts and trades, at least in thick economies filled with buyers and sellers, offered a means to reduce transactional costs by "by embedding their production strategies whether in relationships of trust (which often arose in the context of professional associations), or in relationships of power that bound freed slaves to their former masters."[74] One of the advantages of membership in the *corpus pistorum* is that it increased contact with the state or with powerful individuals and, we have seen, that facilitated forced or penal labor which surely reduced labor costs for entrepreneurial *pistores*. The *collegia* or *corpora pistorum* probably served another economic function for its members, at least those of means: it gave them a way to enact integrated economic strategies and exploit asymmetrical power dynamics within the *corpus pistorum*. A citizen of Ostia, Marcus Cerellius Iazemis, dedicated a small altar at the sanctuary of Hercules Victor in Tibur on which he identifies himself as a *codicarius* involved in the boat transport of goods on the Tiber and as a grain merchant, but he was also *quinquennalis* for life of the *corpus pistorum*.[75]

Iazemis could have enacted a vertically integrated economic strategy without membership in an association of bakers, but as a wealthy member he came into contact with well-connected people whose interests were as diverse as his own. Furthermore, it created an opportunity to outsource components of the production of bread by offering access to a wide variety of *pistores*, both bakery owners and small-scale producers over whom a businessman *pistor* could probably wield significant manipulative power as *quinquenalis* or merely through social capital.

The nature of the *corpus pistorum* at Rome changed at the end of the third century CE as part of certain reforms to the provisioning of the City of Rome. Emerging from the turmoil of the third century, the emperor Aurelian converted the dole from grain to bread.[76] Certainly by 315 CE, commercial baking in Rome and Ostia had become a *munus*. Indeed the duty of the *pistores* to practice their craft in the third century was highly regulated and the *munus* was even hereditary.[77] Members who fled this responsibility could be forced back into their duty as bakers (*consortium pistorum*).[78] This would have been a problem for those members of the associations who were more of the businessman types or for social elites who had agreed to operate a bakery. Sirks notes, however, that there were frequently multiple ways for an heir to evade the *munus pistorium*, and any bakers who were senators were also exempt.[79] Similar efforts are evident at Setifis in North Africa at the end of the fourth century. Under imperial auspices of Theodosius and Arcadius, the governor of Mauretania Sitifensis, Flavius Maecius Constans, restored the bakeries (*furnarias*) which had befallen some disaster and he furnished them and the bakers (*pistores*) with the equipment necessary for the cooking of bread for the annonae (*instrumento pistorio exornatas ad annonae publicae coctionem*).[80] *Pistores* (the bakers) addressed in the plural does not necessarily imply the existence of a *collegium*, but Setifis is also one of the cities where we saw evidence for modes of production and businessman-like *pistores*, suggesting that the necessary ingredients for an association of bakers were present, all of which help explain the direct involvement of imperial authorities. Similarly, king Theoderic had presumably appointed a man named Florentius as father of the bakers (*pater pistorum regis Theoderici*) at Ravenna, a fact that is extolled on his tomb.[81]

Collegia and Collectivity outside of Rome and its Immediate Vicinity

It is often assumed that associations of bakers pervaded wherever commercial bakeries can be identified. Tiinde Kaszab-Olschewski, for example, argues that "professional associations were formed quickly in the provinces. From Roman Cologne, a *collegium pisstricorum* (CIL XIII 8255) is recorded as a professional association of bakers, and there is also evidence for bakeries in Jiilich and Bliesbruck."[82] It is worth noting that Gaius, in *Dig.* 3.4.1, remarks on the presence of similar associations in the provinces (*qui et in provinciis sunt*). The jurist does not specify what association existed where and there is no reason we should assume that he means *collegia pistorum* specifically. The general lack of evidence for associations of bakers outside of Rome, Ostia, and the eastern Mediterranean is also sometimes taken to indicate that bakers did not form associations in the smaller villages, towns and cities of the west. Hawkins, for instance, argues that uncertainty and seasonality in thin markets in rural, extra-urban, or small communities incentivized flexibility and adaptability over stable prices and complicated economic strategies.[83] As such, associations and the regulation and standardization they fostered would have limited the ability of small-scale, small-town bakers to respond to adverse economic conditions. In fact, our one example of a *collegium* outside of Rome, Ostia and the east is at Cologne and is referred to as a *collegium pisstoricium*.[84] The variation in terminology aside, Cologne was a large city, what Hawkins would surely refer to as a thick market, allowing for integrated economic strategies and incentivizing the formation of associations, a relationship with the state, and the exploitation of social relationships fostered by them. We saw that entrepreneurial participants in the commercial baking industry were evident at Cologne.[85]

Even if we lack direct evidence for small-town *collegia*, there is, however, a great deal of evidence for collectivity among bakers and hints that such associations existed, even if we cannot identify *collegia pistorum* in every case. At Pompeii, for example, Tacitus tells us that *collegia* existed and were at times banned, but never with an explicit mention of a *collegium pistorum*.

> et rursus re ad patres relata, prohibiti publice in decem annos eius modi coetu Pompeiani collegiaque, quae contra leges instituerant, dissolute.

> and, the affair being referred back to the senators, the Pompeians were officially prevented from holding gatherings of that type for ten years, and the leagues which they had instituted illegally were dissolved.[86]

The word used for the associations, here translated as leagues, is *collegia*, but Woodman observes that "whether the 'leagues' were fan clubs, supporting the gladiators, or cadet corps, actually performing gladiatorial exercises, seems unclear." Given the context of the passage, it seems likely that *collegia* in this sense refers to gladiatorial fan clubs, as suggested by Woodman, or even local associations that played some part in the Noceran riot. The evidence from Ephesus and Antioch does suggest that craft associations could be involved in unrest, but there is no reason here to assume that the *collegia* indicated by Tacitus were craft-based.

There is, however, other evidence that suggests collectivity among bakers in Pompeii. A number of Pompeian painted *dipinti* indicate that the city's bakers, or at least some of them, cooperated politically by announcing their support for specific candidates. These *dipinti* follow a formula that Henrik Mouritsen calls 'rogantes', a group ostensibly asking for the election of an individual.[87] Two politicians were specifically supported by the city's bakers: Gnaeus Helvius Sabinus and Gaius Julius Polybius. In the case of Sabinus, the *pistores* team up with the *vicini* (the neighbors, presumably of Polybius).[88] Mouritsen observes that the *dipinti* do not necessarily imply the existence of an association of bakers in Pompeii. Certainly the implication is a group, but there is no assurance that the group was universal. Indeed, Julius Polybius enjoyed the support not only of the *pistores*, or at least some of them, but also that of a single ardently supportive *pistor*.[89] In another case, a lone baker also presents his support for Julius Polybius, describing himself as hardworking.[90]

Liu, on the other hand, is less quick to discount the possibility of a professional association of bakers in Pompeii.[91] Even if the *pistores* authoring the *rogatores* dipinti constitute only part of the entire number of bakers at Pompeii, the acts still represent a collective actions that extended beyond a single workshop tying multiple bakers together. One is possibly tempted to see an effort to influence elections or push an agenda, but Mouritsen rejects this notion and instead casts the collective inscriptions within the framework of the patron/client relationship and we have seen that *collegia* and associations often engaged in client-like relationships with elites an state actors, serving as mutual prestige generators. He argues that "the *rogator* inscriptions were posted on the initiative of the electoral agents and not the expression of any particularly strong interest in the election among individual voters."[92] He observes that women, craftsmen, *liberti*, and *clientes* comprised a significant portion of the *rogatores*.[93] He concludes from the "low-status" of such *rogatores* that they would have had an "undesirable effect" on the campaign and election.[94] From this perceived undesirable effect and the low numbers of such *dipinti* he concludes that the *rogatores* had a previous relationship with the candidate and speculates a patron client relationship as the source of their support.[95] Mouritsen developed this idea at time when most scholars agreed that craftspeople suffered under elite disdain for them. More recent work by Nicholas Tran, among others, has shown this to be a misunderstanding that was grounded more in a few texts, notably from Cicero, and not at true reflection of reality, a topic explored further in the next chapters. But this only further serves to further Mouritsen's contextualization of the *rogatores* inscriptions within the context of patronage; *collegia*, as a collective, could take patrons and perhaps informal collections of bakers could do the same. If indeed they were no so maligned as we once thought, supplying their support in political programmata may have been a way to fulfill the obligation of *clientela*, or perhaps a bid to attract a patron. We could, probably, cast this also within the background of mutual prestige and honor creation; indeed, some portion of the fullers of Pompeii collectively dedicated a statue to Eumachia in her eponymous building so we know such things happened at Pompeii.[96]

It is unlikely we will ever understand the *rogatores* inscriptions in terms of their authorship and their intent; the evidence is largely relegated to Pompeii due to its state of preservation. Nevertheless, we might have some corroboration of a social motivation from another inscription that implies that Julius Polybius might have had a specific relationship with bakers or the production of bread. The author proclaims that he brings (or makes?) the good bread (*panem bonum fert*).[97] The use of the word *fert* probably means 'to bring' but it could also potentially mean 'make' and it is sometimes suggested that Gaius Julius Polybius was a *pistor* himself. Other theories maintain that the mention of good bread may be a reminder of previous beneficence or a promise of future generosity.[98] Distributions of bread were common, even before Aurelian converted the dole from grain to bread. The famous depiction of the bread-vendor in Pompeii is now largely thought to be one such distribution (Fig. 5.1).[99] Conversely, the painting needs revisiting because there is a similar scene of bread selling from the Isola Sacra necropolis near Ostia that is almost identical

Fig. 5.1 Distribution of Bread from the Tablinum in the Pompeian House at VIII.3.30 (Museo Archeologico Nazionale di Napoli inventory number 9071)

(Fig. 5.2). No matter the meaning of the painting, which we will probably never know, we should not be surprised if a prominent baker might be so integrated into society that he might even be elected to office; we saw as much in the eastern Mediterranean and in Rome.

Collectivity among Pompeii's *pistores* may have extended beyond associating for patronage or to attract the favor of state actors. We have seen that one of the functions of *collegia* and associations elsewhere is

Fig. 5.2 Funerary Plaque of Bread Vendor with Sieves, from Isola Sacra near Ostia

collective self-commemoration, often funerary, but not exclusively. That may have taken on collective religious worship and procession. A fresco, found along via di Mercurio in Pompeii, outside a shop at VI.7.8 between entrances eight and nine, shows a procession scene (Fig. 5.3); men below carry a bier holding smaller individuals acting as carpenters; one is planing wood (indicted by the green arrow) and the other two are sawing a board (indicated by the orange arrow). John Clarke suggests the smaller figures are in fact statues or idols and identifies this scene as the Quinquatria, a festival in honor of Minerva. Indeed, early accounts of the image report the goddess, now lost, standing behind the man planing the wood and you can still just barely see her shield. Another man at the front of the bier stands over a body and Clarke identifies him as Daedalus, the mythological progenitor of carpenters. The fresco led Mau to conclude that a carpenter operated in the shop at VI.7.8, for which we really have no evidence. More convincingly, Clarke suggests that the men holding the bier are carpenters, which implies that during festivals craftsmen—or at least carpenters—processed with little statues of themselves like medieval icons. A particularly unconventional depiction in fresco of a millstone was found in the macellum at Pompeii (Fig. 5.4).[100] Cupids garland donkeys and

Fig. 5.3 Carpenters' Procession from outside VI.7.8–9 at Pompeii (Museo Archeologico Nazionale di Napoli inventory number 8991)

Fig. 5.4 So-Called Vestalia Scene, from the Macellum in Pompeii (Blümner 1912, fig. 23)

partake of beverages around an abstracted millstone at the fresco's center. Hugo Blümner called the scene a "Mühlenfest" (mill festival) and identifies it as a celebration of the Vestalia.[101] The meaning of such images is impossible to decipher, but one wonders if they represent visual reinforcements of collective worship and expressions of solidarity through procession, ones grounded in craft.

Although Tacitus' passage concerning *collegia* at Pompeii does not specify the nature of the associations, one can at least infer that the state engaged collectively with such institutions. This may well have been true at Pompeii and other places even if formal associations did not exist. This, at least, appears to have been true at Salpensa, in Baetica in Spain, where a second-century inscription records the construction of a dedication by the duumviri from the fines levied on a group of *pistores*.[102] We do not know if the *pistores* were fined as a single unit, with a fine paid from a common treasury, or as individuals. Salvador Ordóñez Agulla and José Carlos Saquete Chamizo identify the types of reasons that bakers might be penalized and speculate that it was probably for some form of collective price increase.[103] But we have no evidence to say what they did to incur the fine nor do we know if all bakers in Salpensa were fined or just a select few, but it is seems significant that the bakers are treated epigraphically as a single unit. At the very least, we saw in Rome and in the East the state actors took great care to manage the provisioning of urban populations. There is no reason to think that local authorities in smaller communities were not also concerned with feeding their cities. Furthermore, we saw at Antioch and Ephesus that when conflict arose between the state and bakers collectively, it tended to be about fluctuating cost of grain and the price of bread, which could lead to unrest.

Conclusion

Bakers associated in the west in ways that were different than those of the east: the *collegium pistorum* in Rome and Ostia had a relationship with the state—and even the Emperor—that was more intense than in any city in the eastern empire with the possible exception of Constantinople in late antiquity. Its status as the capital of a pan-Mediterranean empire and one of the largest cities in the region accounts for such attention in the legal and epigraphic texts. Conversely, among the smaller cities around the western Roman Empire, despite evidence for commercial baking throughout the region, we have almost no evidence for formal associations of bakers and much less evidence for basic collectivity. The one place with evidence for a formal *collegium pistorum*—or in this case *pisstoricium*—comes from Cologne which was itself a large city with a thick market and evidence for integrated economic strategies, making it more similar to

Rome and cities of the east. Some other *collegia* surely existed in similar places, but without documentation in text. It is interesting that the use of words for baker or association differ from city to city and region to region, which suggests that we should expect associations of bakers—or lack thereof—to differ as well.

The differences between the east and the west are probably very much the product of their histories. The large population centers, institutional complexity, and thick-market economies necessary to sustain and incentivize such associations had long histories in places like Egypt, the Levant, Anatolia, and Greece. As such, we should not be surprised that we find less evidence for associations of bakers in the western Mediterranean where urbanism, bureaucratic complexity, and specialized producers had a much shorter history. On the other hand, the difference between the east and west might be overstated to a certain extent. The east had a much longer habit of epigraphy that could serve to artificially inflate the amount of evidence for associations of bakers in the eastern provinces. Furthermore, scholars, we saw, sometimes conflate collectivity in the east with the existence of formal associations, which might be a step too far. Despite any differences, associations of bakers in the east provide valuable sounding board for understanding *collegia* or *corpora pistorum* and collectivity among Roman bakers in the west because we have so much more evidence for their collective actions and their associations. Throughout both areas, collectivity allowed bakers to integrate into society, normalized their profession by generating prestige, and interact with elites and the state. In both the east and the west, associations of bakers in large cities with vibrant markets differed greatly from those in smaller villages, towns, and cities. For example, Rome and Cologne in the west and Ephesus and Antioch in the east had formal associations which had close relationships with the state and local elites and served to generate prestige both for members and state actors through collective euergetism. Such activities integrated bakers into society and probably had a validating effect on their profession and created opportunity for the bakers both individually and collectively. This opportunity allowed for some members of the associations to rise above others and heterogeneity was a defining trait of membership in associations of bakers, in large cities both in the east and the west. One wonders if vertically integrated economic strategies, which we saw were part of the modes of production in places such as Cologne, Ostia, and Rome, might also have been implemented in the east, a possible avenue of further research.

Both in the east and in the west, there is evidence for collectivity among bakers in smaller towns and villages, sometimes with a formal association in the east, but never explicitly so in the west. Such bakers tended to be much more modest in their means and they were more homogenously modest. That is to say, we see no evidence in the small towns for bakers who indirectly participated in the production of bread or implemented integrated economic strategies. Homogeneity and modest means among small-town bakers is corroborated by the material remains of bakeries in such urban centers. They are universally small in size and in productive capacity; never in the small cities such as Pompeii, Volubilis, or Italica do we see the massive bread factories that dominate Ostia and very likely other larger cities. None of this is to say that bakers in small towns could not be integrated into society and participating in generating prestige for themselves and local elites. They may have even held office, as we saw at Aphrodito, Horos the flatbread baker was eligible for *sitologos*. It seems unlikely that any baker at Pompeii was an office holder, but the bakers collectively were interested in generating prestige for themselves and for the local elites who were holding office in an effort to access networks of power and privilege and manage perceptions of their craft.

In some ways, the difference between associations in large cities and whatever collectivity existed in smaller urban centers was a matter of degree. Authorities surely interfered in local baking industries in smaller cities, the bakers at Salpensa were fined by the duumviri for example, but the bakers were engaging with local elites of the *decuriones*, not the Emperor or his direct proxies. Similarly, bakers collectively created prestige for themselves and local elites in smaller urban centers, but without wealthy members they did so in less grand ways with painted rather than carved epigraphic content or with more modest *honoraria*. But the heterogenous nature of associations in large cities and the homogenous nature of bakers in smaller ones means that the difference is also one of kind. An association where members were largely of the same means and more uniformly poor meant that their aims were also fundamentally different. They lacked the access to social networks that more prominent members could provide, thus preventing savings in transactional costs or the enactment of integrated economic strategies.

Finally, it is worth noting that our understanding of associations in general, but particularly those that are craft-based, continues to be founded almost exclusively on legal, epigraphic, and literary texts. The myopia created by our evidence produces a questionable emphasis on the honorific, prestige-generating, and state-negotiating aspects of voluntary associations. Recent work, still grounded largely in epigraphy, has pushed for a more economic function noting the reduction of transactional costs through the facilitation of social networking. Here I also proposed that such networks also allowed members of bakers associations, at least those who held high rank in the institutions, to begin enacting vertically integrated strategies by providing access to resources and individuals who could help connect businessmen with contacts in other industries, men who Liu might say acted as bridges between associations of different crafts and trades. This at least is true in large cities with vibrant economies where we have clearly stated *collegia* or *corpora* whose hierarchy is somewhat clear. One of the remarkable aspects of Roman-period commercial baking is that we have so few overtly stated associations of bakers, even in the eastern Mediterranean. The vast amounts of collective actions taken by bakers does suggest, however, that some form of an association existed in such places and another possible avenue of future research could be to examine why the bakers and possibly other crafts and trades specifically avoided naming their collectivity. One is tempted to argue that they wanted to avoid state attention and anxieties felt about associations of bakers, but that continues to privilege the legal evidence and I suspect their motivations were multifaceted.

Notes

1. Liu (2016, 204).
2. *CIL* XIV 4234; *CIL* VI, 6219, 8998, 8999; *AE* (1923, 76).
3. Ostia and/or Portus In an unusual case, the *corpus pistorum magnariorum et castrensariorum* must be an association of bakers that were elites operated bakers as a *munus* or obligation and maybe for the army. *CIL* VI 1739 and Bakker (1999, 3).
4. *CIL* XIII 8255.
5. *CTh.* 14.17.12.
6. *CIL* XI 317.
7. *CIL* VIII, 8480.
8. *SEG* IV 512.
9. Libanius *Orationes* I.205–10. This is questionable because Libanius describes it as a *sitopoion ethnos* and his account never calls the group of bakers by one of the more traditional names.
10. IDidyma 522 = PHI 247664 = ID# 12332.
11. *SEG* XXXIII 1165.
12. *CIL* IV 886; 7273.
13. *CIL* X, 6494.
14. *HEp*, 18, 389.

15. *SEG* XV 330.
16. *IFayum* III 212.
17. *P.Oxy.* XII 1454
18. Thyatira.
19. *SEG* XXXVII 1309. van Pleket (1984), Nijf (1997: 21– 22), Zuiderhoek (2011, 191) and Venticinque (2016, 153).
20. *IEph.* 2225. Zuiderhoek (2011, 191) and Venticinque (2016, 153).
21. *IEph* 2226.
22. SEG 15330.
23. *IFayum* III 212.
24. *TAM* V 966. Camia (2017, 140) and Venticinque (2016, 193).
25. *I.Eph.* 444, 445, 547, 549, 2076, 2077, 2078, 2079, 2080, 2081, and 2082.
26. Miletus: IDidyma 522 = PHI 247664 = ID# 12332.
27. *P.Oxy.* VI 908. Sharp (2007: 218–30), Lewis (1983: 47) and Venticinque (2016, 144).
28. *P.Oxy.* XL 2892–2940.
29. Rea (1972, 8) and Lewis (1983).
30. *P.Prag.* I 25.
31. *IK* II 215; *SEG* IV 512. *I.Eph.* 215 (II CE), with *SEG* XXVIII 863. Johnson et al. (2012, 213).
32. trans. Buckler (1923: 30–31) and Venticinque (2016, 192–193).
33. Libanius *Orationes* I.205–10. Trans. Norman (1992, 267).
34. *SEG* 33, 1165. ὑρ γ Κενδεας Κενδεου τῇ ὁμόνοίᾳ τῶν συνβιωτῶν ἀλευροκαθάρτες καὶ ἀβακίταις ὁμονοίας χάριν ἀνέστησα τὸ κιόνιν εὐτυχοῦμεν. I Kendeas son of Kendeas have set up this small pillar of *Concordia* so that we the flour-sifters and the dough-kneaders might prosper living together in harmony.
35. Van Nijf (1997, 15 and 236).
36. Van Nijf (1997, 15 n. 57).
37. Mitchell (1993, 64 and 106) and Lau (2010, 100).
38. (*katharourgoi*) *P.Cair.Masp.* II 67147; (*artokopoi*) *P.Prag.* I 25; (*artokollutoi*) *P.Hamb.* I 56.
39. Venticinque (2016, 209).
40. *P.Cair.Masp.* III 67288. Zuckerman (2004: 225) and Venticinque (2016, 220–222).
41. *P.Col.* VIII 230 (200–225 CE). Venticinque (2016, 148–149).
42. Broekaert (2011, 222–4).
43. Gibbs (2011, 299–300).
44. *Dig.* 47.22.4 (Ulpian).
45. Forsythe (2005, 97).
46. *CIL* VI 6219.

47. *CIL* VI 6337, VI 6338.
48. *CIL* X 6494. C(aius) Ruelius C(ai) f(ilius) Tro(mentina) Bassus, M(arcus) V, M(arcus) Papius M(arci) l(ibertus) Epaphra, L(ucius) Tuc, A(ulus) Pomponius A(uli) l(ibertus) Hilarus, Q(uintus) Pacc, C(aius) Caecilius C(ai) l(ibertus) Iucundus, M(arcus) Plot, M(arcus) Arrius ((mulieris)) l(ibertus) Auctus, C(aius) Vocc, L(ucius) Appuleius ((mulieris)) l(ibertus) Ambactus, [L(ucius)] App, C(aius) Terentius ((mulieris)) l(ibertus) Art[e]midor, Cn(aeus) Tanonius Cn(aei) l(ibertus) Plut, M(arcus) Marcius M(arci) l(ibertus) Felix D(ecimus) Antistius D(ecimi) l(ibertus) Philar[g]u, pisto[res].
49. The origins of corpora and *collegia* in Rome has been hotly debated since the nineteenth century. The core problem is a lack of direct evidence for a *collegium or corpus pistorum* before the second half of the first century CE and the first half of the second. The same pattern is evident in the *corpus naviculararum* (the association of shippers), tentative evidence exists for associations of bakers in the first century CE, but extensive evidence emerges for a legal status and a corporate capacity of the association in the second century CE. The *raison d'être* of Roman craft and trade associations has traditionally been explored through comparison of the *collegium* with the medieval guild. Waltzing isolates a number of similarities, such as confraternity, religious devotion, and funerary trusts. But he also notes certain differences; Roman *collegia*, according to Waltzing, pursued none of the self-regulation and collective economic interests that characterized medieval guilds (Waltzing 1895–1900 v. 1, 161–333). Finley concurs with a largely social function of Roman *collegia*, but disagrees with any continuity or much similarity between the ancient and medieval institutions (Finley 1999, 81). On the issue of *collegia*, he writes: The communal activity was restricted to religious, social and benevolent affairs; in no sense were they gilds trying to foster or protect the economic interests of their members, nor did they reveal a trace of the hierarchical pattern of apprentice, journeyman and master that characterized the medieval and early modern guilds. Slaves and free men (chiefly free independent craftsmen) could be fellow-members of a society, precisely because of the absence of any feeling of competition. Ramsay MacMullen, on the other hand, sees the origins of trade associations in the conviviality of local commerce, "a great deal suggests that a friendly, gossipy atmosphere prevailed among people who saw each other every day, worked at the same job in the same neighborhood, and share all the same ups and downs. Trade associations were the result." (MacMullen 1974, 72–77) With regard to the nature of such associations, MacMullen acknowledges the inaccuracy of modern trade unions as an analogy for Roman *collegia*, but he further argues that, "crafts associations

do indeed act as a larger, more influential whole to protect [craftsmen's] economic interests." Yet MacMullen expresses shock not at the ability of craft associations to push an economic agenda, but at how infrequently they pursued one.

50. *CIL* VI 8998.
51. *AE* 1923, 76.
52. *CIL* VI 8999 and Bond (2016, 156).
53. Aurelius Victor *de Caes.* 13.5
54. Sirks (1991, 406).
55. Gaius, *Institutiones*, 1.34. Trans. Poste (1904).
56. *FV* 233. Sirks (1991, 315) translates *centenarium* as 'worth 100 *sestertii*.' Herz (1988, 113), on the other hand, identifies it within amounts of grain, probably counted in the number of *modii*, the measure of grain. Given the stipulation recorded by Gaius, it seems more likely that *centenarium* refers to *modii*, not *sestertii*. D'Escurac (1976, 334).
57. *Dig.* 3.4.1–3.4.1.3 (Gaius). Trans. Watson 1985 v.1, 96–97.
58. Verboven (2002, 278, 284–286).
59. Sirks (1991, 166).
60. *CIL* XIV 4359. [I]MP CAE[SARI] DIVI HAD[RIANI] [FILIO] DIVI TRA[IANI] [PARTHI]CI NEPOT[I DIVI] [NER]VAE PRONE[POTI] [T AELI]O HADRI[ANO] [AN]TONINO AU[G PIO] [P P P] M TR P III C[OS III] [C]ORP PIST.
61. *Dig.* 3.4.1–3.4.1.3 (Gaius).
62. Waltzing (1895–1900).
63. Cracco Ruggini (1971).
64. Broekaert (2008, 697).
65. *CIL* VI 22.
66. *CIL* XIV, 101.
67. *CIL* VI 22. Annonae sanctae. Elius Vitalio, mensor perpetuus, dignissimo corpori pistorum siliginiariorum d(onum) d(edit).
68. *CIL* VI 1002.
69. *AE* (1996, 309). Corpus/pistorum/locus adsignatus a Papirio Dionysio tunc praef(ecto) ann(onae)/decurionumque [permis]su. d'Escurac (1976, 352–353) and Bakker (1994, 138 n. 25).
70. Tran 2006, 73.
71. *CIL* VI 1002.
72. Liu (2016, 224).
73. Verboven (2002), Monson (2006, 221–238), Bang (2006, 2008), Gabrielsen (2007), Kessler and Temin (2007), Venticinque (2010, 2013) and Broekaert (2011, 2012).
74. Hawkins (2016, 5).
75. *CIL* XIV 4234.

76. *HA Aurelianus*.35.1.
77. *CTh* 13.5.2.
78. *CTh.* 14.3.11.
79. Sirks (1991, 326–27). *CTh.* 14.3.3.
80. *CIL* VIII 8480. Fentress (1990, 125).
81. *CIL* XI 317. A similar situation may be attested in a contemporaneous and fragmentary inscription from Pula in Croatia. *CIL* V 307.
82. Kaszab-Olschewski (2019, 205).
83. Hawkins (2016, 103).
84. *CIL* XIII 8255.
85. *negotiator pistoricius CIL* XlII 8338; Rothenhofer (2005, 182), Verboven (2007, 99) and Kaszab-Olschewski (2019, 205).
86. Tacitus *Annals* 14. 17. Trans. Jackson (1937).
87. Mouritsen (1988, 60–64).
88. *CIL* IV 7273. CN(aeum) HELVIVM SABINVM AED(ilem)/PIST(ores) ROG(ant) ET CUPIVNT CVM VICINIS. The bakers, with their neighbors, ask and wish that you make Gnaeus Helvius Sabinus an aedile.
89. *CIL* IV 886. C(aium) IVLIVM POLYBIVM IIVIR(um) O(ro) V(os) F(aciatis)/PISTORES ROGANT. I ask that you make Gaius Iulius Polybius Duumvir; the bakers ask it.
90. *CIL* IV 875. C(aium) IVLIVM POLYBIVM IIVIR(UM)/STVDIOSVS ET PISTOR. I, hard working and a baker, ask that you make Gaius Iulius Polybius Duumvir. The O.V.F is taken as implied or no longer extant.
91. Liu (2008, 57–8) and *AHB* 22.1–4 (2008) 53–69.
92. Mouritsen (1988, 59).
93. Mouritsen (1988, 63).
94. Mouritsen (1988, 64).
95. Mouritsen (1988, 66–67).
96. *CIL* X 813. Flohr 334.
97. *CIL* IV 429. C(aium) IVLIVM POLYBIVM AED(ilem) O(ro) V(os) F(aciatis) PANEM BONVM FERT. I ask that you make Gaius Iulius Polybuis Aedile; he brings good bread.
98. Cooley and Cooley (2004, 114).
99. The painting is from VII.3.30. Fiorelli initially interprets the scene as the municipal distribution of bread. Helbig, on the other hand, identifies the man distributing the bread as a baker selling his products, an idea that proliferated during most of the twentieth century. In the past 20 years, that position has been challenged. The rejection of the individual as a baker is largely based on the work of Frolich, who argues that the modest, but proud house and the vendor's toga suggest a magistrate rather than a craftsman. Fiorelli (1875, 208), Helbig (1868, 366–367) and Frölich (1991, 236–41).

100. Wolfgang Helbig (1868, 154 n. 777) said the fresco was found in the Pantheon, which is what the early excavators of Pompeii called the city's *macellum*, because of its shape. Mau first re-identified the structure as the *macellum*.
101. Blümner (1912, 46).
102. Ordóñez and Chamizo (2009, 199–200). *HEp* 18, 389. Q L OPTATVS ET Q C OPTATVS IIVIR̩ EX MVLTIS̩ PISTORVM POSVERVNT. Multis = mulctis. The duumvirs Q. L. Optatus and Q. C. Optatus build this from the fines of the *pistores*.
103. Ordóñez and Chamizo (2009, 201–2).

References

Agulla, S. Ordóñez, and J.C. Saquete Chamizo. 2009. Una Dedicacion Votiva *ex mvltis pistorvm* hallada en la Betica. *Habis* 40: 197–204.

Bakker, Jan Theo. 1994. *Living and Working with the Gods: Studies of Evidence for Private Religion and Its Material Environment in the City of Ostia: 100–500 AD*. Amsterdam: J.C. Gieben.

———. 1999. *The Mills-Bakeries of Ostia: Description and Interpretation*. Amsterdam: J.C. Gieben.

Bang, P.F. 2006. Imperial Bazaar: Towards a Comparative Understanding of Markets in the Roman Empire. In *Ancient Economies, Modern Methodologies: Archaeology, Comparative History, Models and Institutions*, ed. P.F. Bang, M. Ikeguchi, and H.G. Ziche, 51–88. Bari: Edipuglia.

Blümner, Hugo. 1912. *Technologie und Terminologie der Gewerbe und Künste bei Griechen und Römern*. Leipzig: B.G. Teubner.

Bond, Sarah. 2016. *Trade and Taboo Disreputable Professions in the Roman Mediterranean*. Ann Arbor: University of Michigan Press.

Broekaert, W. 2008. Creatio Ex Nihilo? The Origin of the "Corpora Nauiculariorum" Reconsidered. *Latomus* 67 (3): 692–706.

———. 2011. Partners in Business: Roman Merchants and the Potential Advantages of Being a *collegiatus*. *Ancient Society* 41: 221–256.

———. 2012. Joining Forces: Commercial Partnerships or Societates in the Early Roman Empire. *Historia* 61: 221–253.

Buckler, W.H. 1923. Labour Disputes in the Province of Asia Minor. In *Anatolian Studies Presented to Sir William Ramsay*, ed. W.H. Buckler and W.M. Calder, 27–50. Manchester: The University of Manchester Press.

Camia, Francesco. 2017. The Financing of Public Honours in Greece During the Roman Imperial Period: The Case of Honorary Statues in the Cities of the Greek Mainland. In *The Politics of Honour in the Greek Cities of the Roman Empire*, ed. Anna Heller and Onno Martien van Nijf, 109–148. Boston: Brill.

Cooley, Alison, and M.G.L. Cooley. 2004. *Pompeii: A Sourcebook*. London: Routledge.
Cracco, L. Ruggini. 1971. Le associazioni professionali nel mondo romano-bizantino. In *Artigianato e tecnica nella societa dell'alto medioevo occidentale. XVIII Settimana di studi sull'Alto Medioevo*, 59–193. Spoleto: Presso la sede del Centro.
d'Escurac, H. 1976. *La préfecture de l'annone. Service administrative imperial d'Auguste à Constantin*. Paris and Rome: Ecole française de Rome.
Fentress, Elizabeth W.B. 1990. The Economy of an Inland City: Sétif. *Publications de l'École française de Rome: L'Afrique dans l'Occident romain (Ier siècle av. J.-C. -IVe siècle ap. J.-C.) Actes du colloque de Rome (3–5 décembre 1987)* 134: 117–128.
Finley, M.I. 1999. *The Ancient Economy*. 2nd ed. Berkeley: University of California Press.
Fiorelli, Giuseppe. 1875. *Descrizione di Pompei*. Napoli: Tipografia Italiana.
Forsythe, Gary. 2005. *A Critical History of Early Rome: From Prehistory to the First Punic War*. Berkeley: California University Press.
Frölich, T. 1991. *Lararian- und Fassadenbilder in den Vesuvstädten. Untersuchen zur "Volkstümlichen" Pompejanischen Malerei*. Mainz: Zabern.
Gabrielsen, V. 2007. Brotherhoods of Faith and Provident Planning: The Non-public Associations of the Greek World. *Mediterranean Historical Review* 22: 183–210.
Gibbs, M. 2011. Trade Associations in Roman Egypt. Their "Raison d'tre". *Ancient Society* 41: 291–315.
Hawkins, Cameron. 2016. *Roman Artisans and the Urban Economy*. Cambridge: Cambridge University Press.
Helbig, W., and O.P. Donner von Richter. 1868. *Wandgemälde der vom Vesuv verschütteten Städte Campaniens*. Leipzig: Breitkopf und Härtel.
Herz, P. 1988. *Studien zur römischen Wirtschaftsgesetzgebung: Die Lebensmittelversorgung*. Wiesbaden: Steiner-Verlag.
Jackson, J. 1937. *Tacitus: The Annals 5 5*. Cambridge, MA: Harvard University Press.
Johnson, Allan Chester, Paul Robinson Coleman-Norton, and Frank Card Bourne. 2012. *Ancient Roman Statutes: A Translation with Introduction, Commentary, Glossary, and Index*. Austin: University of Texas Press.
Kaszab-Olschewski, T. 2019. Central and Northern Europe. In *The Routledge Handbook of Diet and Nutrition in the Roman World*, ed. Paul Erdkamp and Claire Holleran, 189–207. London: Routledge, Taylor & Francis Group.
Kessler, D., and P. Temin. 2007. The Organization of the Grain Trade in the early Roman empire. *The Economic History Review* 60: 313–332.
Lau, Te-Li. 2010. *The politics of peace: Ephesians, Dio Chrysostom, and the Confucian four books*. Leiden: Brill.
Lewis, N. 1983. *Life in Egypt Under Roman Rule*. Oxford: Oxford University Press.

Liu, J. 2008. Pompeii and *Collegia*: A New Appraisal of the Evidence. *The Ancient History Bulletin* 22 (1–2): 53–69.

———. 2016. Group Membership, Trust Networks, and Social Capital: A Critical Analysis. In *Work, Labour, Professions in the Roman World*, ed. K. Verboven and C. Laes, 203–226. Boston: Brill.

MacMullen, Ramsay. 1974. *Roman Social Relations, 50 B.C. to A.D. 284*. New Haven: Yale University Press.

Mitchell, Margaret Mary. 1993. *Paul and the Rhetoric of Reconciliation: An Exegetical Investigation of the Language and Composition of 1 Corinthians*. Louisville: Westminster John Knox Press.

Monson, A. 2006. The Ethics and Economics of Ptolemaic Religious Associations. *Ancient Society* 36: 221–238.

Mouritsen, H. 1988. *Elections, Magistrates, and Municipal Elite: Studies in Pompeian Epigraphy*. Rome: L'Erma di Bretschneider.

Norman, A.F. 1992. *Libanius: Autobiography and Selected Letters, Volume I: Autobiography, Letters 1–50*. Cambridge, MA: Harvard University Press.

Poste, E.A. Whittuck, A.H.J. Greenidge, and Francis De Zulueta. 1904. *Gai Institutiones, or, Institutes of Roman Law*. Oxford: Clarendon Press.

Rea, J.R. 1972. *The Oxyrhynchus Papyri* XL. London: London Egypt Exploration Society.

Rothenhofer, P. 2005. Die Wirtscluifisstrukturen im sudlichen Niedergermanien. Untersuchungen zur Entwicklung eines Wirtschaflsraumes an der Peripherie des Imperium Romanum. In *Kölner Studien zur Archaologie der Römischen Provinzen 7*, ed. Thomas Fischer and Eckhard Deschler-Erb, 324–353. Rahden/Westf: Verlag Marie Leidorf.

Sharp, M. 2007. The Food Supply. In *Oxyrhynchus: A City and Its Texts*, ed. A.K. Bowman, R.A. Coles, N. Gonis, D. Obbink, and P.J. Parsons, 218–230. London: Egypt Exploration Society.

Sirks, A.J.B. 1991. *Food for Rome: The Legal Structure of the Transportation and Processing of Supplies for the Imperial Distributions in Rome and Constantinople*. Amsterdam: J.C. Gieben.

van Nijf, O. 1997. *The Civic World of Professional Associations in the Roman East*. Amsterdam: J.C. Gieben.

van Pleket, H.W. 1984. Urban Elites and the Economy of the Greek Cities of the Roman Empire. *Münstersche Beiträge für Antiken Handelgeschichte* 3: 3–35.

Venticinque, P.F. 2010. Family affairs: Guild regulations and family relationships in Roman Egypt. *Greek, Roman, and Byzantine Studies* 50: 273–294.

———. 2013. Matters of Trust: Associations and Social Capital in Roman Egypt. *Center for Hellenic Studies Research Bulletin* 1: 2.

———. 2016. *Honor Among Thieves: Craftsmen, Merchants, and Associations in Roman and Late Roman Egypt*. Ann Arbor: University of Michigan Press.

Verboven, K. 2002. *The Economy of Friends: Economic Aspects of Amicitia and Patronage in the Late Republic.* Brussels: Editions Latomus.

———. 2007. Ce que negotiari et ses dérivés veulent dire. In *Vocabulaire et expression de l'économie dans le monde antique*, ed. J. Andreau and V. Chankowski, 89–118. Bordeaux: Ausonius.

Waltzing, J.-P. 1895–1900. *Étude historique sur les corporations professionnelles chez les Romains depuis les origines jusqu'à la chute de l'Empire d'Occident*, 4 vols. Louvain: Peeters.

Watson, A., T. Mommsen, and P. Krueger. 1985. *The Digest of Justinian. V. 1–4.* Philadelphia: University of Pennsylvania.

Zuckerman, C. 2004. *Du village à l'Empire: Autour du Registre fiscal d'Aphroditô (525/526).* Paris: Association des amis du centre d'histoire et civilisation de Byzance.

Zuiderhoek, A. 2011. The Oligarchs and Benefactors: Elite Demography and Euerget-ism in the Greek East of the Roman Empire. In *Political Culture in the Greek City after the Classical Age*, ed. O. van Nijf and R. Alston, 185–196. Louvain: Peeters.

CHAPTER 6

Crafting an Image

One body of evidence that has factored significantly in the study of Roman bakers and their place in society is the iconography from their tombs and honorific monuments. Images of commercial baking have traditionally been treated in one of two ways: as visual documents of workshop operations or as examples of 'freedman art.' More recently, the discussion has centered on pride, depictions of craft as expressions of pride that a craftsman held for the performance of his craft and the life that it afforded him. Others have pointed out that such expressions are limited in number and probably quite private. There are two broad problems with how we have handled this evidence. First, we have fixated on the iconography of baking—scenes of the production of bread—rather than on the iconography of bakers. Not all bakers made monuments that depicted scenes of baking. Second, we have failed to link the iconography with the reality of production in actual bakeries other than at a technological level. We have succeeded at identifying the processes of production,[1] but such iconography is not a visual record of bakery operations, it is a visual expression of values and aesthetics informed by the bakers, as patrons, and by the artists in their agency as creators. Such iconography is better understood as part of a broader system of interrelated social and economic phenomena and the lived experience of the bakers. And, in fact, one sees that the monuments of bakers differ from one region to the next, with complicated monuments and elaborate iconography more common in larger communities that were home to modes of production exceeding

J. T. Benton, *The Bread Makers*,
https://doi.org/10.1007/978-3-030-46604-6_6

that of workshop production. Simply referring to the depictions as expressions of pride is reductive; they are also windows into the values and ambitions of bakers. A close reading of the iconography of big-city bakers reveals that they were communicating the same traits, even if their monuments differed: trustworthiness, quality craftsmanship, and a distance from actual labor. Moreover, I argue that the millstone, as a motif, emerged as a symbol of the craft and provided a sense of collective identity.

This chapter sets out to accomplish three things. First, regional variation in funerary monuments of bakers is briefly assessed, showing that elaborate iconography was a habit of bakers in larger cities and that the bakers in smaller towns tended to focus on other facets of their life. Second, the iconography of baking is read within the context of Roman perception of bakers, how were bakers perceived and were bakers responding to such perceptions in their iconography. Finally, it is shown that the millstone emerged as a motif in the iconography and even served as a shorthand for membership in the craft, if not in an association specifically.

Framing Our Understanding of Craftsman Iconography

For the study of the monuments of craftspeople, the tomb of the baker, Eurysaces, in Rome looms large and elicits notions of a *nouveau riche* whose wealth was grounded in work and skilled craftsmanship.[2] Despite sustained scholarly interest in the tomb, a coherent understanding of the unique monument has proven elusive, in part because of its bizarre form, but mostly because it lacks any real parallel in the built environment of Rome or among the extant iconographic remains. For literary parallels, many early scholars linked the potential freedman Eurysaces to Petronius' fictional Trimalchio, as a wealthy freedman who earned his wealth outside the traditional aristocratic means.[3] Specific attention is paid to the passage in which Trimalchio and his fellow freedman describe their tombs and to the satirical or mocking message that Petronius clearly intended.[4] Henrik Mouritsen observes that "there is a tendency to pay too much attention to Trimalchio-style monuments, which in fact remain the exception, most freedmen building relatively modest tombs for themselves and their relatives."[5] He further suggests that most of the funerary epigraphy and iconography were never intended for public consumption, that their contexts were secluded funerary precincts and *columbaria*. In other words, craftsmen directly associated themselves with their craft privately and only rarely, not as a prideful boast but rather a modest declaration to one's family.

There can be little doubt that tombs such as that of Eurysaces did not represent the habits and means of the majority of craftsmen. But as the corpus of published funerary monuments continues to expand, there is a growing body of scholarship that has come to cast doubt on the idea that such monuments were ever so hidden from the public view, as Mouritsen suggests.[6] Miko Flohr concludes his seminal book with the conclusion that "the public craftsmanship of the fuller of Pompeii formed a solid basis for a sound dose of occupational pride."[7] Building on Flohr's conceptualization of the workshop, recent work has begun to try to reconcile the pride of craftsmen with the attitudes of Rome's elite toward them. Robert Knapp notes a general lack of animosity toward craftsmen among all levels of Roman society outside the upper echelons. He writes, "We must firmly lay aside any idea that work was not valued in the Roman world; the elite's devaluation of labor does not extend to the vast majority of Roman-Greek society."[8] Similarly, Nicolas Tran makes a compelling case that historians and scholars of the ancient world have focused too intensely on the animosity of elites toward craftsmen and work in general. Tran first establishes the near-universal use of *ars* as a term for, and conceptualization of, the skill that a craftsman or *artifex* acquired. Framing skill as a positive personal quality, argues Tran, provided elites with a way to appreciate craftsmanship and, by extension, craftsmen. In turn, appreciation of skill and quality work created opportunity for craftsmen to express pride in that portion of their life. With regard to the depiction of a slave auction on the funerary monument of a freedman auctioneer, John Bodel writes that, "the representation might belong to either of two well recognized categories of Roman funerary art: scenes of significant moments in the life of the deceased or depictions of the deceased's occupation."[9]

Lauren Hackworth Peterson would contend that these two separate traditions are in fact one and the same; she has shown convincingly that the funerary traditions of freedmen should be viewed within the context of emulation of elite practices.[10] Tran toys with a similar idea, noting that, "although they may be clearly individualized, both value systems should not be considered as hermetically sealed, but rather as being in constant interaction with each other… Furthermore, if professional pride was intense and widespread among Roman craftsmen and merchants, we need to identify which elements and aspects of their work gave rise to such a sentiment."[11] Not only must we assume that the separate ideologies were in constant interaction with one another, we cannot forget that there was a distinct power differential between the elites and the sub-elites (and their respective ideologies). The dialogue between the two ideological groups was not a conversation between peers, but between one group that wielded almost complete power over the other group.

The Monuments of Bakers

Mouritsen and Peterson's goals are to place the monuments of bakers in the context of Roman funerary and social life, particularly that of Roman freedmen. I am more directly concerned with how we should understand the tomb—and the man—within the context of his profession: Roman commercial baking. It is worth beginning with the presentation of the deceased Eurysaces and his wife, Atistia.

> Fuit Atistia uxor mihei,
> femina opituma veixsit,
> quoius corporis reliquiae
> quod superant sunt in
> hoc panario.[12]
>
> Atistia was my wife
> She lived the life of an excellent woman
> what's left of her body is in
> this breadbasket

The inscription bears no mention of Eurysaces, which probably means they did not die at the same time and he may have outlived her. In any event, much attention has been paid to the word *panarium* (breadbasket), which seems both appropriate to the monument and the profession of the man, but also uniquely out of place. As such, a number of scholars have suggested that *panarium* could refer to the shape of the tomb, but more recent work has noted the contemporaneous Roman fad of having funerary urns in the form of baskets.[13]

Eurysaces' own epigraphic presentation comes below the frieze in an inscription that wraps around the three extant sides of the tomb. It reads: *Est hoc monimentum Marci Vergilei Eurysacis, pistoris, redemptoris, apparet* (This is the Monument of Marcus Vergileus Eurysaces: baker, contractor, and public servant).[14] The spelling of the same words differ from one side to the next. Furthermore, *hoc* and *monimentum* are nominative in a predicative relationship with *est*; the verb is not *apparet*, which should probably be read as *apparetor* (public servant). His interests may well have been more diverse than just baking, hence the three different titles. In addition to the sheer size of the tomb and its prestigious location, Eurysaces' self-presentation as a contractor and as a servant of the state strongly suggests that we should view him within the context of a factory-like mode of production rather than workshop one. This is corroborated by the frieze that wraps around the tomb (Fig. 1.1), which shows large teams of workers laboring in specialized tasks to produce massive quantities of bread that are weighed before being shipped out of the scene. This is not a workshop scene; it is industrial-scale bread production. The Trimalchionic lens led us to view Eurysaces and his tomb as eccentricities grounded in the character of the man, but Eurysaces was not craftsman, even if he was an eccentric. Although we often treat the tomb as utterly unique in the built environment of Roman, we have social context for men such as Eurysaces in the likes of Iazemis, Marcus Caerellius Zmaragdo, and Lucius Salvius Epictetus. He was a businessman in a large urban center, operating within an industrial mode of production. In fact, we have hints that other such monuments existed, such as the relief sculpture published by Andrew Wilson and Katia Schorle (Fig. 1.5),[15] the Vigna delle Tre Madonne relief, and a number of sarcophagi and funerary monuments of significant size and opulence.[16]

Depictions of Eurysaces throughout the monument visually reinforce his status as a type of businessman or skilled master rather than a simple craftsman who toils in his shop. In the portrait statue of the man and his wife, Eurysaces is shown togate in a veristic manner, which gives him more the air of a senator than a craftsman. Togate individuals, offset by scantily clad figures, are also present in the frieze and they are sometimes interpreted as Eurysaces: he is part of the production, but not performing labor. He instructs the laborers, he tests the flour for fineness, and he ensures the quality of his product. He is also proud of his technological prowess, which helps to distance him from manual labor. Not only are large millstones, ovens, and mixers evident on the frieze, Peterson has also convincingly demonstrated that the cylinders and roundels, which give the tomb its unique appearance, are actually mixers on their side, an interpretation reinforced by the little squares evident inside the cylinders.[17] Such objects were still a relatively new technology during Eurysaces' time; he may well be highlighting his innovative ways, but within the context of his making of the bread that fed the city, as though he were highlighting the efficiency with which he performed a duty, obligation, or service to the state.[18]

Redemptor and *apparetor* certainly imply that Eurysaces dealt professionally with the state.[19] The scales depicted prominently in the frieze on his tomb are probably some sort of mass measuring device that allowed for the state or customers buying in bulk to ensure they had their full amount. That engagement was almost certainly part of state efforts to ensure the provisioning of Rome which would only intensify in subsequent centuries. Nicholas Purcell argues that, "the Romans themselves perceived the function of the apparitorial posts as providing access to society for those who had been excluded from it: whether they did so or not, the posts did have that function. The complicated history of the apparitorial position in the *res publica* allowed it to provide an excellent *entrée* into the world of patronage which characterized public life."[20] There may have been a *collegium pistorum* to facilitate that *entrée* and those burgeoning relationships, but we have no clear evidence that such an association existed at the end of the first century BCE and none is mentioned on Eurysaces' tomb.

If there were an association of bakers in the later first century BCE or the early first century CE, it would already have had a diverse membership. We have no bakeries of any size in Rome or Ostia from the first century CE, but the bakeries in Ostia do suggest that bakeries operating in different modes of production could exist in a single city. And, in fact, three bakers of much lower means and social status can also be found in the *Monumentum familiae Statiliorum* only 200 m southwest of Eurysaces' tomb at the intersection of via Statilia and via di San Croce in Gerusalemme.[21] Perhaps a generation or two after Eurysaces, dating to the first half of the first century CE, the three *pistores* were buried in the *columbarium* of the slaves and freedmen of the Statilii, a senatorial family in Republican Rome.[22] One of the bakers dedicated a niche in the columbarium to a woman identified as Prima Sura, whose name makes one think she was a slave, but the quality of the dedication suggests their relationship was particularly close.[23] The baker, Alexandros, is identified as a *libertus* in his inscription. The two other bakers, Titus Statilius Anoptes[24] and Titus Statilius Eros,[25] have names following the format of freedmen taking the names of their masters upon manumission, suggesting they were *liberti* as well or at least had servile origins.

These three bakers were almost certainly trained as slaves within an elite household or by a free baker to whom they were apprenticed as slaves. If they were the descendants of a *libertus*, they may well have been taught by a parent or relative without the formality or contractual obligations of apprenticeship. Although their bakeries remain unidentified and their tombs suggest nothing of the nature of their production, the contrast in scale with the tomb of Eurysaces demonstrates the limited nature of their means and scope of their enterprises. They were not businessmen, but craftsmen. Even after their manumission, they probably operated smaller workshops, more akin to those at Pompeii than the Caseggiato dei Molini at Ostia. None of this is to say that they were not integrated into society or had no aspirations, Anoptes is identified as *pistor de conlegio*, which may imply the existence of a *collegium pistorum*, but it is equally likely that it was a more general *collegium* not based in craft. In either case, Anoptes was a man who had friends and engaged with others who had the social capital to help him in his career. He was probably not the *quinquennalis* of his *conlegium*, since such positions were reserved for men of Eurysaces' ilk and the limits of Anoptes' aspirations were far more limited than those of his wealthier counterpart. But that does not mean there was no room for successes and standards of living to rise and fall. The variety of bakers' tombs and funerary monuments in Rome attest to that.

Such variation exists in other places; at Narbonne, for example, three funerary monuments to bakers demonstrate similar patterning, albeit to a lesser degree. A baker named Tertinius Secundus Nervius had a monument made for himself, his dead wife, and one of his freedwomen.[26] In the inscription he identifies himself as a *pistor*, but also a *negotiator*, which recalls the variety of roles claimed by Eurysaces. Similarly, Lucius Decumius Felix set up a small funerary monument for himself and for his patron, Lucius Decumius Hilarus, both freedmen of the same man. The side of the altar reads ET AD SEPTE(M) ARAS (Even at the Seven Altars) which makes one think the monument might be communicating something about his profession and even the location of his workshop.[27] In a remarkable confluence of epigraphy and iconography, a baker at Narbonne named Marcus Careieus Asisa had a monument for himself, his wife, and his child (Fig. 6.1). It reads:

> M CAREIEVS M L ASISA PIS VIVOS SIBI FECIT ET CAREIE NIGELLAE ET CAREIEAE M F TERTIAE []NOR VI MATER CVM GNATA []ACEO MISERABILE FATO QVA[] PVRA ET VNA DIES DETVLT A[] CINERE.[28]
>
> Marcus Careieus Asisa, Baker, freedman of Marcus, had [this tomb] built during his lifetime for himself and for Careiea Nigella and Careiea Tertia,

Fig. 6.1 Funerary Monument of M. Careieus Asisa from Narbonne, Inv. 6903. (Modified from Espérandieu 1925, 190–1)

> daughter of Marcus, six years old. I, the mother, rest with my daughter on account of an unfortunate accident. One fine day dragged them to ashes.

The monument is elegantly carved with a millstone turned by a donkey, a kindly dog looking on, and a small altar evoking the one on which the inscription is carved. Henrik Mouritsen observes that "there is a tendency to pay too much attention to Trimalchio-style monuments, which in fact remain the exception, most freedmen building relatively modest tombs for themselves and their relatives."[29] Tombs such as that of Secundus Nervius—and Eurysaces—foster the impression that bakers were entrepreneurs with investments and ambitions of social mobility. These men were the exception, not the rule. Even the bakers at Rome whose remains were interred in the Colombarium of the Statilii were unique in that they had access to the pan-Mediterranean elite who made Rome their empire's capital. The monuments of Lucius Decumius Felix and Marcus Careieus Asisa point to the more pragmatic interests and ambitions of typical bakers. They wanted successes and to honor the people with whom they had bonds. These could be local elites, but Felix's patron was a freedman, not an emperor or a senator. They also wanted better lives and to remember the ones they loved, honoring and mourning their family.

Narbonne was a major administrative center with a large population and a vibrant economy. The opportunities that existed there may have paled in comparison to those of Rome and Ostia, but the city was capable of supporting economic and political complexity that extended beyond that of most towns and villages. In the smaller towns we see much more modest monuments. For example, the freedmen and freedwomen of M. Acilius Eros, a *pistor*, built a small funerary monument for him in the second half of the first century CE at Dianium.[30] The monument shows many of the same concerns as the other bakers with small monuments, a concern for social relationships and for being remembered. Unlike the monument of Careieus Asisa, that of Acilius Eros does not show a scene pertinent to the profession of the deceased. Instead, the motif of the faceless head and the door represent pre-Roman traditions that persisted despite the Latin of the text and the title *pistor* rather than some Iberian or Punic word.[31] Such a monument is probably a good microcosm for Acilius Eros' career as a baker: living in the Roman Empire had led to a degree of homogenization in the production of bread with masonry ovens and hourglass millstones, but local traditions probably continued to inform what bread was made, how it was made, and how and by whom it was eaten. I think we have to imagine that we have only a fraction of the funerary monuments that once existed for Roman bakers. There were surely also many bakers whose tombs, for one reason or another, did not mention their craft. Moreover, many bakers may not have shared the particular religious beliefs of Greco-Roman society that led to funerary monuments and epigraphy. One could imagine Romanized Berbers, for instance, not commemorating themselves in death the same way a Latin might outside of Rome. Finally, many craftspeople—bakers included—probably had no monument at all. It is telling that at Pompeii we have reference to bakers in political programmata and we have actual bakeries but we have not one funerary monument of a *pistor* from the city. The same can be said for Volubilis, Banasa, and Augusta Emerita, among other cities. Most Roman bakers were probably not epigraphically active. That invisibility is assuredly produced by the modest means of most workshop-level producers.

Crafting an Image

The monuments that do have iconography depicting commercial baking are, almost entirely, from central Italy. There are also indications of professional iconography outside of Italy, but only in central and southern Gaul where we saw there were also large cities and indications of complicated economic strategies and large-scale production. In the smaller towns, the profession is addressed only rarely and usually in the title of the deceased on funerary monuments. When iconography is present on the monuments of bakers in such places it seems focused more on local religious customs than on exalting their craft. But the iconography that does exist is worth discussing because it offers an interesting window into the lives of Roman bakers of the large cities such as Rome or Ostia—not just as visual documents of bakery operations, but as expressions of self, filtered through the lens of the artist's own agency and the ability of the bakers as patron of the work to commission it. We have seen that bakers in large cities—and really those of the smaller towns as well—were savvy actors. They not only enacted complicated economic strategies, they also navigated a world in which they were neither poor and destitute, nor a member of the local, regional, or international elite. Their imagery had to carve out social and actual space for themselves. Petersen, paraphrasing Henner von Hesberg, writes, "the primary aim in funerary art in the mid-first century BCE was to separate or distinguish oneself and one's funerary monument from the crowd."[32] This may have been the only concern for elites such as Caecilia Matella or Gaius Cestius, but sub-elites such as bakers not only had to distinguish themselves from those below them, but also to be careful not to tread on territory that would irk Roman elites. Tran's framework of *artificium* not only provided a way for elites to appreciate craftsmen. It also offered a medium for sub-elites to articulate their standing within society in a way that served to distinguish themselves from menial labor, but also in a way that elites could appreciate. It is worth exploring, therefore, how exactly elites perceived bakers and how bakers responded to the perceptions of elites, both good and bad.

Bakers and bakeries are a frequent subject of discussion in ancient literature as places of commerce and as suppliers of a good consumed by huge swaths of Roman society. They are characterized in a number of different ways, including positive treatment of bakers and appreciation of their skill or the quality of their product.[33] There are, however, a lot of more nuanced or complicated treatments of bakers; it is not really worthwhile to review all of that literature because that work has already been done succinctly by Nicolas Tran and Sarah Bond. But one can begin to categorize the treatment of bakers and bakeries in such literature, and the passages concerning them fall into four broad categories: the profession was one that was inappropriate for elite men,[34] bakers were of low socio-economic status,[35] bakeries were disgusting places,[36] and bakers were untrustworthy.[37]

Roman bakers clearly understood that their skill, or at least the quality of their product, was something that elites (and very likely everyone else) valued about them. Quality of bread clearly mattered. Pliny, with regard to the quality of bread, clearly viewed flour as the critical component determining the outcome of the product, rather than the baking, mixing, or other aspects of bread production. But one type of flour stood out among all others: that which was produced from winter wheat (*siligo* or *similago*).[38] Columella and Celsus also regarded bread made from *siligo* as particularly good.[39] One baker named Olgulnius describes himself in a funerary epitaph as a *pistor similaginarius*, a claim that he was a baker who worked with only the best grain.[40] Columella's esteem for bread is particularly founded on its appearance. One of the other hallmarks of highly desired bread, and one of the traits of *siligo*, was its whiteness. Juvenal describes bread made from *siligo* as soft and snow-white (*tener et niveus*). Although Pliny says that whiteness was sometimes achieved by adding chalk,[41] bread is usually made white through selectivity in what parts of the grain are ground and how finely one grinds the flour. Millstones may be the agent of grinding, but sieves are the tool used to ensure that imperfections are not included, that the wrong parts of the grain are removed, and that the flour is a consistent grade. The sieve, when used as a symbol in the iconography of bakers, serves as the visual equivalent of Olgunius' epigraphic claim. It is a statement of quality product. On the tomb of Eurysaces, two men (both clothed in short tunics) sift flour on either side of a low table (Fig. 1.4). A now-lost fragment from the Bologna

Fig. 6.2 Funerary Urn Holder of P. Nonius Zethus Rome (Musei Vaticani, Museo Chiaramonti, Inv. No. 1343)

plaque shows a similar figure dumping the excess material left in the sieve. On the funerary monument of P. Nonius Zethus are various accoutrements of commercial milling: *modii*, baskets, and a sieve (Fig. 6.2).[42] Similarly, a funerary plaque from Isola Sacra near Ostia shows the sale of bread (Fig. 5.2).[43] Above the vendor two sieves hang, presumably on a wall. The sieve, a seemingly minor component of the *pistrinum*, is elevated to a prominent place in the iconography of *pistores* because it symbolized the quality of the bread and, by extension, the skill of the baker. Driving home this message, a togate man often identified as Eurysaces stands near the sifters on his tomb's frieze, testing the flour in his hands (Fig. 1.1).

Depictions of baking on tombs of bakers in big cities was not simply announcing the quality of their product; the bakers also visually established their trustworthiness, possibly in response to negative perceptions of them. The scales on Eurysaces' tomb are the most obvious example of this. In his role as *redemptor* and *apparetor*, he may well have needed to account for the amount of grain that entered his bakery or bakeries and the amount of bread that left. Mints, which also had close relationships with the state, had similar practices. Mintmarks served as controls to ensure a coin's metallic content, value, and authenticity. They also served to limit fraud and theft within the mint.[44] In fact, the entire frieze on Eurysaces' tomb hinges on two moments in the baking process: the accounting of grain as it enters the production scene and the weighing of bread as it leaves (Fig. 1.1). As a contractor, Eurysaces may well have been under unique pressure to keep careful records about how much grain he received and how much he sold, but on his tomb such imagery is not a contract but a statement that he could be trusted to not swindle his employer.[45] There is some corroboration for this possibility; an inscription, *CIL* IX 2854, records the construction of some sort of weighing or measuring stations (*panarios*) at Vasto on the Adriatic. Wim Broekaert argues that the word serves as an adjective referring to a noun now lost and links *panarios* with the next phrase, which Mommsen read as *ex metr[etis et ponderib]us iniquis* (because the measures and weights had become invalid). If the inscription from Vasto indicates some sort of control on the bread production of state-contracted bakers, then one might imagine that trustworthiness would be something that bakers would need to address. That the scales are meant to demonstrate Eurysaces' trustworthiness seems probable in any event. Smiths, especially those working with precious metals, would mark their works with the actual weight of the metal content[46] and a funerary monument of a metal-worker specializing in gold, *aurifex brattiarius* (gold-leaf goldsmith), prominently displays scales, emphasizing his faithfulness to precision and accuracy.[47] If Broekaert is right about panarios being a reference to giant measures or scales of bread, Atistia's placement in a *panarium* might carry a double entendre: she is both interred in a breadbasket of some sort, but she was also weighed, measured, and found to be *opituma*.

Other indications reinforce this message of trustworthiness. Grain measures, or *modii*, alongside the sieves on the tomb of P. Nonius Zethus (Fig. 6.2) are not integral to the production of bread or even to the milling of flour, but they would be sights familiar to customers who would view them as assurances that one was getting exactly the amount purchased. Being shorted in a purchase was a constant concern in the ancient world and standardized measures served as a way to allay these fears. Officially sanctioned measures could be placed in fora, such as that of Pompeii (Fig. 6.3), at which anyone could certify they had been given the right amount.[48] The funerary monument of P. Nonius Zethus has eight concave cavities carved into the monument ostensibly intended to hold the cinerary

Fig. 6.3 Grain Measure in Pompeii's Forum. (Courtesy of Steven Ellis)

urns of himself, his wife, and potentially those clients, freedmen, or slaves.[49] Although cinerary-urn holders are known from the ancient world, a holder of multiple urns is unattested and the funerary monument bears a striking resemblance to standardized measuring tables from Pompeii's forum. Moreover, each concavity is numbered from L-LIII (Fig. 6.4), which seems as a reference to quantities. The visual is striking: the deceased, as the contents of the grain measure, lives up to what was advertised.

Mirroring the use of certain terminology such as *negotiator pistoricius*, *quinquennalis pistorum*, or *mercator frumentarius*, some of the so-called bakers were much more divorced from the actual labor than most of the craftsman bakers working on workshop bakeries. We saw in Chap. 3 that hierarchy was very clearly indicated in the relief sculpture depicting commercial baking, with lower socio-economic status individuals wearing little clothing and higher status men in togas. The togate men do not perform the actual labor, but are engaged in a number of other activities. These figures have been associated with Eurysaces, specifically the figures who calculate the reception of grain, test the fineness of the flour being sifted, or instruct the kneading group as they look to him for instruction

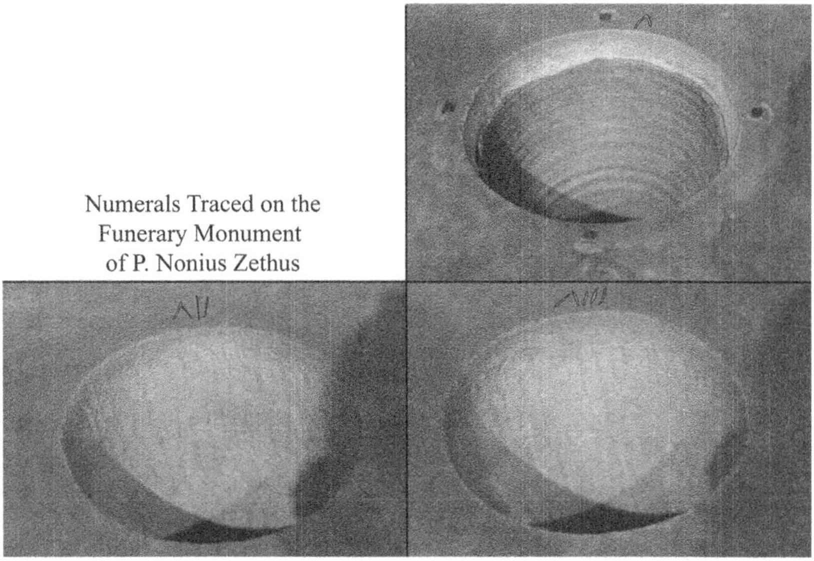

Fig. 6.4 Roman Numerals on the Urn Holder of P. Nonius Zethus (Musei Vaticani, Museo Chiaramonti Inv. No. 1343)

(Fig. 1.9). Groups of togate men cluster around the point where grain enters the scene and at the scales where bread is weighed as it leaves. But one togate man, as observed above, handles the flour as though testing its fineness and ensuring its quality. Another togate man, possibly also Eurysaces, instructs men kneading dough; they look to him and he displays his hands palms facing up as though explaining proper technique. These men are nicely dressed and are not participating in the production of bread, but they are involved in tasks unrelated to labor such as quality control and instruction. Similarly, on the sarcophagus of Annius Octavius Valerianus men in tunics conduct various tasks from reaping wheat to baking loaves in tunics; Valerianus himself stands togate in a central panel with his right hand raised, gesturing to the work around him and holding an object, possibly a scroll, in his left hand.[50] The scroll itself is interesting; Elizabeth Meyer's recent work on such scenes from Pompeii has suggested that they were symbols of *otium*, as opposed to *negotium*, and the women who often accompanied the men with scrolls hold pens adopting a guise of muse, rather than a statement of personal literacy.[51] Reinforcing this message of *otium*, and thus distancing Valerianus from the labor, the epitaph inscribed on the sarcophagus takes the form of a poem:

> D.M.S.L.ANNIVS.OCTAVIVS.VALARIANVS
> EVASI.EFFUGI.SPES.ET.FORTVNA.VALETE
> NIL.MIHI.VOVISCUM.EST.LVDIFICATE.ALIOS[52]
>
> To the spirits of the departed, Lucius Annius Octavius Valerianus.
> I escape. I flee. Goodbye Hope and Fortune.
> There will be no more prayers from me, so have your sport with others.[53]

The poem perhaps alludes to work through the fickleness of fortune and the bitterness of unfulfilled hope, but even if the sarcophagus seems basic against the backdrop of elite tombs and sarcophagi, both in terms of quality and style, it was surely an expense most bakers could not afford. The poem (itself a product of *otium*) further distances Valerianus from the labor taking place in the relief from which he remains visually aloof. A single figure also appears on a relief plaque from Bologna; although not togate, he wears a longer tunic and pants. The figure stands to the side of the oven, not directly engaged with the labor at all, and rather appears to be watching the labor taking place, in a fashion similar to that of Annius Octavius Valerianus.

Although these are idealized depictions of the hierarchy and operation of Roman bakeries,[54] such iconography reveals several important observations about the relationship between social status, labor, and self-presentation. First, workshop or bakery social complexity was very clearly depicted in nearly every scene; this complexity can, to a certain extent, be inferred from the clothing of the figures depicted: some are nude, others are in modest garments, and others are more elaborately dressed. Second, the iconographic hierarchy correlates with different procedures: forming loaves and mixing are performed by individuals of the lowest social status, overseeing the beasts turning the millstones and tending the oven are tasks associated with a second tier of individuals, and tasks such as instruction, management, and sale are all activities saved for to the most elaborately dressed individuals. Third, such a categorization of procedures follows a spectrum of direct engagement with work. The tasks associated with the most modestly dressed figures are those that require actual labor. The still humble but at least dressed figures monitor animals rather than work directly. The least demanding—and arguably highest skill—tasks related to areas of education, oversight, and financial transaction were reserved for the most elaborately clothed individuals. The best-dressed figures are the ones with whom the owners of tombs, those who are crafting an image of self-presentation, are associated. Labor was something with which they avoided direct engagement, perhaps as a way to mitigate the perception of them as being contaminated by work.

The Symbol of an Industry

The millstone is perhaps the most common motif derived from the technologies use in ancient bakeries. There are a large number of monuments and other objects that depict a millstone and no other aspects of commercial baking. Millstones were the most visible component of the bakery, almost always at the entrance to the bakery. I believe that, as a stand-alone motif, the millstone was a sort of visual synecdoche whereby the one process alluded to the entirety of the production.[55] The millstone motif may have arisen also from shop signs, such as one from Pompeii, now lost, which shows a geometric representation of a donkey and mill-stone (Fig. 6.5). But the use of the millstone as a symbol is also found in

Fig. 6.5 Street Sign from Pompeii with Donkey and Millstone. (Modified from Blümner 1912, Fig. 20)

Fig. 6.6 Signet Ring with Donkey and Millstone. (Modified from Blümner 1912, Fig. 21)

a number of other contexts, such a vanished fresco from the *macellum* at Pompeii, which Blümner identified as a "Mühlenfest" (mill festival) and associated with the celebration of the Vestalia.[56] A gemstone from a signet ring, found in Pompeii and also lost, shows a donkey tethered to a millstone (Fig. 6.6).[57] A remarkable graffito from the Palatine hill depicts a donkey with a millstone in the typical fashion (Fig. 6.7), albeit cartoonish, but accompanying the image is an inscription:

> LABORA ASELLE QVOMODO EGO LABORAVI
> ET PRODERIT TIBI.[58]

> Work, little ass, as I have worked
> and you shall profit.

Fig. 6.7 Graffito from the Palatine in Rome. (Modified from Graffiti del Palatino, 1. Paedagogium, a cura di H. Solin – M. Itkonen-Kaila, Roma 1966, p. 223, nr. 289)

The vast majority of the stand-alone millstone motifs are funerary in nature. A relief depicting a millstone was found at the Isola Sacra, part of Tomb 78, leads Eve D'Ambra to suggest that the patron of the columbarium, Tiberius Claudius Eutychus, may have been involved with baking and probably also the transportation of grain (Fig. 6.8).[59] The plaque lacks many details and vestiges of red paint in the upper right corner suggests the relief was painted. The monument of P. Pontius Iucundus from Verona, although heavily damaged, depicts a donkey being led to a millstone.[60] The monument of Marcus Careieus Asisa, discussed above, shows a donkey turning a millstone while a dog looks on with an altar in the background. The funerary urn holder of P. Nonius Zethus, in addition to depicting sieves and *modii*, also shows a single scene of a donkey and a millstone (Fig. 6.1).

This repeated imagery evokes the sense of a collective identity: the visual expression of belonging to a craft. It is hard to know, obviously because one cannot know, whether the signet ring were owned by a baker, someone who owned a bakery, or even someone who just liked millstones but had no relationship with the industry. But there is one example, discussed in the previous chapter, of an honorific monument erected by

Fig. 6.8 Terracotta plaque of a millstone from Tomb 78 at Isola Sacra. (Modified from Wilson and Schorle 2009, Fig. 13)

the *corpus pistorum* on which millstones are depicted and specifically associated with the names of individual bakers. The commemorative monument of the *quinquennales*, Marcus Caerellius Zmaragdo and Lucius Salvius Epictetus, not only indicates their names, but also flanks them with stand-alone millstones.[61] That an industry might generate symbols for itself, albeit relegated to only the most developed urban centers, strongly suggests a collective identity and common sense of belonging among those bakers working in such places. The discovery of such imagery in central Italy and parts of Gaul suggests that this collective identity was being forged between communities, not just within them. This does not seem to be as true of places without the infrastructural advantages and population sizes of places like Rome, Ostia, or Cologne. This is an important point tied to the notion of how people who are neither socially elite nor poor might begin carving out a niche for themselves, a topic addressed in the next chapter.

Notes

1. Wilson and Schorle (2009) and Monteix (2010, chapter 3 fig. 60–66).
2. Thorpe (1995, 30); See Petersen (2006, 1–16; 2011, 84–89).
3. See Mayer (2012, 111–113).
4. Petronius 71. See Whitehead (1993, 319), Bodel (1994, 243–248), Perkins (2005, 139–162) and Petersen (2006, 86–87).
5. Mouritsen (2011, 281).
6. George (2006), Tran (2017) and Lis and Soly (2016).
7. Flohr (2013, 348–349).
8. Knapp (2011, 11).
9. Bodel (2017, 85).
10. Petersen (2006, 100–110).
11. Tran (2017, 248).
12. CIL VI 1958 = CIL I 1206.
13. Peterson (2003, 250–251 and fig. 26).
14. CIL VI 1958 = CIL I 1203-1205.
15. Wilson and Schorle (2009).
16. Wilson and Schorle (2009, 112–119).
17. Toynbee (1971, 128) argued the cylinders might represent grain measures (modii) but the modius was not cylindrical and Peterson's hypothesis is corroborated by the squares and by the novelty of the technology in the first century BCE.
18. Wilson and Schorle (2009).
19. Rossetto (1973), Brandt (1993, 14–15), Curtis (2001, 358–60) and Petersen (2006, 87–88).
20. Purcell (1983, 171).
21. 194–195.
22. There are a number of funerary inscriptions from columbaria in Rome for slaves who are identified as *pistores* and, in one case, a slave *pistor* sets up a monument to others. *CIL* VI 4010, 4011, 4012, 4356; Hasegawa (2005, 45).
23. *CIL* VI 6338 *Prima Sura Alexandri l (iberti) pist(oris)*
24. *CIL* VI 6219 *T(itus) Statilius Anoptes, pistor de conleg(io).*
25. *CIL* VI 9808 T(itus) *Statilius Eros, pistor, Caninianus. Statilia Zotiche.*
26. *CIL* XIII 8338. [Terti]nius Secund(us)/[ci]ves Nervius/[n]egot(iator) pistor/[ic]i(us) vivos sibi et/[Pr]iminiae Sabinae/co(n)i{i}ugi obitae/et Tertiniae/[1]fuae libertae/[s]uae fecit

27. *CIL* XII 4503. V(ivit) L(ucius) Decumius/L(uci) l(ibertus) Felix Roman(us)/pistor sibi et/L(ucio) Decumio L(uci) l(iberto)/Hilaro patrono // Et ad/septe(m)/aras. "In his lifetime. Lucius Decumius Felix, freedman of Lucius. Roman. baker. For him and for the late Lucius Decumius Hilarus, freedman of Lucius, his patron. (On the right side, perhaps we can read the location of the bakery: near 7 altars.)"
28. *AE* 2005 1016.
29. Mouritsen 2011, 281.
30. CIL II 5975. M(arcus) Acilius/Eros h(ic) s(itus) e(st)/pistor lib(erti) libe/rtaeque fac(iendum) cura(verunt)/quisquis in has/partes quisquis percu/rris in illas/precor uti dicas s(it) t(ibi) t(erra) l(evis).

    Here lies Marcus Acilius Eros, Baker. His freedmen and freedwomen have seen to the making of this monument. To anyone who lives around here who goes by here, I ask you to say "may the earth rest light on you."
31. Curchin (2011, 184).
32. Petersen (2006, 99 n. 50).
33. Celsius *Med.* 2.18, 2.28. Cicero *de Fin.* 2.8.23; he echoes the sentiment again in *pro Roscio* 143. Suetonius *Iul.* 48.1.
34. Bond (2016, 145). Seneca *Epist. Mor.* 95.24. Gellius *Noct. Att.* 15.19.2. *HA Pesc. Nig.* 10. Suetonius *Vit.* 16.
35. Cicero *pro Roscio* 134. Suetonius *Aug.* 4.2. Afranius *Tog.* 161.
36. Aulus Gellius *Noct. Att.* 3.3; Martial 12.57. Julian of Ascalon (*Hex.* 14) observes, in practical terms, that bakeries had adverse effects on surrounding spaces with their noise and smoke.
37. Martial 8.16. Suetonius *Iul.* 48.1; Libanius *Or.* 1.206–10. See Wiemer (1996, 527–48) and Bond (2016, 157).
38. Pliny N.H. XVIII.20.85. e siligine lautissimus panis pistrinarumque opera laudatissima (the finest bread and the most esteemed products of the bakeries are made from *siligo*).
39. Columella 2.6.2; Celsus 2.18.4.
40. *CIL* VI 1958. Despite the consensus that SIMI should be read as *similaginarius*, this inscription is very fragmentary and it could possibly be reconstructed to say something else.
41. Pliny N.H. XVIII 29.113-14.
42. Curtis (2001, 362, pl. 28) and Wilson and Schorle (2009, fig. 18).
43. Ciancio Rossetto (1973, 47 fig. 34), Zimmer (1982, 113–14 no. 24) and Wilson and Schorle (2009, 112 fig. 13).
44. Meyboom (1995, 155–58) and Harl (1997, 20).
45. Petersen (2006, 186), Gardner (2011, 410–11), Erdkamp (2013, 275–76) and Joshel and Petersen (2014, 126–27).
46. The Getty conservation team performed an X-Ray scan on a silver cup and found the recording of the weight of the vessel's silver content, but the inscription was inside the cup and unseen to its owner.

47. CIL VI 6939; Burford (1974, pl. 41), Formigli (1985, 104–105) and Treister (2001, 294).
48. Jashemski and Meyer (2002, 10) and Beard (2010, 164).
49. Joshel (2010, 199–201).
50. *CIL* VI 11743; Rostovtzeff (1926, pl. 26), Moritz (1958, pl. 8), Hope (2007, 48) and Wilson and Schorle (2009, fig. 21).
51. Meyer (2009).
52. AE 1980, 767.
53. Trans. Hope (2007, 48).
54. Petersen and Joshel (2014, 126–28).
55. Phalloi, too, are seen on ovens, but they are almost always hidden in more interior parts of the bakeries and the near ubiquitous use of the phallus as an image of luck or power in the ancient world renders it impotent to serve as a symbol of an industry.
56. Wolfgang Helbig (1868, 154 n. 777) said the fresco was found in the Pantheon, which is what the early excavators of Pompeii called the city's *macellum*, because of its shape. Mau first re-identified the structure as a *macellum*. Blümner 1912, 46.
57. Blümner 1912, 45.
58. CLE 1798a.
59. D'Ambra (1988, 98–99).
60. Zimmer (1982: 115–16 no. 26) and Wilson and Schorle (2009, 112 fig. 14).
61. *CIL* VI 1002.

References

Beard, Mary. 2010. *The Fires of Vesuvius: Pompeii Lost and Found*. Cambridge: Belknap Press of Harvard University Press.

Blümner, Hugo. 1912. *Technologie und Terminologie der Gewerbe und Künste bei Griechen und Römern*. Leipzig: B.G. Teubner.

Bodel, John. 1994. Trimalchio's underworld. In *The Search for the Ancient Novel*, ed. James Tatum, 237–259. Baltimore: Johns Hopkins University Press.

———. 2017. Death and Social Death in Ancient Rome. In *On Human Bondage: After Slavery and Social Death*, ed. John Bodel and Walter Scheidel, 81–109. Chichester: Wiley Blackwell.

Bond, Sarah. 2016. *Trade and Taboo Disreputable Professions in the Roman Mediterranean*. Ann Arbor: University of Michigan Press.

Brandt, Olle. 1993. Recent Research on the Tomb of Eurysaces. *Opuscula Romana* 19 (2): 13–17.

Broekaert, Wim. 2008. Bread Baskets on the Marketplace? A Short Note on CIL IX 2854 (ILS 5591). *Zeitschrift für Papyrologie und Epigraphik* 167: 204–206. Accessed November 9, 2020. http://www.jstor.org/stable/20476578.

Burford, A. 1974. *Craftsmen in Greek and Roman Society.* Ithaca: Cornell University Press.

Curchin, Leonard A. 2011. *The Romanization of Central Spain: Complexity, diversity and change in a provincial hinterland.* London: Routledge.

Curtis, Robert I. 2001. *Ancient Food Technology.* Leiden: Brill.

D'Ambra, Eve. 1988. A Myth for a Smith: A Meleager Sarcophagus from a Tomb in Ostia. *American Journal of Archaeology* 92 (1): 85–99.

Erdkamp, P. 2013. The Food Supply of the Capital. In *The Cambridge Companion to Ancient Rome (Cambridge Companions to the Ancient World)*, ed. P. Erdkamp, 262–277. Cambridge: Cambridge University Press.

Espérandieu, Émile. 1925. *Recueil général des bas-reliefs de la Gaule romaine 9 3.* Paris: Nationale.

Flohr, Miko. 2013. *The World of the Fullo.* Oxford: Oxford University Press.

Formigli, Edilberto. 1985. *Tecniche dell'oreficeria Etrusca e Romana: originali e falsificazioni.* Firenze: Sansoni.

Gardner, J.F. 2011. Slavery and Roman Law. In *The Cambridge World History of Slavery*, ed. K. Bradley and P. Cartledge, 414–437. Cambridge: Cambridge University Press.

George, M. 2006. Social Identity and the Dignity of Work in Freedmen's Reliefs. In *The Art of Citizens, Soldiers and Freedmen in the Roman World (BAR International Series 1526)*, ed. E. D'Ambra and G.P.R. Métraux, 19–30. Oxford: Archaeopress.

Harl, Kenneth W. 1997. *Coinage in the Roman Economy, 300 B.C. to A.D. 700.* Baltimore: Johns Hopkins University Press.

Hasegawa, Kinuko. 2005. *The Familia Urbana During the Early Empire: A Study of Columbaria Inscriptions.* Oxford: Archaeopress.

Helbig, W., and O.P. Donner von Richter. 1868. *Wandgemälde der vom Vesuv verschütteten Städte Campaniens.* Leipzig: Breitkopf und Härtel.

Hope, Valerie M. 2007. *Death in Ancient Rome: A Source Book.* London: Routledge.

Jashemski, Wilhelmina Feemster, and Frederick G. Meyer. 2002. *The Natural History of Pompeii.* Cambridge: Cambridge University Press.

Joshel, S.R. 2010. *Slavery in the Roman World.* Cambridge: Cambridge Univ. Press.

Joshel, Sandra R., and Lauren Hackworth Petersen. 2014. *The Material Life of Roman Slaves.* Cambridge: Cambridge University Press.

Knapp, Robert C. 2011. *Invisible Romans.* Cambridge: Harvard University Press.

Lis, Catharina, and Hugo Soly. 2016. Work, Identity and Self-Representation in the Roman Empire and the West-European Middle Ages. In *Work, Labour, and Professions in the Roman World*, ed. K. Verboven and C. Laes, 262–290. Boston: Brill.

Mayer, E. 2012. *The Ancient Middle Classes: Urban Life and Aesthetics in the Roman Empire, 100 BCE-250 CE*. Cambridge, MA: Harvard University Press.
Meyboom, P.G.P. 1995. *The Nile Mosaic of Palestrina: Early Evidence of Egyptian Religion in Italy*. Leiden: Brill.
Meyer, Elizabeth A. 2009. Writing Paraphernalia, Tablets, and Muses in Campanian Wall Painting. *American Journal of Archaeology* 113 (4): 569–597.
Moritz, L.A. 1958. *Grain-Mills and Flour in Classical Antiquity*. Oxford: Clarendon Press.
Monteix, N. 2010. *Les lieux de métier: Boutiques et ateliers d'Herculanum*. New edition [online]. Naples: Publications du Centre Jean Bérard.
Mouritsen, H. 2011. *The Freedman in the Roman World*. Cambridge: Cambridge University Press
Perkins, J. 2005. Trimalchio: Naming Power. In *Metaphor and the Ancient Novel. Ancient Narrative: Supplementum 4*, ed. Stephen Harrison, Michael Pachalis, and Stavros A. Frangoulidis, 132–168. Eelde: Barkhuis.
Petersen, L.H. 2003. His Tomb, His Wife and Her Breadbasket: The Monument of Eurysaces in Rome. *Art Bulletin* 85 (2): 230–257.
———. 2006. *The Freedman in Roman Art and Art History*. New York: Cambridge University Press.
Purcell, N. 1983. The Apparitores: A Study in Social Mobility. *Papers of the British School at Rome* 51: 125–173.
Rossetto, P.C. 1973. *Il sepolcro del fornaio Marco Virgilio Eurisace a Porta Maggiore*. Rome: Istituto di studi romani.
Rostovtzeff, M.I., and J.D. Duff. 1926. *A History of the Ancient World*. Oxford: Clarendon Press.
Thorpe, M. 1995. *Roman Architecture*. London: Bristol Classical Press.
Toynbee, J.M.C. 1971. *Death and Burial in the Roman World*. Ithaca: Cornell University Press.
Tran, N. 2017. Ars and doctrina: The Socioeconomic Identity of Roman Skilled Workers (First Century BC-Third Century AD). In *Work, Labour, and Professions in the Roman World*, ed. K. Verboven and C. Laes, 133–146. Boston: Brill.
Treister, M.Y. 2001. *Hammering Techniques in Greek and Roman Jewellery and Toreutics*. Leiden: Brill.
Whitehead, J. 1993. The Cena Trimalchionis and Biographical Narration in Roman Middle-Class Art. In *Narrative and Event in Ancient Art*, ed. P. Holliday, 299–325. Cambridge: Cambridge University Press.
Wiemer, H.-U. 1996. Der Sophist Libanios und die B.cker von Antiocheia. *Athenaeum* 74: 527–548.
Wilson, A., and K. Schorle. 2009. A Baker's Funerary Relief from Rome. *Papers of the British School at Rome* 77: 101–123.
Zimmer, G. 1982. *Römische Berufsdarstellungen*. Berlin: Mann.

CHAPTER 7

Conclusion: The Question of the Roman Middle Class

In light of the observations made in this book about the regional nature of commercial baking and the various modes of production evident in different communities, it is worth deploying these lessons against the backdrop of Roman social life more broadly. One of the recent debates, in which Roman craftsmanship has played a critical role, is the question of the Roman middle class. Resistance to the application of class, as a categorization of human society, to antiquity has reemerged follow renewed efforts to identify a middle class in the cities and towns of the Roman Empire, most notably by Emanuel Mayer.[1] Motivated by the new debate, a number of studies have begun trying to frame this debate in a way that captures the nuance of sub-elite life in the Roman world.[2] Commercial bakers and craftspeople have much to reveal about this issue because it is precisely the sort of profession that might have sustained a sub-elite middle class or fueled social mobility.

Early efforts to address class and social mobility in the Roman world focused almost entirely on the upper *ordines*, particularly the equestrians and whether they could become patrician. Herbert Hill, for example, positioned the equestrians as a sort of urban bourgeoisie whose wealth resulted from professional activities and whose access to power was limited.[3] Hill was by no means an outlier and others interested in social mobility were consumed by evidence *novi homines*, men who became senators despite equestrian roots, such as Cicero. An early focus on social mobility and stratification among elites was perhaps a natural result of the

J. T. Benton, *The Bread Makers*,
https://doi.org/10.1007/978-3-030-46604-6_7

histories of Classics and Mediterranean Studies as disciplines. Literature, in which elites appear so clearly to us, formed the evidence base for the writing of nearly all Roman history. Moses Finley, however, shifted the debate by observing that both equestrians and the senatorial orders were wealthy beyond measure, positioning either as a middle class failed to recognize their immense power and wealth.[4] Moreover, Finley argued that detailing social mobility between the two groups was merely parsing different types of international elites. Real efforts to identify social mobility continued to focus on becoming elite, but now on becoming local elites (mostly at Pompeii) rather than international elites in Rome. Such studies found it was rare for there to be new decurions.[5] Thus, for forty plus years, the consensus was that Roman society consisted of an international elite in Rome and a local elite at places like Pompeii or Italica; everyone else was not only poor, but powerless. The means of subsiding for the masses, craftsmanship and services, were both entirely geared toward the production of prestige goods for elite consumption and simultaneously maligned by the same people. The opportunity of craftspeople and other economic actors was limited by the social power of the elites through institutions such as slavery, manumission, *clientele* and rents because land ownership was consolidated among the few. This model for the workings of Roman society has found its most concise expression in the *Rome's Cultural Revolution* by Andrew Wallace Hadrill and it is a powerful and often quite accurate model for Roman civic and social life.

A number of studies have been systematically dismantling some of the core tenets of this model over the last 15 years. Nicholas Tran, who was much discussed in the last chapter, definitively shows that attitudes toward craftsmanship and craftspeople were more complicated than the largely elite-produced literature would suggest. Moreover, a growing body of scholarship on craftsmanship, such as that of Miko Flohr, Elizabeth Murphy, and Nicolas Monteix, among others, demonstrates that real opportunity existed for craftspeople to enact complicated economic strategies thereby bettering their living conditions.[6] Perhaps the most direct challenge to the traditional narrative about Roman social life has come from Emanuel Mayer, whose book revives the question of a Roman middle class and the application of class analysis to the ancient world. He acknowledges that Romans never had a concept of a middle class, but rightly argues that it could still provide a useful heuristic for the study of Roman society. Mayer first defines the middle class as sharing "similar economic opportunities, and, at the same time, social and cultural conditions."[7] He then lays out an argument for a middle-class Roman aesthetic, replete with its own mythological preferences and tastes, the wealth for such art generated by commercial activity.

Mayer's book is ambitious with implications that could change how we view and study the very fabric of Roman society and thus it has solicited direct and sometimes scathing criticism. Much of the criticism focuses on his use of evidence; he sometimes uses examples of visual culture from villa estates or the behavior of Cicero to corroborate an ideology distinct from elite culture.[8] Methodological problems aside, the problem at the heart of Mayer's work is in part one of semantics. Middle class is a loaded term that evokes early modern European mercantilism or an Industrial-Revolution bourgeoisie. Moreover, it feels to many as a reversion to a 'modernist' interpretation of Roman social life not seen since before Finley's seminal work. Indeed, most of the criticism of Mayer's work centers on his blurring of the lines between elite and sub-elite and the occasional conflation of wealth and social status. Flohr notes, for example, that Mayer's conceptualization of middle classes would deprive the small towns of the Roman world of their local elites.[9] Similarly, Henrik Mouritsen, in his review of Mayer's book, marks a distinction between people of middling means and those of a "middle class", the former he finds uncontroversial and the latter he views as unproven and inconsistent in the evidence provided by Mayer.[10]

Following Mayer's work, a number of studies have begun equivocating on this point, making a claim for a middle class but often choosing other terms, such as "ordinary people."[11] These terms diverge from Mayer's middle classes in name only and often try to find a concept of a middle class emic to the Roman world, with mixed results.[12] On this I agree with Steven Ellis, who avoids a semantic debate in his recent book on Roman retail, taking issue with the monolithic conceptualization of sub-elites in general. He writes that:

> Terms like "commoners" and, perhaps worse still, "ordinary people" are appealing to some cycles of scholarship but are to my mind less helpful: these definitions tend to strip our subjects of their diversity, complexity, and interest. And while we can list a good many instances of ancient authors referring to sub-elites as a singular group, in reality they constituted an enormous but disparate proportion of the urban demographic, certainly socially stratified, but flexibly so.[13]

This desire to capture the more prosaic nature of sub-elites mirrors our increasingly complicated understanding of inequality; class as a division in society was always about inequality. A laser focus on class as derived from Marxist thought elides past the much more complicated nature of oppression and asymmetries in society, both modern and ancient. It is here that I hope observations in this book might be able to contribute to the debate, by adding in some of that granular analysis of different ways of living and how they intersect with industry and craftsmanship. Three lessons learned from this book have bearing on the question of social stratification among Roman sub-elites: the heterogenous nature of commercial baking, the difference between bakers in small communities and those of larger communities, and the crafting of a collective identity with symbols of that collectivity.

The first observation made in the book is that Roman-era baking and the lives of bakers varied widely from community to community and that local traditions continued to inform later baking even as homogenization of baking practices occurred in a Mediterranean basin unified under the Roman Empire.[14] Work on slavery and other social institutions has concluded much the same; slavery or something akin existed among most ancient cultures in the region, but it differed from culture to culture.[15] I think we have to imagine that social stratification and the opportunity to change the quality of one's life also differed from one town to the next and they were determined by a variety of local traditions and habits, in addition to economic and political pressures. There are some traits that seem relatively homogenous in Roman-era commercial baking, such as millstones which were traded widely, but in general the bakeries are fairly different from city to city. The small workshop bakeries at Pompeii and Herculaneum, for example, sometimes have indicators of elite domesticity such as triclinia, lararia, or elaborate wall paintings. The intertwining of elite such trappings and commercial production are not evident elsewhere. Part of that might be variation in the state of preservation in places other than the Vesuvian cities, but it seems equally possible that a certain privilege or unique opportunity for craftspeople existed in central Italy, much as it did further east.

We also saw that that there were broader trends within the largely heterogenous baking traditions of the Roman world: commercial baking in small towns was fundamentally different from that of larger urban centers, not only in scale of production, but also in the hierarchical composition and in the economic strategy of practitioners. In cities such as Rome or

Cologne, businessmen divorced from the actual labor owned massive bakeries with complicated hierarchies.[16] They had thin profit margins made sustainable by high production levels within the thick markets of the cities to earn sizable profits; these men—and we only know of men—could attain vast wealth. Eurysaces is the most prevalent example, but we saw that he was not as unique as his tomb might suggest. I think we also have to infer that the wealth of such men was not inherited, suggesting intergenerational elasticity in wealth. That is to say, one generation could become wealthier or poorer than its predecessors. With names such as Iazemis and Eurysaces, it is unlikely that such families were always prosperous or powerful, at least in central Italy, which certainly implies a change in living conditions from some modest family origin, however distant. Moreover, they are unlikely to have held high social status themselves. These businessmen navigated a complicated social and professional word in which they wielded little social power and might have to contend with elite disdain, but could also generate prestige for themselves individually through monuments and through the collectively proferred by *collegia*. Much like the later Medieval and early Modern urban traders and craftsmen, they varied widely even within one community.[17] Some of the bakers were like Eurysaces, but not all. Some were less successful or produced on a smaller scale, possibly filling a niche market.

Throughout many of these large urban centers there is also a clear use of imagery and symbolism by bakers, particularly the use of the millstone as a symbol of the craft and possibly as a symbol of collective identity. It is perhaps not coincidental that the same regions from which we have the most evidence for professional associations of bakers in the western Mediterranean are also the areas where we have such iconography. One is tempted to infer from the deployment of millstone imagery a manifestation of a middle-class consciousness. This is problematic because nearly all the millstone imagery—deployed as a symbol of the craft—comes from central Italy with a few found in southern and central France. But it also only ties bakers to other bakers, if indeed the representation of a millstone were a symbol of collective identity; the symbolism does not link bakers to other craftspeople except in the broadest terms of pride in one's craft. In Mayer's conceptualization of "middle classes," bakers would comprise one of many sub-elite but not poor classes that overlap but do not comprise a single unit in Roman society. That is one way to see it; I tend to view both the pride in craft and the unity manifested visually through the millstone as linked to proto-guild structures and proto-mercantilism, which is why it is found primarily in the large urban centers. I think there is a real argument to be make that later mercantilist traditions have their roots in a Roman mercantilism evident among the Empire's larger cities and the businessmen who amassed wealth but lacked high social status. Rather than retroject a notion of middle class or bourgeoisie onto these people, it might be more enlightening to work forward and attempt to link Medieval mercantilism with its ancient predecessor, not only in Europe but also in North Africa and western Asia, viewing *collegia* and apprenticeships as proto-guild activities.[18] The two modes of production, separated by centuries, can be fundamentally different and part of the same development trajectory, just like one species evolving into another.

The small-scale producers scattered among the smaller urban centers of the Roman world should be treated separately from their big-city counterparts; these are not mercantilists or capitalists. Some small-town workshop bakeries are in large homes, suggesting slave bakers, but many bakeries had no definable relationship with elite housing and our evidence suggests that many were freeborn and that most were at least freed. Take, for example, the House of the Chaste Lovers at Pompeii in which the donkey stalls (complete with their skeletons), the millstones, the oven, and the other features are interwoven with indicators of elite domesticity, such as a triclinium between the donkey stalls and the mills, fourth style wall painting, and lararia. An elegant painting of Venus and Cupid even adorns the room with tables and shelves where loaves were shaped and proofed.[19] Some bakers, particularly in the eastern Mediterranean, held civic positions and participated in politics through programmata painted on walls and through their relationships with local elites, albeit to a lesser extent than their counterparts in the larger urban centers.[20] Their success, like the bakers of Newark New Jersey, was likely predicated on their skill and charisma as craftspeople, as well as their ability to navigate local social and political realities.[21] As such, the fortunes of one family could rise and fall within a generation or two, as we saw with the small-scale bakers of nineteenth century Newark. One could lift their family out of poverty through work, but without a social safety net, the bakers of the Industrial Revolution and those of the Roman world were probably very vulnerable to adversity and misfortune. One bad growing season or one expensive equipment failure and the fortunes of the family could shift quickly. This vulnerability probably kept them neatly tied to elites through whom they could mitigate risk through clientele or similar vertical institutions specific to local social structures.

Notes

1. Mayer (2012).
2. Ellis (2018) and Rosenfeld and Perlmutter (2020).
3. Hill (1952).
4. Finley (1973, 49).
5. Mouritsen (1988, 70–124) was responding to past efforts by Gordon (1927) and Maiuri (1942) to isolate extensive social mobility. Pavo Castren (1975), who saw the advent of Roman colonists and the principate of Augustus as precipitating a local bourgeoisie who accessed wealth and power directly through holding magistracies. Mouritsen effectively showed that the same families who ruled Pompeii in the first century BCE still ruled it when Vesuvius erupted in 79 CE.
6. Flohr (2013), Monteix (2010, 2016) and Murphy (2016).
7. Mayer (2012, 2).
8. Petersen (2013) and Taylor (2013).
9. Flohr (2013, 309).
10. Mouritsen (2012).
11. Knapp (2011).
12. In a very recent publication on social stratification among the Jewish population of Roman Palestine, Ben Zion Rosenfeld and Haim Perlmutter parse Roman-era Jewish society largely into different classes based largely on terminology from the Torah, the New Testament, and Rabbinic literature. The poor and rich are delineated as obvious categories, but Rosenfeld and Perlmutter subdivide the a "middle-class" group: low middle class (craftspeople) and modest landowners.
13. Ellis (2018, 12).
14. The bibliography reviewed in Chap. 2 on bakeries from around the western Roman Empire and on local baking traditions demonstrate the heterogeneity in baking habits and technologies. Leduc (2008, 2011), Monteix (2010), Sidi Mohammed Alaioud (2010, 579–83), Mauné, Monteix and Poux (2013), Domínguez and Álvarez (2014), Amraoui (2017) and Benton (2020).
15. Katharine Huemoeller (work in progress) acknowledges in her work that Roman-style slavery should not be projected onto all regions of the Mediterranean, even if comparable institutions existed in most cultures. Moreover, the local social hierarchies and institutions continue to impact the fabric of society even after Roman conquest. She notes that the social status of captives informs their treatment and their place in society for generations.
16. Silver (2009) and Broekaert (2011).
17. Epstein (1991, 86).

18. Medieval scholars seem less worried about seeing ancient origins for later commercial and economic phenomenon. Epstein (1991, 10–21) and Ogilvie (2011, 20–23).
19. Ciarallo and Lippi (1993) and Sica et al. (2002).
20. Mouristen (1988) and Liu (2008).
21. Epstein (1991, 126).

References

Alaioud, S.M. 2010. Les activités artisanales à Banasa: témoignages archéologiques. In *L'Africa romana: i luoghi e le forme dei mestieri e della produzione nelle province africane: atti del XVIII convegno di studio, Olbia, 11–14 dicembre 2008*, ed. Marco Milanese, Paola Ruggieri, and Cinzia Vismara. Carocci: Roma.

Amraoui, T. 2017. *L'artisanat dans les cités antiques de l'Algérie: 1. siècle avant notre ère – 7. siècle après notre ère.* Oxford: Archaeopress.

Benton, J.T. 2020. The Bakeries of Volubilis: Process, Space, and Interconnectivity. *Mouseion* 62: 1–31.

Broekaert, W. 2011. Partners in Business: Roman Merchants and the Potential Advantages of Being a *collegiatus. Ancient Society* 41: 221–256.

Castrén, P. 1975. *Ordo Populusque Pompeianus. Polity and Society in Roman Pompeii.* Rome: Acta Instituti Romani Finlandiae VIII.

Ciarallo, A., and M. Lippi. 1993. The Garden of 'Casa dei Casti Amanti' (Pompeii, Italy). *Garden History* 21 (1): 110–116.

Domínguez, J.S., and M.B. Álvarez. 2014. *Pistrina Hispaniae: Panaderías, molinerías y el artesanado alimentario en la Hispania Romana.* Montagnac: Mergoil.

Ellis, S.J.R. 2018. *The Roman Retail Revolution: The Socio-Economic World of the Taberna.* Oxford: Oxford University Press.

Epstein, S.A. 1991. *Wage and Labor Guilds in Medieval Europe.* Chapel Hill: The University of North Carolina Press.

Finley, Moses Immanuel. 1973. *The Ancient Economy.* Berkeley: University of California Press.

Flohr, Miko. 2013. *The World of the Fullo.* Oxford: Oxford University Press.

Gordon, M. 1927. The Ordo of Pompeii. *Journal of Roman Studies* 17: 165–183.

Hill, Herbert. 1952. *The Roman Middle Class in the Republican Period.* Oxford: Blackwell.

Knapp, Robert C. 2011. *Invisible Romans.* Cambridge: Harvard University Press.

Leduc, M. 2008. Les Pistrina Volubilitains, Temoins Majeurs du Dynamisme Economique Municipal. In *L'Africa Romana. Le Ricchezze dell'Africa Risorse, Produzioni, Scambi. Atti del XVII Convegno di Studio. Sevilla, 14–17 Dicembre 2006*, 475–505. Rome: Carocci.

———. 2011. L'artisanat au Coeur de la ville: l'exemple des pistrina de Volubilis. In *La ville au quotidien: regards croisés sur l'habitat et l'artisanat antiques:*

Afrique du Nord, Gaule et Italie: actes du colloque international, Maison méditerranéenne des sciences de l'homme, Aix-en-Provence, 23 et 24 novembre 2007, ed. Souen Fontaine, Stéphanie Satre, and Amel Tekki, 181–189. Aix-en-Provence: Publications de l'Université de Provence.

Liu, J. 2008. Pompeii and *Collegia*: A New Appraisal of the Evidence. *The Ancient History Bulletin* 22 (1–2): 53–69.

Maiuri, Amedeo. 1942. *L'ultima fase edilizia di Pompei*. Roma: Istituto di studi romani.

Mauné, S., N. Monteix, and M. Poux. 2013. *Cuisines et boulangeries en Gaule romaine*. Paris: CNRS.

Mayer, E. 2012. *The Ancient Middle Classes: Urban Life and Aesthetics in the Roman Empire, 100 BCE–250 CE*. Cambridge: Harvard University Press.

Monteix, N. 2010. *Les lieux de métier: Boutiques et ateliers d'Herculanum*. New edition [online]. Naples: Publications du Centre Jean Bérard.

———. 2016. Contextualizing the Operational Sequence: Pompeian Bakeries as a Case Study. In *Urban Craftsmen and Traders in the Roman World*, ed. Miko Flohr and Andrew Wilson, 153–182. Oxford: Oxford University Press.

Mouritsen, H. 1988. *Elections, Magistrates, and Municipal Elite: Studies in Pompeian Epigraphy*. Rome: L'Erma di Bretschneider.

———. 2012. Review of *The Ancient Middle Classes: Urban Life and Aesthetics in the Roman Empire 100 BCE–250 CE*, by E. Mayer, BMCR 2012.09.40.

Murphy, E.A. 2016. 7 Roman Workers and Their Workplaces: Some Archaeological Thoughts on the Organization of Workshop Labour in Ceramic Production. In *Work, Labour, and Professions in the Roman World*, ed. Koenraad Verboven and Christian Laes, 133–146. Leiden/Boston: Brill.

Ogilvie, S.C. 2011. *Institutions and European Trade Merchant Guilds, 1000–1800*. Cambridge: Cambridge University Press.

Petersen, L.H. 2013. Review of *The Ancient Middle Classes: Urban Life and Aesthetics in the Roman Empire 100 BCE–250 CE*, by E. Mayer, *American Journal of Archaeology* 117(4), October. DOI: 10.3764/ajaonline1174.Petersen.

Rosenfeld, Ben-Zion, and Haim Perlmutter. 2020. *Social Stratification of the Jewish Population of Roman Palestine in the Period of the Mishnah, 70–250 CE*. Leiden: Brill.

Sica, M., S. Aceto, A. Genovese, and L. Gaudio. 2002. Analysis of Five Ancient Equine Skeletons by Mitochondrial DNA Sequencing. *Ancient Biomolecules* 4 (4): 179–184.

Silver, M. 2009. Glimpses of Vertical Integration/Disintegration in Ancient Rome. *AncSoc* 39: 171–184.

Taylor, R. 2013. Review of *The Ancient Middle Classes: Urban Life and Aesthetics in the Roman Empire, 100 BCE–250 CE* by E. Mayer, *CAA.reviews*, August 2013. Online only.

Index[1]

A

B

[1] Note: Page numbers followed by 'n' refer to notes.

J. T. Benton, *The Bread Makers*,
https://doi.org/10.1007/978-3-030-46604-6

The manufacturer's authorised representative in the EU is Springer Nature Customer Service Centre GmbH, Europaplatz 3, 69115 Heidelberg, Germany. If you have any concerns regarding our products, please contact ProductSafety@springernature.com

Printed and bound by CPI Group (UK) Ltd, Croydon, CR0 4YY
30/09/2026
02225450-0004